MY AMERICAN HISTORY

By the same author

Empathy (1992)
People In Trouble (1990)
After Delores (1988)
Girls, Visions and Everything (1986)
The Sophie Horowitz Story (1984)

My American History

LESBIAN
AND
GAY LIFE
DURING
THE
REAGAN/BUSH
YEARS

Sarah Schulman

Foreword by Urvashi Vaid

ROUTLEDGE NEW YORK

Published in 1994 by

Routledge
29 West 35th Street
New York, NY 10001

Copyright © 1994 by Routledge

Printed in the United States of America on acid free paper

Library of Congress Cataloging-in-Publication Data

Schulman, Sarah, 1958–
        My American history : lesbian and gay life during the Reagan/Bush years
 / Sarah Schulman.
        p.   cm.
 Includes index.
 ISBN 0-415-90852-3
 ISBN 0-415-90853-1 (pbk.)
    1. Homosexuality—Political aspects—United States. 2. Lesbians—United States—Political activity. 3. Feminism—United States. 4. United States—Social policy—1980–. I. Title.
 HQ76.3.U5S38   1994
 305.9'0664'0973—dc20

                             94—9261
                                CIP

Colophon

The main text of this book was set in Diotima, designed in 1953 by Gudrun Zapf von Hesse and named for Diotima of Mantinea, the earliest female philosopher on record. Heads and commentaries were set in Futura/Futura Condensed, an early modernist typeface designed in Germany in 1924–26 by Paul Renner.

Interior design by Leslie Sharpe.
Lesbian Avengers Handbook consultation and graphics from Carrie Moyer.

Dedicated to Peg Byron
Inspirational Journalist
and Loving Friend

LIST OF PUBLICATIONS

Womanews Monthly feminist newspaper, with an emphasis on the lesbian community. Volunteer collective. Writers include Jewelle Gomez, Peg Byron, Paula Martinac, Vendora Corazon, and many others.

Gay Community News Boston-based weekly newspaper. One of the first and only to serve men and women. News from a gay left perspective. Writers include Michael Bronski, Sue Hyde, Liz Galst, Scott Tucker, Elisabeth Pincus, Eric Rofes, Urvashi Vaid, Richard Burns, Cindy Patton, and many others. Minimal paid staff. Always on the verge of bankruptcy.

The New York Native The oldest gay newspaper in New York City, published by Charles Ortleb. Highly controversial for its political conservatism and white, male hegemony. Long a hotbed of contested views about AIDS. Early opponent of AZT and of ACT UP. Writers have included Marcia Pally, Daryl Yates Rist, Patrick Merla, Sally Chew, Anne Christine D'Adesky, David France, Craig Harris, Anne Fettner, and many more.

Off Our Backs Oldest surviving feminist newspaper in America. Based in Washington, D.C. Known for conference coverage and disorganized design. In the late seventies and early eighties it served as a forum for national feminist debate. Writers include Charlotte Bunch, Adrienne Rich, Tacie DeJanikus, Carole Ann Douglas, and many, many more.

Seattle Gay News Community-based weekly newspaper for women and men.

The Village Voice Weekly newspaper with progressive origins, now straddling both sides of the balance sheets. Entrenched, stratified, gay and lesbian staff often at odds with community activists and community-based publications. Often the only available forum for discussion of gay and lesbian issues. Only mainstream publication to take gay and lesbian artists seriously.

The Nation Left newsweekly with token (at best) gay and AIDS coverage.

Outweek Short lived but controversial weekly magazine—first to combine gay politics with popular design due to art director Maria Perez. Failed to represent women and people of color. Driven out of business due to dubious financing. Writers included Michelangelo Signorile, Gabriel Rotelo, Sarah Petit, and Vicki Starr, among others.

Interview Glossy, groovy, up-scale gossip sheet founded by Andy Warhol.

Outlook Quarterly gay and lesbian cultural publication out of San Francisco, attempting to address gender and racial issues as well as generic gay ones. Had its great moments. Writers included Jackie Goldsby, Jeff Escoffier, Alan Berube, Cherrie Moraga, and many more.

The Guardian The last of the Marxist weeklies. Scattered and peripheral gay and lesbian coverage until the last minute when it became unavoidable. Folded.

Cineaste Quarterly progressive film magazine

The Guardian of London One of Britain's three daily newspapers.

QW Gay weekly that replaced *Outweek*. Even more upscale—competing with *Details* and *GQ* for the white male gay reader. Later called *NYQ*. Writers included Maer Roshan, Avril MacDonald, Walter Armstrong, Helen Eisenbach, Ann Northrop, and many others.

Lambda Book Report Gay book review published by Lambda Rising Bookstore in Washington, D.C. Sponsor of the Lammies—the only book awards available to openly gay and lesbian books.

Contents

PART TWO — THE LESBIAN AVENGERS

ACKNOWLEDGEMENTS

I am very grateful to Norbert Buller and Carl Owens for the gift of my first computer, on which this book was composed. Thanks also to Ruth Karpel, Marie Honan and Su Friedrich for the use of their printers, Debby Karpel, Lesly Curtis, Carrie Moyer, and others who read the manuscript and gave helpful and supportive advice and encouragement, especially Maxine Wolfe, David Robinson, Jacqueline Woodson and Beryl Satter. For financial support during the development and preparation of this book, I am grateful to the Author's League Fund, PEN Writer's Fund, the Carnegie Fund for Authors, and my agent Diane Cleaver at Sanford Greenburger Associates.

FOREWORD

by Urvashi Vaid

For lesbians, gay men, bisexuals, and transgendered people, the Reagan-Bush years were the worst years of our lives. Their only value was the stimulus and urgency that repression gave to the (still) unfinished project of building a gay and lesbian movement. To be a movement activist during Reagan/Bush was to work in the Resistance. We waged a daily, low-tech, guerrilla war to influence policy and widen the public space to live as lesbian, gay, and bisexual people. Glimpses of freedom were won with posterboard, spray paint, press releases, and banners; with legislation, litigation, lobbying, and most importantly, with our bodies on the street.

It is exhausting to remember the many battles the lesbian and gay movement fought in this time: from the Moral Majority and the Family Protection Act in 1980 to the Oregon and Colorado fights of 1992, from the anti-porn sex wars of the early 1980s; from the smug denial of the huge problem of anti-gay violence which pervaded in 1982, to the passage of the federal Hate Crime Statistics Act in 1990; from less than $100 million in AIDS Funding in 1985 to more than $3 billion in 1993. Every victory had a body count.

It is this experience—of activism and resistance—that grounds Sarah Schulman's work. *My American History: Lesbian and Gay Life During the Reagan/Bush Years* not only collects the political articles of an extremely talented American writer, it documents a radical political history that most people—gay or straight—never knew happened. This book is an absorbing journey through a remarkable writer's nonfiction, and it is a unique chronicle of the debates that shaped the radical lesbian and gay movement in the 1980s and early 1990s.

My American History collects selected news articles and speeches written by Schulman for feminist and gay publications (some defunct like *Womanews* and the old *Gay Community News*), as well as pieces prepared for conferences and meetings. Most of the events covered were largely unnoticed by the "mainstream" press and poorly reported even by "alternative" media. The succinct commentary after each piece updates the events discussed, and provides a broader context for them. This book collects only a fraction of Sarah's actual nonfiction work—some 50 of more than 200 pieces.

Schulman's reporting takes us back to the lesbian-led Seneca Women's peace encampment, the raid on the New York City bar Blues in 1983, the closing of the bathhouses in 1985, the dyke-baiting and defunding of the National Coalition Against Sexual Assault by Ed Meese, the direct action in Congress in 1983 to protest the Human Life Amendment restricting abortion, the 1991 Outwrite conference, the Dyke March at the 1993 March on Washington, and much more.

Reading these pieces is both energizing and sobering. It's energizing because Sarah's writing is so provocative. It provoked me to underline emphatically ("in a way the sex wars really saved the grass-roots from total co-optation"), to disagree furiously (with her analysis of the NEA battle), and to question old assumptions (that direct action may have had its heyday). The work is full of opinion, and powerfully argued. Sarah is an original and rigorous political analyst. She writes with a confidence that leaves her insights ringing like bells in your head.

The book is also sobering, because in the act of remembering the past, Sarah Schulman exposes how much of it is lost forever. Yesterday's political activists are remembered today only by the handful of us who happened to work with them. Organizations come and go, activists die, and defeats or internecine battles burn passionate people out.

Queer, lesbian, and bisexual radicals especially have a skimpy historical context in which to place themselves. There are only a dozen histories, and even fewer which cover the direct action, street activist, lesbian-feminist, or left gay movements. We have little record of the fact that every city has a significant gay American history—tales of individuals who fought the police, the media, the government, and the church in virtually every town in this nation. This book makes a huge contribution to closing this gap.

In these shifty times, when conservative values monopolize all cultural discourse, when a theocratic state is embraced by Bill Clinton and the religious fanatics on the right, when it feels like the gay and lesbian movement slouches towards Republicanism to be reborn, Sarah Schulman's writing is bold, and refreshingly unrepentant in its progressive moorings.

The poet Muriel Rukeyser wrote, "Pay attention to what they tell you to forget." This is an admonition Sarah Schulman heeds. By paying attention while these events were happening, she created a record, a history, that is invaluable. By gathering these pieces in this collection, she reminds us of what lesbian and gay people continue to face—both what has changed and what remains still to be transformed.

PREFACE
MY LIFE AS AN AMERICAN ARTIST

I was born in 1958 in New York City. From childhood I was emotionally a social realist. My mother was a social worker and a modernist. She had reproductions of Diego Rivera and Moses Soyer on the walls. My sister and I put on leotards and the three of us did modern dance on the floor of our apartment. The first books I read had memorable lines like "Good Night, Moon. Good Night, Red Balloon." and "What Do Daddies Do All Day? Daddies Work While Children Play." I was read to at night before I fell asleep. We received books as rewards.

My grandmother Dora Yevish gave me unconditional love. In Tarnopl, Austro-Hungary she had been a Zionist and a Socialist. She came to America at the age of twenty-one and married my grandpa Charlie three months later. She spent the rest of her life working in laundries, theirs and other people's. My grandmother had lost two sisters and two brothers to a combination of Nazis and Russians. The tailor sewing in the window across the street had a number on his arm. We bought our clothing in a store in Brooklyn run by people who had all been in the same concentration camp. I was only size 6X so the numbers on their forearms were eye level for me. One of the first real books I remember receiving was *The Diary of Anne Frank* purchased at the Eighth Street Bookshop. It was intended, I think, to remind me of my historical burden, my place as a Jew. But, simultaneously, it taught me that Jewish girls can be writers. In my diary, at the age of six, I wrote, "When I grow up I will write books." I threw that diary away.

I wrote all through my girlhood. I wrote a history of baseball. I wrote plays for Hanukkah which my younger brother and sister enacted, often under duress. I made newspapers about the family, about the neighborhood. I only read books from the history section at my school library. I was an intellectual and a leader from the age of four. I was a troublemaker, an underachiever, creative, a behavior problem. I took myself seriously. In kindergarten Peter

Pope and I played Rocketship to Mars. But when education students from Hunter College came to observe us we determined that we were not representative of other five-year-olds and decided to play house instead. Only, he stayed home with the children and I went off to work. My mother was mortified; she thought the teacher would think it was really like that in our house.

My mother had been at Peekskill for the riot surrounding a concert by Paul Robeson. Her father was afraid of being deported. She took us to Washington for peace rallies on buses sponsored by the National Association of Social Workers. My father, the doctor, waited at home by the window for us to return at three o'clock in the morning.

In high school I fell in love, had my first girlfriend, read *The Bell Jar*, attended consciousness raising, read *The Female Eunuch*, read Jean Genet's *Funeral Rites*. My lover and I got caught by my father who continues to punish me to this day. I was emotionally ejected from my family and never allowed back in. I found out about Patti Smith and Prufrock, got my first job as a theatrical lighting technician, and saw Robert Altman's *Nashville* all at the same moment. I attended my first gay event, a lecture at the Firehouse on Lesbian Witches. I tried to go to Gay Youth but got scared and turned back.

In college I had boyfriends and girlfriends. Found out about Jack Kerouac, Sun Ra, Archie Shepp, Blondie, *The Protestant Work Ethic and the Spirit of Capitalism*. There were two women's groups on campus, the gay one and the straight one. I was in the straight one. I wait-ressed, sold records, worked as a secretary, a file clerk. I got arrested when Robert McNamara received an award for International Under-standing, got put in a cell in Cook County Jail with prostitutes. One had burned, scarred hands underneath her leather gloves. One asked me if we were "no-nukers." I dropped out.

Back in New York I became a journalist, continued to be politically active. In 1980 I found out about a theater company called "More Fire! Productions" run by a bunch of waitress/artists. "More Fire!" is what you call to the kitchen if the burger isn't done enough. "More heat for the meat." The directors were Robin Epstein and Dorothy Cantwell, a lesbian and a straight woman who were best friends. Their play was called *Junk Love* and I was hooked. I went back night after night until they let me be their stage manager, and soon after, Robin and I started collaborating on plays. Our first was called *Art Failures* about two lesbian stand-up comics trying to make it in New York City. Our second play was called *Whining and Dining* and starred Jennifer Miller and Susan Seizer as

God and the Devil. My grandmother died. I wrote extensively on the new right. Our third play was called *Epstein on the Beach*.

When the Hyde Amendment passed depriving poor women of Medicaid funding for abortion, I attended a community meeting in the West Fourth Street Church. In the middle of the usual combination of rhetoric and panic that accompany political catastrophes, a small woman with a New York accent stood up and proposed that we not repeat any strategy that had not worked before. This, believe it or not, was heresy in the old/new left which fears change more than they fear stagnancy. In the days before VCR's and personal computers, she suggested that instead of long boring leaflets, we should be on street corners with video monitors because they would attract people's attention. I was hooked. Her name was Maxine Wolfe, and now, fourteen years of friendship and political comraderie later, she remains the singularly most creative, caring, visionary, and committed political person that I have ever encountered. If the lesbian and gay movement has produced its Emma Goldman—i.e., someone with unique clarity and effective independent thought rooted in real experiences—that person is Maxine. Inspired, I joined a reproductive rights group, wrote political articles, organized locally and nationally, and learned more and more about alternative modes of activism. I was arrested for interrupting an anti-abortion hearing in Washington, D.C. and was later convicted, with five others, of "Disruption of Congress."

I started learning more and more about theater and performance art, about dance, about improvisational new music. I covered the robbery of a Brink's truck and wrote a novel about it called *The Sophie Horowitz Story*, the third lesbian detective novel on the face of the earth. It had twenty-five rejections. My brother Charlie dressed up like a messenger and hand-delivered it to various editors but I kept getting letters like "This would offend conservative librarians." I got kicked out of my political group in a lesbian purge. I started reading Wilhelm Reich. A lesbian named Rebecca Sperling was a temp at Scribner's when my manuscript came across her desk. She sent it to a lesbian publisher, Naiad Press, in Florida, with a letter on Scribner's letterhead. They thought they were getting it from Scribner's. Naiad published my first novel in 1984.

I started writing for the *Native* and trying to get into other publications. I studied Yiddish at the YIVO Institute and took a class at Hunter College with Audre Lorde. It was officially listed as "American Literature After World War II," but the first day of class she changed the name to "The Poet As Outsider." She told us, "That you can't fight City Hall is a rumor being circulated by City Hall." I applied for a Fulbright in Jewish Studies to Belgium because I had a lover in Belgium. Maxine told me to check "Yes" next to the question "Do you have a BA?" So I did. I got the Fulbright. I went to Empire State College, desperately trying to get a BA, submitting my novel and articles for credit. I went to Belgium and was miserable. I broke up with my girlfriend and wrote another novel. This time the writing was different. I suddenly realized that word order had some meaning and wrote *Girls, Visions and Everything* which is still my favorite. It was all about the lesbian boyhood, identifying with Jack Kerouac and life in New York City the summer before Reagan's re-election. Naiad hated it because it had no plot. Somehow all that theater, performance, postmodern dance and improvisational new music had had its impact. It was published by Seal Press in 1986.

I came back to New York and resumed working as a waitress with Robin at Leroy's Coffee Shop in Tribeca. I waited on Meredith Monk, Yvonne Rainer, and David Lynch. Meredith was doing a cabaret piece called *Turtle Dreams*, and she invited the waitresses at Leroy's to be the waitresses. I watched that piece every single night. Someone told me to apply to the MacDowell Colony, so I did. I waitressed until the day I got there and I waitressed the day after I returned, but those two weeks absolutely changed my life. I was in the middle of my third novel and had still never really met another novelist. I had no idea that I was an artist. At MacDowell I met composers, painters, and fell in love with an experimental film-maker. I came home and watched films for the next seven years. Jim Hubbard and I founded the Lesbian and Gay Experimental Film Festival. I joined ACT UP. I started to write for the *Voice*.

A girl I didn't know stopped me in the health food store and told me that a friend of hers was an out lesbian and a senior editor at a big publisher and I should call her. I went to the corner and called her. She told me to come over and bring my manuscript. Three days later she called me and said she wanted it. Her name was Carole DeSanti. The novel was *After Delores*. Writing that book was an exercise in honesty. I admitted to the full range of human emotions—including jealousy and rage. I also admitted that words could be put together in a way that replicates emotions instead of describing them.

When Dutton published the novel in 1988 I surpassed every dream and goal that I had ever set up for myself. I was not born into a world where openly lesbian novels could be the stuff of careers. It was a choice between the two, or so I thought, and I made that choice without question. I remember sitting down at the breakfast table at MacDowell with three other gay writers and each one told me that as long as I had primary lesbian characters I would never be able to get a general audience. They were from the old school of primary straight characters and secondary fey ones. "Oh, you can have your fabulous fags and your fabulous dykes," one said to me. "But you have to throw in some blahs or they'll never publish you."

Carole DeSanti and I were from the same generation. We had both always been out. I discovered that smart women who were not apologetic about their lesbianism could have an enormous impact—to a degree. Understanding the limitations of that degree was the subtext to our relationship over the next seven years as we worked together on four books. So, I wrote successful novels, got *New York Times* reviews, continued to be obsessed with experimental film, theater, performance art, Kathy Acker, Carla Harryman, postmodern dance, discovered opera. Tried to write an opera. Continued to write plays. Stayed in ACT UP. Started to experience death of the young on a regular basis. Felt helpless. Saw how alone we are. Lived with dying, participated in denial, felt uncontainable grief. Learned to contain my grief. Wrote on social aspects of AIDS. Grew angrier and angrier at the passivity of artists when it came to politics. Began to hate the avant-garde. Got more involved in ACT UP. Realized that personal homophobia becomes societal neglect. That there is a direct relationship between the two. Wrote a social realist novel *People in Trouble* trying to explain this idea. Tried increasingly to close the gap between politics and art. Could not believe how sexist gay men were. Read poetry (Edwin Denby, Jimmy Schuyler, Eileen Myles, Sapphire, Joan Larkin, Bernadette Mayer, more Carla Harryman, Frank O'Hara, Theresa Cha, Bob Gluck, Frank Bidart, Nicole Brossard, William Carlos Williams, Kenny Fries, Ponge, Zukofsky, Larry Eigner, Muriel Rukeyser, more). Read Jane Bowles three times. Read Reich's *Mass Psychology of Fascism*. Watched experimental films (Su Friedrich, Abigail Child, Jim Hubbard, Carl George, Roger Jacoby, Cecilia Dougherty, Michael Bryntrup, Peggy Ahwesh, Jennifer Montgomery). Got arrested with ACT UP when we occupied Grand Central Station at the Day of Desperation Action three days after the beginning of the Persian Gulf War. Wrote more articles about AIDS.

By 1992 I discovered that I was in a ghetto as a lesbian novelist. My fifth novel *Empathy* was published. I got reviewed in *Entertainment Weekly* but still could not get one straight bookstore in New York City to let me read there except during Gay Pride Month. The best-selling

books by lesbian writers had no lesbian content. When that content
was introduced, the books plummeted in the esteem of critics, book
buyers, and the general public. My books were translated into eight
languages. Straight people never heard of me. I went to my high
school reunion. I could tell who was straight and who was gay
because the gay people said, "Oh Sarah, you've been doing so much."
and the straight people said, "Oh Sarah, what have you been doing?"

Five friends and I founded the Lesbian Avengers. I read Taylor
Branch's *Parting the Waters* about Dr. King and his movement. How
each strategy was carefully chosen and orchestrated. Some girls
from LA called me up at home to option one of my novels. They
flew into town and took me out to the Tribeca Grill. I had a twelve
dollar cheese sandwich. They bought the option. Nothing ever
happened. I went on a book tour through the American South,
reading at twenty-three bookstores and founding four Lesbian
Avenger chapters. In many cities not one man or straight person
came to see me. I was/am still a novelty act. I was/am not part of
the intellectual life of the nation. I wrote more plays, screenplays,
began my sixth novel, *Rat Bohemia* with Carole. No male editor has
ever even bid on any of my manuscripts. I got arrested with the
Irish Lesbian and Gay Organization on Saint Patrick's Day when a
court order took away their right to have a counterdemonstration
against the Saint Pat's parade that officially excluded them.

I started putting this collection together and had a crisis of
confidence about taking my own work seriously. I realized that few
of the people I mention or the events or organizations that I
describe have ever made it into the history books. I realize that I
am proposing a re-periodization and re-conceptualization of the
lesbian and gay community as a protest from below. I admit that I
am not typical. My view is not a typical view. I am thirty-four years
old. This is, I suppose, volume one.

—June 15, 1993

Author's note: Some articles have been slightly changed for clarity, readability, or to reinstate initial drafts before they were dramatically altered for publication by a variety of anonymous editors.

Introduction

In 1979, at the age of twenty-two, I took on my first journalistic writing assignment. A newly founded feminist newspaper called *Womanews* sent me out to cover a demonstration by Women Against Pornography at the Playboy Club on Valentine's Day. *Womanews,* Women Against Pornography, and the Playboy Club have all passed out of this life, but that emblematic assignment was the beginning of an ideal training for this young reporter.

History has revisioned seventies feminism as either dominated by dogmatic and prudish lesbians or deeply homophobic. While the larger organizations, like NOW, were the site of well-known lesbian purges, the version of feminism that I had inherited at the end of the seventies, and that many lesbians identified with, was a vibrant, activist movement, engaged in re-evaluating and re-imagining every aspect of social life. Its practitioners opened up new venues for the imagination as they asserted women's lives and lesbian lives as justifiable terrain for autonomous political organizing, challenged male power and hegemony, raised con-sciousness, and learned to re-conceptualize the social and physical functions and the desires of the female body.

The seventies was still a time in America where it was possible to challenge traditional roles in general. Androgyny among lesbians, to the extent that it existed then more than any other time, was as appropriate to the historical moment as ponytails on men. The transformative influence of international freedom movements increasingly broadened radical feminism's visionary field. And despite the crippling legacy of McCarthyism on the American left, there was a growing determination in the feminist movement(s) to articulate an economic basis for women's political power. The political maturation of global and economic components of a social movement rooted, initially, in the private sphere, seemed imminent as feminism articulated its goal of rescuing the United States and the world from minority rule.

Yet, Ronald Reagan was just around the corner. The starting point for this collection is the week of Ronald Reagan's inauguration into the presidency of the United States—January 20, 1981. Despite the youthful enthusiasm of my early writing, reviewing these events from the perspective from which they were experienced provides dramatic evidence, almost twelve years and three presidential terms later, of how unprepared we were for the ravages of Reaganism. Cold War high school history classes had convinced my generation to expect neat scenarios, somewhat along the lines of *Invasion of the Body Snatchers,* in which oppressive regimes come to power overnight and are just as easily replaced. I don't think that many of us anticipated the systematic deprivation of services, the increasingly precise determination of who would live and who would die. Nor did we understand the massive propaganda campaigns that were to be conducted through the corporate media to normalize these conditions in the mind of the public. The manipulation of the public through advertising is as American as home-ownership and housewives, but the movements for freedom did not really articulate an understanding of the impact of advertising and T.V. "news" on American "opinion" until the sixties. This critique was still primitive when Reagan came to power.

ABORTION, THE LEFT, AND THE MEDIA

Of course, anyone who has ever participated in an act of political rebellion only to see it ignored or distorted in the next day's newspaper learns quickly about the role of the media in maintaining a status quo of power. But the selling of Reaganism becomes particularly obvious as I read over these early pieces on the tactical developments in the anti-abortion movement. In the television and print press throughout the Reagan/Bush years, anti-abortionists were portrayed as sincere people, devoted to their own personal understanding of human life. Abortion, the media continues to convince us, is simply a matter of opinion. In reality, however, the anti-abortion movement has proven repeatedly that it is composed of maniacal fanatics, under the thumb of the organized religions who have consistently funded them. The period discussed here illuminates the historically crucial coming together of the right-to-lifers and the Catholic left. Their shared strategies of civil disobedience have become the norm in the nineties as abortion clinics are bombed, practitioners murdered, and women harassed on a regular basis. As Reagan's policies provoked broader and broader opposi-

2

tional coalitions, abortion rights were sacrificed repeatedly for the "sake" of generic progressive organizing. In my years in CARASA (Committee for Abortion Rights and Against Sterilization Abuse), it was a regular occurrence for the abortion issue to be dropped from anti-Reagan coalitions in order to not "offend" Catholics, keeping the entire abortion issue on the margins of the left. This strategy was later used by heterosexuals in CARASA to keep lesbian issues equally marginal. During the 1983 antinuclear march of one million people on Central Park, the official platform included the broadest possible range of progressive issues with the exception of abortion and lesbian and gay issues because of the participation of the Catholic left and the canonization of the Church as a representative of "the masses" by a perennially deluded left. In fact, it wasn't until ACT UP (AIDS Coalition To Unleash Power) and WHAM (Women's Health Action Mobilization) demonstrated at and inside of Saint Patrick's Cathedral in November 1989, that the left directly took on the church, in a form it did not own and would not consider to be "the left."

THE RISE OF THE RIGHT AND THE ATTACK ON FEMINISM

When I came out in the 1970s, I came out into a feminist movement of lesbians and heterosexual women working together for women's liberation. Abortion was legalized in this country in 1973 when I was fifteen years old. And, my first real activist commitment was to keep abortion safe, legal, and funded. Reagan's coalition with ruthless right-wing political and religious cults had changed the way political organizing was being done. We were suddenly subjected to a bizarre, extremist line of attack that was already computerized and heavily financed through direct mail campaigns when these tactics were virtually unknown among progressives. The economic conservatives had gotten in bed with right-wing zealots such as Phyllis Schlafly and Jerry Falwell in order to get elected. Overnight this vicious fringe was in the White House, and we were being hit with both a devastating economic agenda and a hypocritical "family values" agenda. But the liberal abortion rights movement was unable to adjust their organizing style. They were caught up in feigning normalcy by using euphemistic words like "choice" instead of sticking to the moral ground of a woman's right to control her own life. At the same time the direct action roots of gay liberation were also being traded in for assimilation as many gay men focused on trying to access heterosexual men's social advantages.

3

By the early eighties, feminism, as an activist grass-roots movement, was on the verge of collapse. Reaganism had severely disempowered our constituency. The cuts in social services primarily affected women and children, making political mobilization more difficult in terms of time, financial resources, and attention. The fashion of conformity that accompanied Reaganism was one of strict sex roles and little counterculture. Few alternatives to mass media images of masculinity and femininity were in general circulation.

In addition, the relentless mediazation of "feminism" insisted that it was a movement of white middle-class women striving for success in the corporate world. These distortions began to overwhelm the grass-roots definitions and ultimately the media-created myth became the defining understanding of feminism for most Americans. On the left, the need for working in broader coalitions often meant that lesbianism and/or abortion were hidden. I remember absurd battles with heterosexual leftists where they insisted that using the word "lesbian" would "alienate Hispanics"—or claiming that homosexuality and abortion were fringe, lifestyle, or middle-class issues. And, conflicts within the movement over racism, homophobia, and sexual practice began to obstruct organizing. The kind of confusion reported in my coverage of the Reproductive Rights National Network convention in 1982 was indicative of national trends.

Meanwhile abortion rights were being dismantled piece by piece. First, the Hyde Amendment deprived poor women of Medicaid funding for abortion, then, in a "States' Rights" environment, individual statutes obstructing access to abortion services began to appear more quickly than the small national abortion lobby could respond. In particular, parental consent and "spousal" (euphemism for husband) consent laws played into false fantasies about American family life as a place where individuals were protected and nourished instead of abused and isolated. These right-wing strategies pushed highly charged emotional buttons in the press. The rapidly enacted restrictions of women's most fundamental rights became blasé standard news items provoking no response except for that of a small group of obsessed women who spent the eighties trying to mobilize their constituency.

Interestingly, the handful of committed abortion-rights activists in the early eighties ran a broad political spectrum from Catholics For a Free Choice to the population control advocates of International Planned Parenthood to left groups like CARASA. Even

4

though legality had been threatened since 1981 by such proposed bills as the Human Life Amendment, and outright dissolution of Roe v Wade seemed imminent with the Reagan court, it wasn't until around 1990 that large groups of women began to respond to the attacks on abortion. A decade of apathy seems to have been a mixture of callous indifference towards abortion access for poor women and minors as well as the reluctance of most liberal organizations to take the lead. But I also think that the collapse of activist feminism left heterosexual women in a state of ambiguous political purpose. Heterosexual men never really got on board with abortion rights. As a result, heterosexual women could not, outside of the context of feminism, muster the enthusiasm necessary to build a powerful movement.

PREPARATORY POLITICS AND THE RETREAT FROM ACTIVISM

By the end of Reagan's first term, the women's movement was separating into identity groups which focused more on cultural expression and less on direct action. Lesbians' increasing insistence that homophobia was no longer acceptable forced a breakdown between lesbians and heterosexual women that seemed to be permanent. The rise of twelve-step programs, the primary emphasis on cultural activities such as women's music festivals, bookstores, and women's studies programs—combined with organizing that was ethnically instead of ideologically based—changed the face of the community with an emphasis on personal and cultural growth projects. When direct organizing dispersed, heterosexual women were more able to assimilate while lesbians built a counterculture.

Often these divisions were articulated as preparation for creating activist groups and in some rare cases they did provoke new kinds of direct action, mostly from ethnically based organizing. For example, the campaign against the Broadway play *Miss Saigon* was a direct result of work by activists such as June Chan, founder of Asian Lesbians of the East Coast, who had been purged out of the reproductive rights movement **as** a lesbian. There were also the actions of various ethnic gay groups like the Irish Lesbian and Gay Organization, the South Asian Lesbian and Gay Association and others who fought prohibitions to march in their national parades. Men of All Colors Together participated in anti-Apartheid organizing, and Jewish women's groups against Israeli occupation of the West Bank and Gaza evolved from a wing of the Jewish Feminist Movement. These acts could not have occurred in the 1990s without ethnically based organizing in the mid-eighties. However, in most cases, self-awareness and identity politics of this period remained primarily cultural, protective, and social.

Of course people have to be able to identify into constituency groups of common needs or experiences in order to be able to organize together for social change. And when a person is a member of a demeaned constituency like people with AIDS, or a denied constituency like lesbians, there is an entire personal process that takes place before the similarity with others can even be spoken. So it is not identity politics, per se, that became an alternative to activism, but rather, the specific rhetoric of the seventies and early eighties which claimed that the process of cultural bonding on the basis of identity was a necessary "first" step before political action. This rhetoric was also used by New Age movements, therapy movements, and some twelve-step movements: that people have to heal themselves "first" in order to be able to take political action.

The problem with this theory of progression is that it provides an ideological reason not to participate in direct action at the same time that it posits self-awareness as a time-limited occurrence, which it is not. Besides, new people come into political movements all the time, and a group of people does not move in stagnant consensus. This theory had, as one of its assumptions, some idea of people moving identically together, which is actually undesirable and contrary to how people really live. As we returned to activism in the late eighties, a broader range of opinion was tolerated within the movement's ranks. The fact is, as Maxine Wolfe has pointed out, that people can only be where they are at, and a movement has to be flexible to provide access to activism for everyone at every stage of their personal and political development. A consensus model inhibits this possibility.

The second half of the eighties saw, instead, the evolution of movements more reliant on praxis (the application of theory to practice) so that identity issues and personal development questions were more likely to be addressed in the process of organizing instead of as a preparatory substitute for organizing. For example, instead of stopping the activism of ACT UP to do consciousness raising on sexism, or developing a women's caucus inside the organization principally to provide support (which would have been the old identity politics model) the question became one of application. How can the entire organization address women's access to AIDS services in the practicalities of our organizing? One of the answers was a three-and-a-half-year campaign started in

1989 to change the official definition of AIDS so that more women would qualify for disability benefits and services. This was a successful campaign that won a substantial victory for women with AIDS, which would not have been achieved without direct action by ACT UP working in coalition with groups like Lifeforce, ACE, Healthforce, and other community based activist organizations for people with AIDS. These were not won by cultural organizing.

In fact, the ticking clock in the lives of AIDS activists was really the most significant factor in pushing aside this laborious idea of a one-step, two-step approach. It enabled people to organize by community (gender, HIV status, geography, etc.) in a flexible way when it was more efficient to organizing, but it defined activism as something available to everyone, immediately. I'm not implying that ACT UP ever overcame its sexism, but they could have spent those three-and-a-half years doing preparatory consciousness raising and never would have done what was necessary to change the definition. Or perhaps, two years later we would have been ready to start the work at hand, but so many women with AIDS would have died without benefits in that interim period.

THE SEX WARS

For a short time in the early eighties, the Women Against Pornography position was unchallenged. Their analysis said that pornography is the propaganda for the subjugation of women and that both the pornography industry and the actual materials produced by that industry cause violence against women. And when it was first introduced, this view seemed comfortable to many feminists. I remember attending their first New York conference which was absolutely packed and featured many prominent leaders. Even Joan Nestle, of the Lesbian Herstory Archives—later one of their most virulent opponents—led a workshop featuring a slide show of images of lesbians used in heterosexual pornography with a cogent analysis of what these images meant about the position of lesbians in the larger society.

But by the second half of Reagan's first term, the right wing seemed so entrenched that the segment of the anti-porn movement calling for protective legislation appeared to have far too much in common with the new right's agenda on sexual imagery. As they became increasingly isolated within the movement, the feminist anti-porn leadership began to critique sexual practice,

7

singling out butch-femme lesbian sexuality and sado-masochism for particular attack. This inspired a backlash of anger and resentment by activists and academics who questioned WAP's analysis and tactics. The anti-WAP contingent held control over the historic Barnard College Scholar and Feminist Conference on sexuality and excluded anyone associated with WAP from speaking. The lines were drawn.

Even though many, many women are troubled in some way by different aspects of pornography or its accompanying industry, the official anti-pornography wing articulated a critique that was unacceptable to the rest of the movement. Their underground credibility was irreparably damaged by a short-lived effort to condemn various groups of women based on sexual practice or presentation. Ironically, that condemnation became the basis for notoriety and many of their targets went on to achieve mainstream recognition and reward while most of the anti-porn activists (with the exception of Andrea Dworkin and Catharine MacKinnon) changed their tune or went off into obscurity. The "community" of lesbians and feminists (that is to say women who identified with other women or lesbians in opposition to the state) was broader than ever before, even without an activist wing. It now included increased visibility for a wider variety of sexual practices and a broadly divergent relationship to pornography and sexual imagery. Feminist intellectuals were increasingly more influenced by postmodernism than by Marxism and so became increasingly complex in their understanding of representation of sexuality. To top off all the emerging contradictions, the male-owned liberal media was far more interested in a pro-porn feminism than an anti-porn one and gave a lot of space and attention to the burgeoning schism in the ranks. Finally the feminist backlash against the anti-pornography movement erupted into a full civil war that put any remnants of united organizing to rest.

In a way the sex wars really saved the grass roots from total co-optation, even though it contributed to the de-mobilization of the movement. For, while the dominant culture, during the Reagan/Bush years, went firmly in the direction of repressing sexuality and sexual imagery, the "sex radicals" won control of the lesbian community. For years, the highest circulation commercial lesbian magazine in the world was *on our backs,* a sexual quarterly published in San Francisco and founded by Susie Bright.

With the sex wars came a revisionist analysis of the feminist agenda, criticizing the focus on "victim" issues such as rape, abortion, and sexual harassment. Instead it emphasized a more upbeat sexuality discourse—one that was more fun and more palatable to the liberal press in that it presented an image of what a feminist could be that also incorporated more elements of dominant culture desirability. This contributed to a temporary stigmatization of political activism as "boring" and sexual practice issues as more hip and contemporary. Only recently have these two elements been able to re-unite with the rise of groups like Queer Nation, the Lesbian Avengers, and other activist groups that are both sex positive and politically engaged at the grass-roots level.

Interestingly, the sex wars also deeply influenced the self-image of lesbians. It provoked a desire among lesbians in language, clothing, entertainment, and art to appear to be sexually adventurous and provocative. A new uniform look and presentation appeared, advertising lesbians as uninhibited, sexually skilled, and sexually fearless. Aesthetically, of course, this was a lot more pleasing to the eye for girlwatchers like myself, and gave an illusion of excitement based on traditional American codes of what is daring and seductive. However, it was accompanied by a distastefully dishonest rhetoric in which particular clothes or sexual stances were interpreted to mean that the bearer enjoyed her sexuality more than people who did not conform to this style. And this line was backed up by an amazingly distorted revisionism on seventies feminists and lesbians claiming that *they* were sexually inhibited and prudish, when all the documentation from that period points in the opposite direction. Indeed, lesbian writings from the time are obsessed with sexual pleasure, the body, non-monogamy, etc.

One crucially important factor in understanding this trend had to do with the increasingly close relationships between lesbians and gay men as a result of the AIDS crisis. The influence of gay men's fashions and sexual styles was huge. This may have contributed to the sudden distaste for seventies feminism insofar as that was exclusively a women's movement. The late eighties/early nineties version was definitely co-ed and the influx of men's material resources and visibility made seventies feminism look shabby and powerless.

In the end, I still don't believe that the nineties dyke enjoys sex more than Catharine MacKinnon. And it would have been more interesting to separate the ideas behind the two factions from aspersions on people's relationships to their own sexuality. But this conflation could be seen as an expression of lesbians' sense of themselves as sexually inadequate and their need to position themselves *relationally* to the dominant culture, which is a classic sign of disempowerment. Ironically, by the nineties the *dominant* aesthetic is to claim to be a "bad girl," a "sexual outlaw," and a "deviant." And while it is true that in relation to the right-wing Christian influence on culture and policy, we are still perverts—in underground lesbian culture, the "bad girl" is the norm.

AIDS HYSTERIA AND THE CLOSING OF THE BATHS

By 1985 I had begun writing regularly for the *New York Native*, a gay newspaper that actually paid its writers, although they did pay men more than they paid women. Peg Byron, one of the founders of *Womanews*, had gotten a job there as one of the only women staffers and was desperately trying to bring women writers onto the paper. The AIDS crisis had begun in 1979, but it wasn't until 1982 that someone I knew personally had died. My first AIDS-related writing assignment was to cover a small gay investment firm that had faced intense AIDS-phobia when they placed an advertisement for their financial services in a straight publication.

The *Native* was at the forefront of AIDS coverage until its editorial direction deteriorated into a style usually associated with screaming tabloids like the *New York Post*. After too many headlines about AIDS being caused by dolphins and, more importantly, a complete intolerance for other opinions, the *Native* lost its credibility for more than a decade. Ironically, many of its arguments proved to be of value in the long run, especially its critique of AZT and its assertion that HIV may be only one of a series of co-factors required to produce AIDS. But for a number of years, since the *New York Times* continued to completely ignore the crisis, it was up to the gay press to define AIDS, thereby injecting a new note of urgency into our responsibilities as reporters.

Peg Byron published the first article, anywhere, on women and AIDS in 1985 in the *Village Voice*. There were other women reporters like Ann Fettner, Anne-Christine D'Adesky, Cindy Patton, Celia Farber, and more who did and still continue to do ground-breaking reporting on medical and political elements of the crisis. But, for the most part, women stayed out of AIDS, with the exception of the many individuals who were involved as service providers, and a few organizers like Dr. Suzanne Phillips, one of the founders of the People With AIDS Coalition. Lesbians never made up the majority of ACT UP members. And to be a woman in ACT UP meant you had to be politically confident. It was not a place where politically inexperienced lesbians could easily learn organizing skills. Many of the women in the group were tough and most had previous political experience, which accounts for our significant representation in the leadership of the movement. But ironically AIDS service organizations were training grounds for a lot of women, because we could be politically active in them and not violate the prescriptions of the female role.

In 1985 I was City Hall reporter for the *Native* and just happened to be on assignment when Governor Cuomo handed down the guidelines for public sexual establishments that led swiftly to the closing of the bathhouses that were situated in the gay ghetto. As is clear from the articles reproduced here, the events surrounding the closings were completely chaotic and the community was unprepared. We divided, once again, along the lines of sexual practice. One faction of the gay male community invited the state in to regulate or close bathhouses and the others insisted on the community's right to sexual territory. As the potential scope of the epidemic began to come into focus for some, the community became increasingly overwhelmed emotionally. It also became obvious that the kind of intra-Democratic Party bargaining that had been the staple of homo-cratic (to use a phrase coined by Peg Byron) life was completely inadequate to this huge and incomprehensible disaster.

THE FOUNDING OF ACT UP

Contrary to the recent periodization of the history of AIDS activism, there was resistance and political rebellion before the founding of ACT UP. In this collection are several articles documenting civil disobedience by people with AIDS, and calls for direct action and street activism from lesbians, people with AIDS, and drag queens, over a year before ACT UP was founded. However, its creation was a direct manifestation of gay men becoming increasingly fed up with government inaction and the hesitancy of their leaders. At the same time a number of experienced lesbian and straight women activists were moved by their own relationships with gay men, by compassion, and by political understanding of the anti-gay, anti-sex rhetoric that was mushrooming around the epidemic to join the newly formed ACT UP by the spring of 1987.

The coming together of feminist political perspectives and organizing experience with gay men's high sense of entitlement and huge resources proved to be a historically transforming event. Necessity was the best motivator for efficiency, and for the most part ACT UP was able to function with a wide coalition and broad divergence of opinion. Despite the efforts of the gay press, the straight press, and the government to control the AIDS agenda, ACT UP produced the largest grass-roots, democratic, and most effective organizing in the history of both the gay and feminist movements. Of course, the flaws of ACT UP can also fill volumes, as can the many ways in which the U.S. government is able to obstruct a mass movement, no matter how clear their vision is.

I think it is safe to say that most of the substantial progress that has been made in this country on behalf of people with AIDS can be traced to ACT UP. For implementation of needle exchange pro-grams, condoms in the schools, faster mechanisms for releasing new drugs, development of alternative treatments, standards of care for pediatric cases, insurance reform, changing the official definition of the disease so more women can receive benefits, etc., etc., ACT UP was there. But ACT UP also changed many of the ways that gay people do organizing. Most of ACT UP's work was painstakingly detailed and behind the scenes, but when these proposals were backed up by street organizing and actions, we had a much higher rate of success. But the media only put out the most superficial images of our methods. To this day many people only think of ACT UP as those people who disrupted mass at Saint Patrick's Cathedral.

Unfortunately the area of treatments was, for a number of years, the committee of ACT UP least in favor of direct action. In the early years we did treatment actions. For example, when Sloan Kettering was not drawing patients into experimental drug trials during the summer of 1987, we held a round-the-clock silent vigil. We did major actions at the Food and Drug Administration (FDA) and at the National Institute for Health (NIH). Affinity groups often did actions at pharmaceutical headquarters and New York offices—even going so far as to interrupt trading on the floor of the Stock Exchange to demand a cut in the price of AZT. But as we increasingly worked within government agencies and pharmaceutical companies, using their language and their tactics, our direct actions on treatments became fewer and further between. Of course these agencies and companies responded much more to the upper-class white men of ACT UP than they did to the women and people of color, and so our good old boys often became their good old boys. As treatments relied more and more on negotiation, by the end of the Bush years, it was clearly the area in which we had made the least progress.

Another time-tested and true tactic of ACT UP's was the use of Zaps—small actions of four or five people with a very focused target. This had been a tactic of the early gay movement: I'd employed it myself with the Women's Liberation Zap Action Brigade in 1983. And ACT UP used it many times and well. My favorite ACT UP Zap involved five people, including two of the hardest working and most respected members of the group—Ron Goldberg and Amy Bauer. They and three comrades decided to Zap Bill Clinton when he was campaigning in the New York primary in 1992. In true ACT UP style, they got a print-out of the entire itinerary of his visit and managed to be at every one of his speeches, meetings, meals, and hand-shakes. When Clinton went to the bathroom, ACT UP was there. In fact, a local TV broadcast that night called "A Day in the Life of the Candidates" revealed that every shot of Clinton in New York fea-tured an ACT UP sign in the background. Finally they caught him on camera being interviewed by a TV crew and the intrepid Zap team challenged Clinton to promise that a person with AIDS would speak at the Democratic Convention. Clinton agreed, before the cameras, and that is how Bob Hattoy came to make his historic speech as a gay man with AIDS at the nominating convention that summer. Two years later the newly formed New York Lesbian Avengers used the same tactic to Zap Denver Mayor Wellington Webb one month after the anti-gay ballot measure Amendment 2 was passed in Colorado.

Clinton's election, which should have been a huge victory for ACT UP, turned into organizational quicksand. Clinton's promises were so enticing that ACT UP stood by and waited, too patiently, for them to be fulfilled. In the meantime, the most conservative elements of the gay movement picked up the bandwagon by emphasizing military issues over AIDS. The gap in time was damaging to the credibility and momentum of the group, and, as of this writing, ACT UP is trying to recover full enthusiasm with ideas like the Barbara McClintock Project—a structured approach to the basic science of AIDS.

CLINTON'S MILITARY FIASCO AND THE RETURN OF THE HOMOCRATS

There is a new visibility now, under Clinton, and with it come new danger zones. President Clinton's choice of the military as the arena in which to argue gay civil rights was one that the gay community would never have made on its own. It was determined instead by gay people inside the Democratic Party and businessmen who came out only recently and positioned themselves as powerbrokers for a community they do not know and cannot represent. But, as "Friends of Bill" they have access to the White House and an inordinate influence on policy. Not only is there great dissension within our community about the role of the military (which has made grass-roots organizing on the issue difficult and low key), but it seems clear that the community's own priority is AIDS, a subject Clinton has done nothing about. So, while provoking a national public debate on homosexual rights which can only benefit us, Clinton simultaneously usurped control of the gay agenda from us. And it is unclear to what extent we will have to go to gain control, if that is possible at all. Historically this reflects a classic problem for gay people. Once our fate is debated at a level in which most lesbians and gays with access are closeted, like government, we have a weak voice in determining the terms of discussion.

As exciting as it has been to see gay issues in the national spotlight, there is also something profoundly depressing about watching the debates unfold on the nightly news. It quickly became clear that very few openly gay people were permitted to be full participants in the discourse. Instead we were treated daily to supposedly straight generals, newscasters, and government officials deciding whether or not we should have basic civil rights. The exclusion of openly gay or lesbian people from power became excruciatingly obvious.

Clinton needs a far more complex understanding of gay life than he currently holds to avoid trading one step forward for one step back. Unfortunately his comments in March of 1993 that he might favor segregation of gay and lesbian troops in the military revealed that he has not got a clue about how gay people live. He sees "gay" and "lesbian" as permanent, static, and easily definable states that would enable easy separation. He also does not have a clue that the vast majority of gay men and lesbians are already in the closet and would not be detectable through a voluntary admission and segregation system. His friendliness towards the "Don't Ask. Don't Tell" proposition of Senator Sam Nunn revealed even further his ignorance about gay life and gay politics and his complete lack of interest in defending the rights of homosexuals. Unfortunately, the gay leadership wasn't much better. Tom Stoddard, of the Campaign For Military Service, told the *New York Times* in June 1993 that forbidding homosexuals to hold hands or kiss on an army base was acceptable to him.

The media contributed strongly to the downfall of Clinton's initial plan to lift the ban by reporting the issue as though gay people were not already *in* the military. The gay press was not very helpful either, since for years they had been misreporting the issue. Lesbians and gay men of color were forced out of the military for their homosexuality at higher rates than white men, but the gay press is so racist that all its model cases were white officers. These soldiers were equally abandoned by the homophobic black press which also ignored their cases.

THE RELIGIOUS RIGHT'S ANTI-GAY AGENDA

Clinton came to office at a time when the religious right was making dramatic strategic shifts in their attacks on lesbians and gay men. When Clinton reinstated some access to abortion rights through a presidential order, he undid a substantial portion of fifteen years of effort by the anti-abortion movement. As the result of this defeat the religious right is putting all their money and enthusiasm into a massive national campaign against lesbians and gay men using tactics and strategies similar to ones they had developed in the anti-abortion movement. They are mass-producing video cassettes filled with misinformation and mailing them to people's homes. Throughout the nation they are running highly financed campaigns town by town and county by county in hand-to-hand combat trying to pass anti-gay propositions and amendments through direct vote ballot measures. Attempting to duplicate the way abortion rights were stripped away piece by piece through local ordinances, the anti-gay movement is funding a variety of local campaigns. Small gay communities throughout the country are now being asked to fight these ballot measures alone.

Unfortunately, like the state-by-state approach on restricting abortion, many of these areas do not have the resources to put up a good fight. Often there are not enough people who are even out of the closet to speak out publicly against the right. The communities often do not know how to use the media nationally and are not sophisticated about new technologies of political organizing. Clinton's office has a crucial role to play offering federal support to the most oppressed gay communities by sponsoring a federal civil rights act that would make the local statutes moot. Otherwise many of these areas will not be able to stand up to the highly financed religious campaigns.

But, in the meantime, the Christian right has replaced preachers with scientists in their propaganda videos and are basing many of their attacks on the assumption that homosexuality is either a choice or else the result of reversible environmental factors. This perspective enables them to justify punishing gay people by depriving us of housing, job protection, and the like because our homosexuality is within our control, and so, if it is socially undesir-

15

able and voluntary, we do not merit protection. The "liberal" media has responded with a huge campaign asserting that homosexuality is biological in origin, a concept they find very comforting when anticipating being more integrated with openly gay people. Publications which have barely ever mentioned gay people, like *The Atlantic,* suddenly run cover stories on homosexuality and biology. A recent poll in the *New York Times* showed that more people would be willing to support gay rights if they believed that gay people genetically could not help their orientation. Intrinsic to this approach is the insistence that heterosexuality is obviously superior and preferable and homosexuality is only acceptable if biologically determined and therefore beyond the free will of the practitioner.

I am concerned that a biologically determinist explanation for homosexuality will be the point around which general cultural agreement on gay rights is cohered. And the military may be the laboratory for the surfacing of this argument. Since the most important element of any concept is that its originating question be appropriately framed, any theory demanding an explanation for homosexuality is a problematic one because it maintains our existence as a category of deviance. I mean, no one is running around trying to figure out why some people like sports, for example. So, a liberal agreement on homosexuality as biological and therefore the basis for civil rights is, I predict, imminent and will bring the debate even further out of the hands of our community. Without anti-gay stigma and oppression, the origins of homosexuality would not be an issue. What really needs to be interrogated is the nature and causes of homophobia and why it is so rampant in our culture.

AMERICA'S ABANDONMENT OF LESBIANS AND GAYS

When I turned twenty, I thought I was growing up in the world of women's rights, gay liberation, and a viable future. Instead I entered adulthood in a world dominated by Reaganism and AIDS. Yet, gay and lesbian people have managed to build an extremely humane political movement out of our own sense of necessity. But, for all our heroism and valor, gay people are coming into the fifteenth year of the AIDS crisis feeling angry and alone. While the Clinton administration's nod is clearly more than gay men and lesbians have ever had before, its complete inaction in the face of the AIDS crisis and bungling of the gays in the military issue is a good indication that none of Clinton's promises to our community are going to be fulfilled. And in the very few areas where he has taken action, it has been against us—for example, his restriction on people who are HIV-positive coming into the country. Even more outrageous was his placing of HIV-positive Haitians in a quarantine camp in Guantanamo after having won the presidency with the support and money of the AIDS community. It is shameful that the gay and lesbian leadership has not mobilized to condemn Clinton's neglect of AIDS and has, instead, been busily faxing their resumes to the White House.

During the Republican National Convention in August 1992, Americans were subjected nightly to the most vile and hateful homophobia ever broadcast in the history of commercial television. And still I was surprised that no straight people, no family members, straight friends, or students called me just to say, "This must be so awful for you." Personally, there is a way that gay men and lesbians have been abandoned. We've lost so many lives that giving into grief seems an impossible luxury and still so many of our closest friends and relatives see AIDS as only an issue on television. Our fate is now being debated in the national media without our full participation and in a manner that distorts our existence.

Recently two friends and I got into a weepy conversation about the whole military phenomenon. The fact that Clinton so naively introduced these changes, never anticipating or preparing for the wave of hatred and distortion was quite revealing. It showed how little he knows about what we face every day—how little he understands what our lives have been like. Just as legal racial segregation may be gone, officially this country has not even begun to try to come to terms with what we have done to black people—there is little acknowledgement in this "changing America" about what the country has done to lesbians and gays. Gay people so often speak freely in private about things that we never dare say in public. Either because we are too busy explaining, trying not to offend, or because it is too painful to face or simply because, like now, the debate is taking place at a level at which we do not have a voice. These are some of the legacies of the eighties and challenges of the nineties that will continue to live with us during the years to come.

—July 1, 1993

ESSAYS 1981-1994

1

FEAR AND LOATHING
ON THE HALLELUJAH TRAIL

Excerpted from
an address at
the Conference of
Women in Economic
and Political Crisis
at the New School
for Social Research,
January 1981

Now that the shock of Ronald Reagan's ascent to power has reverberated across the land, progressive people have a lot of work ahead if we are to understand and then defeat the new right coalitions that brought him to office. Acting on a number of different fronts, the new right is not a monolith but rather a collection of diverse reactionary movements with a wide variance of agenda.

Take for example the National Right-to-Life Party, the electoral wing of the anti-abortion movement. This year marked their first foray into legislative races in which they endorsed fifty candidates, sixteen of whom were victorious. Right-to-Life may be the largest grass-roots, single-issue political force in the nation. Their sole goal is the passage of the Human Life Amendment to the Constitution which would outlaw abortion in all cases.

> The Right To Life applies to all human beings irrespective of age, health, function or condition of dependency including the unborn offspring at every stage of their biological development.

Their strategy is to pass this amendment via state-by-state ratification or by convening a constitutional convention on the issue. Nineteen states have already called for a "con-con" on abortion.

Right-to-Life is rigorously single issue and devout about their version of anti-abortion politics. Here in New York State, 26,000 people decided that Ronald Reagan was not anti-abortion enough for them. Instead they cast their presidential ballots for Ellen McCormick, the RTL candidate. This move was partially a reaction to Reagan's selection of George Bush as his running mate. Bush has gone on record as opposing a constitutional amendment against abortion but recently changed his position in the name of party unity.

RTL's views are so extreme that even the most virulent anti-abortion politicians avoid their full agenda. For example, even

21

Henry Hyde of Illinois, sponsor of the amendment to end Medicaid funding for abortion, disagreed with RTL's opposition to abortion in cases of rape and incest. In 1975 their president, Dr. Carolyn Gerster wrote

> By allowing abortion for rape we would be abandoning the only principle by which we can resist abortion on demand.

She claimed that the number of women impregnated during rape was minimal due to such factors as "increasing numbers of rapists with vasectomies." Gerster continued in this vein citing experiments conducted by the Third Reich "proving" that women's fertility is affected by trauma. She cites "research" conducted by Nazi scientists who sent ovulating women into mock gas chambers. Many failed to ovulate during their next cycle. Gerster also argues that unwanted pregnancies resulting from rape can be eliminated with DES (the "morning after pill"), a synthetic hormone known to be carcinogenic.

On the other side of the right-wing coin are a bunch of hard-core politicos with a much more opportunistic attitude towards their own quest for power. One of their most visible leaders is Terry Dolan, head of NCPAC (National Conservative Political Action Committee). A former Young Republican, Dolan's organization is responsible for the infamous "hit-list" which contributed to the surprise defeat of a number of liberal senators last November. NCPAC's first substantial victory was the election of Gordon Humphreys as the Republican senator from New Hampshire. Humphreys, a former airline pilot, had rarely voted in any election before his own.

Another figure in the movement is Paul Weyrich, who is responsible for bringing beer magnate Joseph Coors into new right circles. Coors has been funding the movement since 1971, and, with Weyrich, co-founded the Committee for the Survival of a Free Congress, one of the top ten spenders in political action committees (PACs) for 1980. Their first victory was the election of Orrin Hatch to the Senate from Utah in 1977.

Howard Phillips, the token Jew of the Moral Majority and head of the Conservative Caucus, went to Harvard where he was student body president. He favors a return to biblical law and told a Washington newspaper that he didn't understand why women need to own property or vote.

Phillips and Richard Viguerie, editor of *Conservative Digest* and direct-mail king, both got their training in Young Americans for Freedom, a right-wing youth corps founded in 1960 by William Buckley as a protest against Rockefeller liberalism. Later, as a fund-raiser for George Wallace, he used his now famous direct-mail solicitation method and raised a then unheard of six million dollars. George McGovern wanted Viguerie to work on his 1972 presidential bid, but Viguerie, being more principled than McGovern, refused. He now maintains a staff of 300 nonunion employees and a computerized mailing list of over twenty-five million names. His clients include Conservative Books for Christian Leaders, No Amnesty for Deserters, National Rifle Association, and Gun Owners of America. In 1971 his associates started an organization called Friends of the FBI to express support for J. Edgar Hoover. They got Efrem Zimbalist, Jr., star of the TV series *The FBI*, to sign a fund-raising letter which netted close to $400,000. Over half went to operating expenses. In 1977 he raised funds for the Children's Relief Fund, a program of the Korean Cultural and Freedom Foundation—part of the worldwide operation of Reverend Sun Myung Moon. His magazine has proposed Phyllis Schlafly (president of STOP-ERA) for the Supreme Court and argues that abortion should be illegal in cases of incest because "women participate voluntarily in incest." *Conservative Digest* runs full page ads for Krugerrands.

This gang of four and more are worried that Reagan will leave behind the "moral agenda" that they represent and carry out his presidency primarily on a traditionally conservative economic platform. "Main Street won the election," says Howard Phillips, "but Wall Street is running the country." Jerry Falwell told *US News and World Report* that, "If Mister Reagan turns out to be like all the other presidents we've had lately, our people are so committed, they wouldn't hesitate to turn against him and find another candidate in 1984." In this scenario, Reagan comes out looking like a moderate and, therefore, more credible.

The divisions between old time Republicans and the new right may have a lot to do with class. The new right hates big business, international corporations, and the families that run them as much as they hate labor unions. The right-wing coalition is a fragile joining of both sides of the conservative track. The factions appear in the public imagination as a wedding between Lester Maddox and William Buckley. Can the marriage survive beyond the ceremony?

According to the *New York Times,* a 1980 study by the Connecticut Mutual Life Insurance Company showed that religious commitment, more than age, race, sex, education, geography, political conviction, or income level, determined how people respond to a wide variety of questions on moral and political issues. Religious respondents were primarily interested in abortion, homosexuality, national defense, and women's rights. Approximately forty-five million Americans believe that God loves them.

COMMENTARY

Here, as a rather cocky twenty-three year old, I imagined that simply by understanding the origins of the new right we would be able to defeat them. Their political genealogies showed them to be the same old thing—that crazy bunch of religious fanatics that my generation had never taken seriously. Even with Reagan freshly inaugurated, the idea of an anti-abortion political party still seemed absurd. Still, the left spent the next decade chasing after the right trying to imitate all their best tactics. What we couldn't bring ourselves to face, however, was that it did not all boil down to good mailing lists, but rather that we were unable to stand by our most radical and dramatic demands in the way that they stood by theirs. The most bizarre aspects of their program often became law while we watered down our visions until we ended up without a clearly articulated platform. It was the capitulation to fear that cleared the pathway for the American right in the eighties more than any computer program. In this speech at the New School I think I chose to quote from their most extreme positions as a way of mocking them. Yet, at the same time it reveals now what I could not understand then—that their "single-issue" veneer actually contained a longhand detailed agenda about the social role of women which depended on the maintenance of such institutions as rape at its core. Twelve years later the confrontation between Anita Hill and Supreme Court nominee Clarence Thomas would be the fulfillment of the oppositional relationship between anti-abortionism and women's right to challenge sexual harassment.

An interesting sidebar has to do with Terry Dolan, one of the masterminds of the right-wing offensive. He was known to be gay among the Washington fag elite and actually frequented gay bars. But in these days before a concept like outing was even imaginable, gay people never thought to blow his cover. Ironically, he ended up dying of AIDS early on in the epidemic.

AN OPEN LETTER

Womanews,
November 1981

by Stephanie Roth and Sarah Schulman

As right-wing forces in this country gain strength and control over our lives and more people begin to organize to fight the attacks, lesbian feminists have to make some difficult decisions about how to proceed as a movement. While we must join with others we must also retain our vision of a world where women's lives truly matter and where the fight for control of our lives is understood to be central to any politics claiming to be progressive.

In the past year progressive groups and coalitions have been mobilizing people to become involved in fighting the right. Because the women's movement had been consistently active and often successful in organizing women to take their own lives and oppression seriously, many groups recognize that they need to include us in their organizing.

Clearly lesbians and feminists share much common ground with other progressive forces. But in deciding to work together we have to ask what the terms of the relationship should be. For us to join with other sectors of the progressive movement without having our issues and perspectives subsumed by theirs, there must be a substantial change in both their analysis and their practice of integrating feminist perspectives into their work.

One of us recently attended a meeting of ACARP (Ad Hoc Coalition Against the Reagan Program) a loose coalition of various progressive groups. The original draft of their platform had *no* mention of any aspect of lesbian or gay rights. Nor did it mention child care, sterilization policy, or any issue of violence against women even though Reagan is cutting funds for battered women's and children's programs. Later, at the same meeting, a representative of the left group Line of March said that the attacks on gays and lesbians are coming from the new right, not the

White House and are therefore not an appropriate focus for an anti-Reagan coalition.

Since Reagan's inauguration, liberal feminist groups have also taken giant leaps to the right. Betty Friedan wrote in the *New York Times* that women should disassociate themselves from the movements for abortion and lesbian rights in order to win the ERA (the Equal Rights Amendment to the Constitution). On a national level NOW (National Organization for Women) has conducted a large, expensive campaign for the ERA to the exclusion of other rights that women are fighting for. ERA "Walk-a-thons" have featured such hosts as Betty Ford and Maureen Reagan. National NOW's support for the drafting of women and for the appointment of Sandra Day O'Connor to the Supreme Court further reveals their move to the right.

We fear that unless progressive movements can challenge compulsory heterosexuality and recognize lesbianism as a positive choice for women our issues will be rendered secondary and peripheral.

COMMENTARY

For the rest of 1982, the left scrambled to find some kind of unified approach to action. For those of us who had been active in the feminist movement in pre-Reagan America, the newly re-surfaced left seemed like a real dinosaur, and a dangerous one at that. Having been essentially inactive since the Viet Nam War, they were far behind social movements organized by women and by lesbians and gays. As is clear from this concerned plea many wanted to pick up where they had left off almost a decade before.

For the first time I found myself having to make decisions about giving up portions of my own sense of self in order to work with people who could not or would not accept women or gay people or both as fully human. So many of our efforts to construct lives outside traditional female roles involved not allowing women's lives to be made secondary to men's lives. That was a broadly understood fact of feminism at the time, even though it was not included in the media depiction of the movement. But almost no other social grouping was able to see us as multidimensionally as it saw itself. So, to demand full reciprocity meant to demand the impossible. It was a decision that we made differently each time, trying out a variety of rationales as the political situation steadily worsened.

Participating in the political movements of the day inherently meant—at some point—stepping back from our full vision of feminism. It was a personally debilitating choice that many of us were not prepared to make, choosing to demobilize instead. Quite a shocking change for someone like me who had come out in the seventies when feminism and gay liberation were the two most vibrant contributions to American radicalism.

As a girl educated under the Cold War, and a second generation American, I was still raised with the old fashioned concept of progress—that things got better, and society became more free, over time. To be twenty-three and suddenly be plunged into a dramatic detour from this tidy myth, was shocking. It became ever so much more so as things deteriorated steadily throughout my entire twenties and early thirties. As a teenager I had watched rapid changes for women and for lesbians and gays. To suddenly be stuck in rooms with men and straight women who had never even noticed these changes was shattering. Reagan's election didn't create them, but it did create a situation in which I had to deal with them and their arrogance. That was the level of desperation we felt in those early years.

I have to laugh at how shocked I was at the ignorance of the left and also at what radical demands Stephanie and I posited as "the bottom line." By 1992 "compulsory heterosexuality" and "lesbianism as a positive choice for women" would be replaced with begging the government to tell people how to use condoms and a desperate attempt to salvage even the most restrictive abortion laws. The political losses were so great that threats to the most basic sexual rights of heterosexuals (seemingly resolved in the sixties) now obliterated complex understandings of lesbian existence. The latter seemed to be dependent on certain social assumptions about heterosexuality in order to be understood.

It is a telling sign of the times that when an activist lesbian movement did re-emerge, it was focused on resisting the right and winning basic freedoms. And even in the midst of the reactionary nature vs. nurture debates, our community could not articulate a radical re-conceptualization of how to understand the origins and meaning of lesbian life.

TENSIONS RUN HIGH AS REPRODUCTIVE RIGHTS ACTIVISTS FORM COALITIONS

off our backs,
January 1982

For the first time since Roe v Wade, there is a national network of radical reproductive rights organizations. Yet, differences in analysis and approach were evident at the annual conference of the Reproductive Rights National Network (R2N2). The conference, which was wheelchair accessible, interpreted for the hearing impaired and provided child care, was something like a family reunion with all the familiarity and unavoidable tensions. But that did not minimize the accomplishment of bringing together seventy organizations on the common principles of birth control, abortion rights, an end to population control, and lesbian rights.

Marlene Fried (Massachusetts Childbearing Rights Association and Solidarity: A Socialist-Feminist Network) gave the opening speech as a representative of the national steering committee.

> The struggle for reproductive freedom is a struggle to empower women.
> . . . We see ourselves as part of the larger women's liberation movement. We want a movement that has class consciousness, that is anti-racist, that is deeply committed to lesbian liberation.

Fried's perspective was partially contradicted the next morning by the presentation of a slide show prepared as an organizing tool for the Network by Pat Rush (Chicago Women Organized for Reproductive Choice) and Carol Travis (WORC and The Sojourner Truth Organization). The slide show carefully documented the history and impact of population control. It also discussed the takeover of women's practice of medicine by male institutions. But it never asked the question *why women?* Why are women the targets of sterilization when it is cheaper and medically easier to sterilize men? There followed a heated and complicated discussion about what kinds of perspectives we wanted to have represented in our organizing materials. Many people commented that population control cannot be presented uniquely as an act of imperialism, but also must be discussed as a symptom of women's vulnerability to the medical establishment. They identified sterilization policies as a sign of the government's belief that they have the right to invade women's bodies for the purpose of social control. This conversation brought to the surface some of the difficulties within an array of conflicting perspectives when we try to come up with common tools with which to organize.

The second day was just as difficult. It began with presentations on abortion strategy. Vicki Alexander (Oakland Coalition to Fight Infant Mortality and the Alliance Against Women's Oppression) called for the Network to have a specific focus on stopping the Human Life Amendment. The idea of a single-issue focus was not popular with most members who see R2N2 as a place to offer a broad, multi-issue reproductive rights platform. They prefer to leave single-issue organizing to more conservative groups like Planned Parenthood.

Although the Network is primarily white and heterosexual, a few groups led by women of color, like the Oakland coalition, have recently joined. Because of issues they have raised and because discussions of race are taking place nationally throughout the women's movement, the afternoon was reserved for a plenary on racism. But people came with a wide variety of expectations. Some wanted to discuss anti-racist *theory*. Others focused on anti-racist *work*. Others wanted a discussion of how racism plays itself out in the Network. The session began with a panel discussion.

Maria Rodriguez (Mexican-American Education and Legal Fund and the Chicano Legal Rights Project of Los Angeles) spoke of some of the realities in the lives of Chicanas that organizers must be aware of when dealing with issues like abortion. She spoke of high pregnancy rates among Latina teenagers even when contraception is available. "They may resort to pregnancy as a source of identity," she said. "Latinas use abortion in high numbers, but they have a negative attitude about it and will not take a stand publicly." She suggested that the best way to reach Latinas was through health care provision.

Miyesha Jenkins (Oakland Coalition and the Alliance) analyzed how Reagan's cuts were affecting people of color. Food stamps and welfare are cut while social security, which serves mostly white people, is not as severely cut. She warned us against ghettoizing population control as *the* issue of primary concern for women of color while falsely assuming that abortion is a white women's issue.

29

Dolores Nolan (Director, Chico Feminist Women's Health Center) spoke about organizing women of color for reproductive rights. "There are still women," she said, "who believe that abortion is genocide and that it is a white women's issue."

Rafita Anderson (American Friends Service Committee and the Black United Front) was the last speaker. "The bottom line is self-determination . . . . What brought me to this work was hearing about another woman's experience, a black woman who had to get illegal abortions twice. Your personal experience—whatever got you here—is an organizing tool for getting someone else here."

So, it was clear, as we broke up for small group discussion, that there is an enormous diversity of opinion among women of color in the Network about how to approach these issues.

By the end of the weekend, however, there was enough agreement to continue the Network and approve some resolutions:

1) R2N2 will participate in the July 16th demonstration against the National Right to Life Convention in Cherry Hill, New Jersey.
2) All work and publications of the Network will include specific anti-racist perspectives and affirm the Network's commitment to lesbian liberation.
3) The next R2N2 conference will include a panel on lesbian oppression and experience.
4) R2N2 members will work in local coalitions against the Family Protection Act.
5) Work on teenage sexuality will be incorporated into the Network's commitment.
6) The Network will incorporate an understanding of infant mortality into its work.

COMMENTARY

Although this may look like one of the dirty laundry moments of the eighties' feminist movement it actually reveals quite a lot of poignant information. One of the reasons that so many women from very diverse political agendas came together in R2N2 was that there was not an activist response to attacks on abortion coming from their own communities and movements. It is clear from Marlene Fried's tentative opening statement that she was trying to walk a tightrope between women inside the Network from leftist organizations who rejected feminism and a women's movement outside the

Network that was not willing to take a multi-issue approach to abortion.

This conference was, in many ways, typical of the old, pre-AIDS way of organizing. People from various political perspectives tried to hammer out "unity" on a variety of principles and came together to make proposals from their specific perspectives with the intention of lobbying for a particular analysis. In the case of R2N2 a lot of actual organizing was going on and for a couple of years R2N2 played a unique role influencing the left, the women's movement and the single-issue abortion organizations. But with AIDS, ACT UP instituted a new, more efficient and flexible organizing style that was not predicated on agreement. And subsequently the most successful organizations in the gay community focused their discussions on concrete application of specific events, projects and actions instead of on theoretical unity.

But R2N2's conference occurred one year after Reagan's inauguration, and the confusion was appropriate to its historical context. At that time we were busy trying to build broad coalitions quickly as women's rights lost ground with dramatic rapidity. That same month a U.S. Court of Appeals upheld a Florida law requiring that a woman's husband be notified prior to her abortion. Agreeing with arguments by attorneys for Americans United for Life Legal Defense Fund, the court said that the law was justified by the state's interest in protection of the marriage relationship and in protection of the husband's right to have children.

> The marital relationship between a couple could be maintained without a husband ever discovering why or how his aspirations for a family have been frustrated. This is surely a perversion of the institution of marriage as conceived in our society and as instituted by this state. If his aspirations include his desire for children, it is a small concession for him to have the right to know that his wife is considering an abortion.

Feminism in this period has falsely been called a "white women's movement." Although primarily white, it is clear from the organizational affiliations of the speakers at the R2N2 conference that the racial and political spectrum was very broad. All through the history of grass-roots feminism there has been a division between predominantly white groups, a few rare truly integrated groups, and women-of-color groups. But there have always been women of color who have been willing consistently to work with predominantly white organizations, and their existence and their leadership or just hard work is clumsily erased by referring to these organizations as "the white women's movement." When I studied with Audre Lorde at Hunter College, she made it very clear that she had been willing to be the person who

31

defies categories. Throughout her life she was willing to place herself in predominantly straight black organizations, in predominantly white lesbian organizations, in predominantly male gay organizations, in homophobic black arts contexts, or racist white arts contexts or sexist white or black arts contexts. And it was clear that the individual refusing to follow the prescription pays a high personal price. So it is crucially important that women of color who have worked hard and organized brilliantly in predominantly white groups do not have their existence erased.

CRITICAL HISTORY OF BLACK WOMEN

Womanews,
February 1982

Ain't I a Woman
by bell hooks
(Boston: South End Press, 1981)

With the advent of new publications featuring women of color—
like *This Bridge Called My Back* edited by Cherrie Moraga and Gloria
Anzaldua, *Towards a Black Feminist Criticism* by Barbara Smith, *Conditions
Five: The Black Women's Issue* edited by Lorraine Bethel and Barbara
Smith, and the upcoming *Home Girls,* race, racism, and racial
identity have become the most widely and heatedly debated
concerns in the radical women's movement.

By publishing in the feminist presses, by speaking in women's
bookstores and to feminist audiences, these writers are placing
themselves firmly within the context of the feminist movement.
For this reason I was drawn to a new book that has appeared from
a left press without much promotion—bell hooks's *Ain't I a Woman.*

hooks is black, heterosexual, and feminist. She embraces
feminism as an ideology but strongly condemns the practice that
has been developed by white women.

> Prior to slavery, patriarchal law decreed white women were lowly
> inferior beings, the subordinate group in society. The subjugation of
> black people allowed them to vacate their despised position and
> assume the role of superior. Consequently it can be argued that even
> though white men institutionalized slavery, white women were its most
> immediate beneficiaries.

hooks does not reveal much about her own personal history,
but the reader does assume she has experience in the black power
and civil rights movements because she analyzes the anti-feminism
and sexism of both. She also draws parallels between the sell-out of
black women by the early suffrage movement and then later by

second wave feminists. In all cases she posits insightful, eclectic, and creative psychological and historical explanations of these events.

hooks asserts that the higher standard of living for 19th-century whites was accompanied by a drift away from fundamentalist Christianity to a different perception of women. White women were both de-sexualized and elevated to "the nobler half of humanity." At the same time, the sexualization of the powerless was imposed on blacks.

> White women held black slave women responsible for rape because they had been socialized by 19th-century morality to regard women as sexual temptresses.

In a chapter entitled "The Imperialism of Patriarchy," hooks examines social and political relations between black women and white men.

> In a class I taught at USC, black female students discussed their anger and rage that white men approached them at jobs, in restaurants etc. . . . They also acknowledged that many aggressive sexual overtones . . . were casually dismissed or seen as positive when made by black men.

She claims that the black movement has not been honest about the sexual exploitation of women because it does "not want to acknowledge that racism is not the only oppressive force in our lives."

In her discussion of bonding between white and black men in the left, hooks emphasizes the idolization by white leftists of black power leaders, claiming that the whites

> responded favorably to the demands of the Black Power advocates with their emphasis on restoring Black men their lost manhood precisely because their sexism enabled them to identify.

There were a number of areas in hooks's book that could be challenged. For example, she criticizes the attempt of white women to draw analogies between their condition as women and the condition of black people. hooks says, "If they had been poor and oppressed they would not have been compelled to appropriate the Black experience." But what she does not recognize here is that these white women were appealing to white men to acknowledge the validity of their freedom fight. These men had, theoretically at least, accepted blacks as a category of oppressed people, an under-standing they often rejected in the consideration of women's lives. Even today in 1982, white women are forced to draw parallels with racism to assert the existence of their oppression.

Second, hooks's heterosexual bias is really inexcusable con-sidering how smart she is and how well read in feminism. She never mentions the existence of black lesbians, and she closets Audre Lorde as "a Black woman poet." In her discussion of misogyny among black nationalist men, she does not address its impact on lesbians' ability to function in that movement. Nor does she con-front the homophobia in the work of black male supremacists.

Although problematic in its heterosexism, this book raises fascinating questions about the ways we have historically approached the juncture of sex and race. As a book of historical theory it complements recent experiential writings by feminists of color and opens another road towards new imaginings for us all.

COMMENTARY

I followed bell hooks's exciting intellectual development for the next twelve years. She emerged into one of the most original and risk-taking of America's intellectuals. Her 1992 book *Black Looks* provided unique interpretations of the Anita Hill affair, the movie *Paris Is Burning,* and the otherwise exhausted subject of Madonna.

hooks worked really hard to overcome the silence in her first book about the lives of lesbians and gay men. Her book *Breaking Bread* (South End Press), an exciting conversation with her close friend Cornel West, is the only example I can think of where two heterosexual intellectuals seriously consider homo-phobia and gay life as part of public discourse. In fact, she was invited to be the keynote speaker, along with Angela Davis, at the Black Lesbian and Gay Leadership Conference in California in 1993.

Because her views are eclectic, unpredictable, and hold no sacred cows, hooks ended up being firmly placed within the postmodernist school of cross-cultural and multicultural examination more than in the feminist movement or black movement per se.

THE CONVENTION

Womanews,
September 1982

Two thousand anti-abortion activists came to Cherry Hill, New Jersey, in mid-July to attend the National Right-To-Life annual convention, "A New Birth of Freedom." They met at the Cherry Hill Hyatt to exchange literature, fetal slide shows, "I Love Life" comic books, and "precious feet" lapel pins "identical in size and shape to the feet of a ten-week-old unborn baby boy."

The rank and file of the Right-To-Life are women. Most have never been politically active before they became "pro-life"—usually through their churches. Each chapter still does its own fundraising through basketball-a-thons, swim-a-thons and selling candybars. As a result, they perceive themselves as financial underdogs in comparison with groups like Planned Parenthood who still receive federal funds.

But something is changing in the country's largest single-issue anti-abortion organization. It is becoming more radical. While many of the older members, particularly men, are happy with lobbying, writing letters to the editor and waiting for Reagan to make good on his promises, younger activists are taking a new approach. Heavily influenced by the anti-nuclear Catholic left, they are encouraging civil disobedience, picketing, and getting arrested—anything to disrupt abortion clinics.

Every Saturday, Anne Gilmartin, chairman of Life in First Essence (L.I.F.E.), from Woodside, New York, stands in front of abortion clinics with photos of aborted fetuses shouting to entering women that they are "killing their babies." Mrs. Gilmartin calls this "sidewalk counseling." Pro-abortion activists call this harassment.

"The thing is to go up to the abortion clinics outside and convince these women to save their babies," Mrs. Gilmartin said. "Every day we go there we save one or two babies."

Olga Fairfax of Methodists for Life, Maryland, also goes to the clinics.

"There are some weapons I have to have with me," she

explains. "First, a seven-by-five foot billboard of an aborted unborn child. It costs $22.95. I fold it up and carry it with me wherever I go. Then, I have a twelve-week-old fetus in a jar. I had it on my desk for four days but now—that poor poor precious unborn baby boy—now I keep him in my car. Also, the Lord gave me a free xerox machine. I prayed and I got one."

Although no one claims responsibility for the fire-bombing of clinics that has occurred over the last decade, right-to-lifers are interested in learning civil disobedience. Some groups, like Shield of Roses, run into clinics and scream the rosary. Others look to more secular methods. Many attended a workshop on "Non-Violent Direct Action" lead by Mary O'Malley of People Expressing Active Concern for Everyone (P.E.A.C.E.).

"Our most successful demonstrations have been focused on themes—Mother's Day, prayer vigils, days of rescue, funeral services. You can use hearses and infant caskets which are quite easily made at home. Bring pictures of dead babies and tapes of the little unborn baby's heartbeat," she said, encouraging her comrades to more militant activity. "In the words of Dr. Martin Luther King, 'We will wear them down by our capacity to suffer,'" she said.

Quoting King and Gandhi and making references to slavery and the Holocaust have become commonplace in the language of the new anti-abortion organizer. In fact, much of the recent anti-abortion rhetoric has taken on phrases and vocabularies usually associated with progressive causes. Jack Wilke, president of the National Right-to-Life Committee, a "pro-family" Catholic who opposes sex outside of marriage, refers to his organization as "an equal rights movement." "We are civil libertarian," Wilke says. "We are largely a movement of women. . . . If the ERA included the wording *all women born or unborn* we would support it."

Another example of the adoption of progressive strategies is the recent use of "speak-outs" as an organizing tool. Feminists have often spoken out publicly about their experiences with illegal abortion. This year the right-to-life responded with Women Exploited By Abortion (WEBA). Their members have had legal abortions and feel permanently damaged by the experience. Their spokesperson told the press, "We see abortion as the most exploitative thing that has happened to women in the entire history of mankind. Abortion is diametrically opposed to feminism."

Although WEBA does not support any feminist issues, new groups such as Feminists for Life and Pro-Lifers for Survival have started to make an impact on the left and the right. Pro-Lifers for

Survival is an anti-nuke, anti-abortion group that favors funded child care and supports gay rights. Their common denominator with the right-to-life movement is their opposition to abortion and their Catholicism. The activism of anti-abortion leftists such as Daniel Berrigan in the disarmament movement resulted in the elimination of abortion rights from the program of the enormous disarmament rally in New York last June. Speakers represented issues from gay rights to El Salvador but abortion was absent.

"The peace movement and the pro-life movement were made for each other," says Feminist For Life Julie Loesch. "If they don't work together they may both deserve to fail." These groups co-exist on the basis of single-issue unity with right-wing groups such as Phyllis Schlafly's Eagle Forum. Schlafly's ad in the convention souvenir book reminded her comrades that "The winning team of Eagles has a proven record of success in . . . defeating the women's lib plans to draft women and assign women to combat, establish federal child care for all children, and give lesbians the rights of wives." One woman told me that even though she is a devout Catholic, she would welcome the Ku Klux Klan or a homosexual group as long as they were "pro-life."

Slavery and the Holocaust were used as themes at this convention. Abortion was often compared to black slavery. Pro-abortion Pennsylvania assemblywoman Ruth Harper spoke against this imagery at a press conference sponsored by the Reproductive Rights National Network. "This comparison," said Harper, "is wrong and deeply offensive to women, particularly to black women. In fact, one of the most terrible aspects of slavery was its exploitation of black women through coerced childbearing. During slavery, black women were advertised for sale as breeders and their children were taken from them and sold. . . . If comparisons are to be made at all, the anti-abortion movement has much in common with the slave owners and nothing in common with the struggle for freedom."

The Holocaust was the primary metaphor at this year's convention. An Auschwitz survivor gave the keynote speech calling abortion the "American Holocaust."

"Abortion is far worse than what the Nazis did as far as I'm concerned," said Father Thomas Crusak, a Colombian priest. "The unborn are more helpless." Mrs. Becker of Pennsylvanians for Life told me that "It was the fact that abortion was legal in Germany in the 20s and 30s that made Nazism acceptable. It laid the groundwork for a Holocaust/abortion mentality."

But, according to Rabbi Rebecca Alpert, professor of Holocaust Studies in the New Jersey University system, this is not historically valid. "I find it difficult to believe that the so-called right-to-life movement has the audacity to compare the genocide of six million Jews and others in Nazi Germany with the current American policy supporting abortion as a woman's right of choice. The Nazis opposed abortion rights. Hitler considered abortion and contraception a "violation of motherhood" for those he deemed fit to live—members of the Aryan race. Hitler favored sterilization and death for those deemed unfit: Jews, Communists, homosexuals, Gypsies, the mentally and physically handicapped. As a woman and a Jew, I feel a personal obligation never to allow another Hitler to dictate what I should believe or how I should live my life."

As the anti-abortion forces enter what may be the final phase of activity before Congress votes on three bills that could severely limit or completely eliminate legal abortion, they are becoming more militant. When housewives from West Virginia are willing to be arrested twenty-two times a year to "save a baby's life," it seems obvious that the right-to-life is very committed and willing to take greater risks.

COMMENTARY

Looking back on my own reporting I can see with hindsight I was so taken with the kitsch of the anti-abortion accoutrement and iconography that I overlooked the more important fact that their speech is composed of incredible lies. Throughout, people used twisted logic, false facts, and manipulated vocabulary to construct a convoluted justification for subjugating women. By focusing on nonentities like "the unborn" and developing an entire rhetoric designed to establish them as a class of people needing rights, the anti-abortionists managed to engage in a complex and extended discussion without ever addressing the real issue at the core of their actions.

Through all this mumbo jumbo about slavery, the Holocaust, lapel pins, and appropriations of the language of liberation, no right-to-lifer who I met ever addressed why they thought that women should not be able to make their own decisions.

I also missed a hugely important historic transformation taking place right before my eyes—the introduction of massive civil disobedience techniques by Catholic leftists into the anti-abortion vocabulary. This enabled them to transform single acts of harassment into what we now know in the nineties as

Operation Rescue—a professional gang devoted to depriving rights at abortion clinics all across the nation.

Back in the early eighties, while we were busy trying to build the broadest possible multi-issue coalitions, the anti-abortion groups were busy doing the exact opposite. They were steadily constructing a single-issue movement, uniting a wide diversity of political perspectives around the unified goal of ending abortion rights in this country. These choices were more than purely strategic. The selection of tactics is not an arbitrary decision but rather one that must accurately reflect the values and experiences of the constituency in question.

Examining the strategic choices of the anti-abortion movement reveals clearly that single-issue organizing cannot work for people fighting for their freedom. For the people whose rights are being taken away, in this case women, single-issue organizing quickly becomes impossible because your reason for being politically active has to do with your actual life and how it is concretely lived. The forces united to deprive us of our rights were primarily ideological and theological. Since they were on the offensive, anti-abortionists had the luxury of acting systematically. In other words, if you need an abortion you need it right away. This involves a whole set of issues that must be addressed immediately from funding to your sense of expectation for your own life as a woman. This range of factors must be broached and dealt with within a matter of days. Furthermore, the stigma around abortion makes it an issue that many women want to avoid until the moment that it affects them personally, or they may want to forget about it after having accessed their own legal rights. For the people trying to stop abortion, a twenty-year plan to revoke Roe v Wade is a lot more efficient. Additionally, it is important to remember that the constituencies most brutally damaged by Reagan era policies came to this historical moment already in great need. Most of us had never had full citizenship. We didn't have basic civil rights and we had no economic power. Furthermore, we had no visibility in the dominant culture and could only organize and agitate from the underground. As a result, we began our fight from a place of deprivation. In short, those under attack had a much more complicated reality of defense than the ones attempting to deprive us of our rights.

Finally, the contradiction for women of the right wing organizing enthusiastically for their own enslavement became clear for me at the convention. The right enabled women to engage in the political arena, escape the private sphere, and travel and work in a community without stepping out of their prescribed female role. They could be activists, organizers, lobbyists and fundraisers but only in the capacity of "saving babies," the one thing that women are supposed to do.

Nyack and a History
of Strategies Disputed

Womanews,
March 1982

Eve Rosahn's arrest posed a big problem for the feminist movement. While her political development is part of our history, her
current analysis and choice of tactics are sharply contested. Most
agree that it is possible to support her resistance to a grand jury
subpoena without having to endorse her politics. Others say that
Eve's decisions are incompatible with feminist ethics. A letter in this
week's *Womanews* even went so far as to state, "I will not support a
newspaper that chooses to grant credibility to Eve Rosahn."

This essay concerns the aftermath of an aborted robbery of a
Brink's truck last October and the murder of a Brink's guard.
Arrested on site were a number of white and black activists including Kathy Boudin, a former Weatherman who had been
underground for a decade. Others, like Judy Clark, were members of the self-described "white anti-imperialist movement" as
represented by groups such as the John Brown Anti-Klan Committee, May 19th Communist Organization, and Moncada Library.
As a member of these same organizations, Rosahn was called to
testify against her colleagues by a grand jury and was then imprisoned as a result of her refusal to cooperate. All of these dramatic
events have been further distorted by the irresponsible coverage
offered by the left, liberal, and mainstream press. We have been
glutted with "I Remember Kathy Boudin" stories and *New York Post*
headlines screaming about "Cop Killers."

Meanwhile the grand jury has called a number of white and
black activists and then imprisoned them for contempt. They
include Fulanni Suni-Ali, a member of the Republic of New Afrika
(an organization founded in Detroit in 1968 that calls for the
formation of a black nation in five southern U.S. states) and Yasmin
Fula, a black legal worker. Suni-Ali, along with eleven children, was
originally arrested by soldiers, police, tanks, and a SWAT team
because police said she had been involved in the robbery.

Witnesses later placed her in New Orleans at the time and all charges have been dropped. Rosahn was then charged with having been a criminal accomplice at Nyack. Her car was used in the attempted robbery and police claimed that, under the name Judith Schneider, she rented the van used in the "expropriation."

At her grand jury hearing Rosahn was refused counsel and questioned in a closed courtroom where she was found in contempt for refusing to give hair and handwriting samples. As a result she spent nine weeks at Metropolitan Correctional Center, sometimes in twenty-three hour lock-up and solitary confinement. The government claimed she was a high security risk. Nonetheless she was released on only $23,000 bail and on January 28 all related charges were dropped.

The dismissal was based on the inability of the car rental clerk to positively identify her as well as handwriting samples indicating that she was not the one who filled out the car rental forms. When her attorney Maurice Sercaz argued that her right to counsel and to an open hearing had been violated, the DA responded that "If Eve Rosahn was called to testify in Yankee Stadium before 65,000 people the result would have been the same," revealing his understanding that she would never have given information under any circumstances.

Eve still faces two more grand jury subpoenas and charges resulting from a demonstration last fall against the South African rugby team's tour of the U.S. Along with Brink's defendant Judy Clark, she is also a plaintiff in Clark v U.S., a $100 million lawsuit charging the government with misconduct. It focuses on COINTELPRO's (a counter intelligence program) illegal wiretaps, infiltration, surveillance, and harassment of the black, anti-war and women's movements during the Nixon administration.

Rosahn calls herself part of "the anti-imperialist women's movement." She cites the root of the oppression of women, blacks, and third world peoples in U.S. imperialism. She believes that U.S. global power can be ended by supporting movements in third world countries trying to oust U.S.-controlled governments. She points to the Vietnamese War as an example of how a national movement can force the U.S. from power in their own country. She refers to the combination of communist forces in Vietnam and the anti-war movement at home as "a war on two fronts." Eve also believes that the liberation of women is related to women taking leadership roles in national liberation movements. Eve's organizations argue that the "role" of white people is to organize other whites to do support work under the leadership of specific black and third world movements.

Compared to feminism, these beliefs seem precise and deterministic. But it is not just in theory that feminists diverge. Since Eve is a lesbian and has had some presence in the women's community, the feminist press has been closely watching her case, although not always with support. *off our backs*, the Washington, D.C. feminist newspaper, accused her of "male ejaculatory politics." Perhaps a look into her own history will clarify the roots of some of these contrasting views.

As a Barnard freshman in 1967–68, Eve worked with SDS (Students for a Democratic Society) and a campus women's group. Later she joined the December Fourth Movement, a group named for the late Black Panther leaders Fred Hampton and Mark Clark who were killed in their beds by Chicago police. D4M did support work for the Black Panthers. In New York, the Panther 21 were in court for several months and acquitted after ninety minutes of jury deliberation. Sekou Odinga and Donald Weems, two current defendants in the Brink's case, were defendants in that trial as well. At the same time in New Haven, fourteen Panthers were also on trial. The prominence of Panther leader Erika Huggins (whose husband John had been killed by police) helped bring together the women of the white and black left. In November 1969, a large women's demonstration in New Haven linked support for Panther women to issues of women's liberation. Speakers included women from the Panthers, the Young Lords, and New Haven Women's Liberation.

On April 10, 1971, 2,500 women in face paint, wearing t-shirts saying "Madame Binh—Live Like Her" (Madame Binh was a Vietnamese leader) marched on the Pentagon. They called themselves "the anti-imperialist women's movement." They were different from the women's movement against the war (such as the Jeanette Rankin Brigade or Women Strike For Peace) because they supported a military victory for the National Liberation Front of South Vietnam instead of only calling for U.S. military withdrawal.

Eve says that the march on the Pentagon "targeted imperialism as an enemy in women's daily lives." Like other women interviewed, she vividly remembered an inspiring speech by a Vietnamese woman on the Pentagon's lawn. Another veteran of the march recalled that "to be a total revolutionary in the early

43

seventies you gave up your life. The model of complete commitment came from the third world."

Some participants helped found a women's school in pre-gentrification Park Slope, Brooklyn in 1973. It was a coalition of left feminists in which the current May 19th women were heavily involved. Many of them made a commitment to live and work in Park Slope where their community center, the Moncada Library, still functions. The breakdown of that coalition and the subsequent isolation of this small group from other sectors of the left has been attributed by others to their increasingly inaccessible level of rhetoric, cult-like group behavior, intimidation tactics towards those who disagreed, and political conflicts with feminists over the role of police in fighting rape and the politics of self-defense for women.

These conflicts continue to this day. For example, the Women's Committee Against Genocide, one of Eve's organizational affiliates, distributes leaflets at New York Women Against Rape's annual Take Back the Night March accusing the marchers of "working with killer cops."

Eve and many of the women in her group, although openly lesbian, are closeted politically. Unlike, for example DARE (Dykes Against Racism Everywhere) which has chosen to make a lesbian presence in the anti-racism movement, the Women's Committee has, it seems, decided to keep lesbianism out of their politics. I asked Eve why she chose to do support work for seemingly homophobic and male supremacist groups instead of, for example, third world lesbians.

"My struggle with imperialism," she said, "is stronger than any contradiction over lesbian liberation."

One woman active in the 1971 Pentagon march offered this perspective.

"It was hard for women to participate in SDS. The men ran the movement and there was no place for lesbians. The fact that they [Eve and her colleagues] came out together contributed to them never going their separate ways."

This woman tried to start a defense committee after Nyack but the old radicals she contacted wanted no part of it. "Even those active in D4M didn't want to have anything to do with them. But when we look back we will see that the Weathermen were the first underground revolutionary group that survived."

In *off our backs* Janis Kelly accused the Nyack defendants of endangering the women's community by taking violent actions which made the movement vulnerable to grand jury investigation. She also accused them of implicating feminists by taking shelter in women's communities under aliases when underground. In response, women from the DC Feminist Alliance wrote

> It is essential not to accept the accusation that activists cause repression. We must remember that there is no action or belief which warrants the suspension of constitutional rights.

In the same issue Joan Gibbs and Linda Backiel of the Grand Jury Project in New York City wrote

> Neither will we survive by accepting the government's invitation to blame its opposition for either terror or repression.

COMMENTARY

The Brinks robbery and murders sparked a broad investigation culminating in sentences of seventy-five years to life for a significant portion of the leadership of May 19th and their various organizational affiliates. Some of the women were placed in a sensory deprivation unit in Lexington, Kentucky expressly constructed for political prisoners. Judy Clark and Kathy Boudin continued their activist work inside Bedford Hills women's prison, founding a number of organizations and programs including ACE, an advocacy group for women with AIDS. One of ACT UP's most tireless and effective organizers, the late Katrina Haslip, was a former prostitute and drug addict who was politicized by ACE inside Bedford Hills .

May 19th and its various affiliates, including The Prairie Fire Organizing Committee, dropped out of sight for a while. Some of its members worked inside ACT UP, not in their traditional oppositional pose, but as independent, constructive participants. In 1990 they re-emerged as QUISP (Queers United in Support of Political Prisoners), gay and lesbian associates of the former May 19th plus people on their periphery doing support work for the same set of political prisoners (straight and gay) that had dominated their political activities for the previous twenty-five years.

Eve Rosahn went to law school and remained politically active. In 1993 she published a retrospective article in the journal of Movement Research (an arts organization). Speaking quite candidly Rosahn wrote

> We were so focused on refuting the separatist view that being a lesbian was somehow inherently revolutionary that we didn't really explore how

lesbianism was subversive of mainstream culture and sexuality. We usually collapsed the category lesbian into that of women, without investigating the difference among us. And in our desire to build relationships with organizations of people of color, we often let homophobia go unchallenged. Most seriously we didn't see the obvious need to build ties with lesbians of color. . . . We were trapped by our own rigidity and our own conflicts.

In 1993, another former sixties radical emerged with very different repercussions. Katherine Ann Power had gone underground in 1980 with her Brandeis roommate Susan Saxe after they participated in a bank robbery in which a policeman was killed. Neither of the women was ever accused of having actually murdered the policeman but as accomplices they were legally responsible. Powers and Saxe had spent a number of years in lesbian communities in New Haven and Kentucky and the FBI search had directly targeted those people. Lesbians from New Haven actually went to jail in defiance of court subpoenas rather than testify against Saxe and Powers. And the New York City lesbian community circulated leaflets "What To Do When the Man Comes To Your Door" to prepare women for FBI activity.

When Saxe was caught she made no effort to hide her lesbianism. In fact, she made an enormously powerful and influential speech when sentenced stating that "the love between my sisters is stronger than any power the state can muster. I intend to fight on as a lesbian, and an Amazon." She served eight years in prison during which time she organized visitation programs for incarcerated mothers and computer-training programs for women inmates.

But in 1993, when Powers voluntarily turned herself in to the police, the media went out of its way to obscure the lesbian chapter of her history. Her motherhood, marriage, and entrepreneurial abilities were emphasized. While *Newsweek* made blithe references to her time in "women's communes," the jailings, contempt charges, and FBI investigations into lesbian communities went entirely unmentioned.

THE PRO-FAMILY LEFT

Womanews,
May 1982

For the right and the left both, the question was not women's reproductive freedom or individual right to determine their own lives, but
rather the central function of their reproductive work as bearers and
socializers of children and nurturers of the family unit.

—Atina Grossman, on the 1930 German abortion rights
movement in *New German Critique*

In the August 30, 1978 edition of *In These Times* (a democratic
socialist newsweekly from Chicago), former new leftist Michael
Lerner wrote an article called "Sanctify the Family Since New Forms
Prove Useless." He suggested that the critique of the family by
feminism and the gay liberation movement was "misguided and
personally destructive." He knows this because his friends tried
to live communally and failed. Now that they've "grown up" he
realizes the importance of the family. Lerner suggests that a pro-
family politics for the left would be strategically sound because it
would be "an approach to the family that actually speaks to the real
daily lives of people who can be our allies if we don't automatically
write them off as enemies." He proposes that "socialist feminists
and other progressives should campaign in defense of the family."
Finally he asks, "What in the program of the right speaks to needs
that are legitimate and reasonable?"

In 1981 Lerner proposed a "Family Bill of Rights" and "National
Family Day" announcing the formation of his new organization,
Friends of the Family. According to Kate Ellis, a professor at Rutgers,
"The point of the feminist critique of the family was not to tell
those who had husbands or wives or children or aunts or
grandparents that they were ipso facto reactionary. It was to investigate the fissure between the family as an ideal and the family as a
lived experience and to deal with the sense of loss created by the
fissure by deconstructing and analyzing the ideal."

Lerner's question "what is legitimate and reasonable" about the right got answered in February 1982 by John Judis, the editor of *In These Times*. Judis, like Lerner, invoked the mythical family where rape, child abuse, and violence against women barely exist—where nurturing for all is the norm instead of the occasional exception. He wrote, "The family provides a home and security for its members, introducing initial education for infants and children and providing a protected space for love and sex." Later in the article he exposes what many of us expected all along from the left pro-family movement—their base anti-feminism and hostility towards the principles of gay liberation. Judis writes, "Society does not have the same responsibility towards homosexuality as it does toward the child-bearing family." Not only is he saying that homosexuals don't have children—but by using the words "child-bearing family" (which means women, since men are never identified as child-bearers) he is putting out a pro-natalist politics. Judis is thereby maintaining that the left's first commitment should be to heterosexuals who have children within the confines of the conventional family. How does this differ, really from the right wing's Family Protection Act?

In the March 27 issue of *Gay Community News*, Scott Tucker wrote that "According to Lerner people are mistaken to think gays are a cause of family insecurity or of relationships being less stable today. . . . In this case, the left is wrong and the right is right. Gay liberation aims to make all people freer to be gay. Gay people are blatant contradictions to the patriarchal order of things; the right understands this. That's why it wages war against us."

COMMENTARY

By 1982 the debate about sex, sexuality, and the family was really heating up. Patriarchal socialists like Michael Lerner were proclaiming ideologies that would insure male heterosexual control, but justifying them in the guise of coming up with a strategy that could beat the right. What is shockingly absent from his discourse is any kind of empathy or compassionate understanding of the real effects of oppression on the lives of women and homosexuals. This is a clear example of a group of people developing and choosing a strategy without regard for its impact on people's real lives, which is only possible when the theorists have nothing really personal at stake. Gay life became expendable in Lerner's worldview because gay people were not fully human to him. They were, as for the right, only an ideological football. It wasn't until the 1992 Republican convention, a decade later, that even the most mainstream Republicans gleefully spouted a pro-family line as the mainstay of George Bush's failed re-election campaign.

Scott Tucker's response in *Gay Community News* also represents the end of an era. Tucker, one of only two men in the Reproductive Rights National Network and an active socialist, was one of the first to spot and speak up against the liberal version of the family values campaign. He was still willing in 1982 to dialogue with the left, albeit on the pages of a gay publication that straight leftists probably never knew existed. *Gay Community News* from Boston was the first and only truly co-gender gay publication. It was also the only overtly socialist gay newspaper with any credibility. From the ranks of its staff emerged some of the country's most influential gay and lesbian leaders like Urvashi Vaid, Sue Hyde, Eric Rofes, Richard Burns, cultural critic Michael Bronski, AIDS theorist Cindy Patton, etc. Soon after this piece appeared, Scott Tucker got completely disgusted with the left and took time off to become International Mister Leather. He then re-emerged some years later as an AIDS activist and a contributor to *Z Magazine*, a publication of the democratic socialist left, edited by Diedre English.

Michael Lerner went on to become the editor of *Tikkun Magazine*, a progressive Jewish quarterly. In their pages he articulated his theory of the politics of meaning, a rather vague discourse claiming that Americans had no meaning in their lives. He was very influential for Hillary Clinton, who quoted him in her public speeches.

RIDING THE GO-GO BUS HOME
AN INTERVIEW WITH DIANE TORR

Womanews,
November 1982

I first met Diane Torr when I walked into a cafe about a year and a half ago with a copy of Andrea Dworkin's *Pornography: Men Possessing Women* under my arm. She came up to me and said she was a go-go dancer in New Jersey. There, between sets, she would go into the bathroom and read Andrea Dworkin books. Since then we've had a series of discussions about the sex industry and feminism. Here we address the logistics of go-go dancing, the vulnerability of women in the sex industry, and the relationships between women in and out of the business.

DIANE   I first got into go-go dancing when a friend told me she could make fifteen dollars an hour. I started in Passaic and Patterson, New Jersey. At first I didn't really give them what they wanted because I didn't understand very well what was required of me. But gradually I learned from watching the other girls.

SARAH   *Why did you stick it out?*

DIANE   Money. The amount of money that you can make in a go-go club is about ten to fifteen dollars an hour for a five hour shift, and you can get tips on top of that. So, if you work nine to two, you can come home with a hundred and twenty dollars. But in some clubs, being a good dancer means that you're doing something more than just dancing. Like, New Jersey is not a topless state, so you flash your breasts or show your pubic hair.

SARAH   *How do you get your tips?*

DIANE   Men give tips for all kinds of reasons. Sometimes they're just feeling generous. Sometimes they're drunk. Sometimes you just remind them of somebody. Sometimes they feel sorry for you or you really do turn them on. What really makes tips is giving the men something that's not allowed, like walking the bar and letting them touch you.

SARAH   *How do you choose your costumes?*

DIANE   Well, you have to assess your body and see what your best lines are. After all, it is your commodity. You find out what it is that you have to accentuate and what it is that you have to cover up. If you don't take these things seriously you are ignoring what is necessary to make a living in this trade. If you have large hips, which a lot of men like, you wear a G-string that accentuates the curviness.

SARAH   *How do the women relate to each other?*

DIANE   Oftentimes we catch the same bus home—the go-go bus it's called. It leaves Patterson, New Jersey at three in the morning, and then it picks girls up at Passaic and Secaucus. On that bus people are often in high spirits and just talk. There's a lot of exchange about different clubs and how they're treating girls, which club has been raided recently, which club owners should be avoided. For instance, there's one bar in Passaic called Stagecoach Lucy's, and they have a habit of deducting money from your night's wages if you have a run in your stockings. You have no redress. What can you do short of producing a gun and saying "Give me my money"?

SARAH   *Do many women carry guns?*

DIANE   Some. If you perform in a place which is really isolated, you really have no protection. It is assumed that because you're doing this kind of work that you are up for grabs. The idea is that women working in the skin trade are somehow less than anybody else. How many times do you see a prostitute interviewed on television to find out what she thinks of Ed Koch's new development policy?

SARAH   *How do you feel about your customers?*

DIANE   Men come for all different reasons. Sometimes you

find yourself acting like a mother or a psychiatrist. Then there are other guys who try to get your phone number. Quite a surprising number are Vietnam veterans who want to describe their experiences to me. Some have said that they never share these experiences with anyone else.

SARAH   *Do they have a fantasy that you are a fallen woman?*

DIANE   Yeah—I had one man like that. He's a psychologist. He offered me a job as a secretary to get me out of the business.

SARAH   *But not at fifteen dollars an hour?*

DIANE   No (laughs).

SARAH   *Last year you performed for an audience in New York that was mostly lesbian. What was that like?*

DIANE   I was very curious as to how women would respond to a performance that is mostly done for men. I was also interested in presenting a documentary of the dancers' backgrounds so that the reality of their lives would accompany the illusion. Also, some of the dancers are really good, and it is a shame that they should only be seen by men and under such awful conditions. Well, some women responded just like men, cat-calling and giving us tips. Some women were really turned on. But there was a sort of controversy. I remember reading a review in *Womanews* last year in which the author said that she could see no reconciliation between striptease and feminism. I would say to her that the common ground is the dollar bill. You can't have pure morality without a trust fund. Also, you have to remember that a lot of women who were in women's studies in 1972 could be go-go dancers in 1982 because of economics.

SARAH   *What ideas do you have about organizing women in the sex industry?*

DIANE   If this industry came above ground there would be advantages and disadvantages. For example, now we get paid in cash with no deductions. But clubs can just fuck you over and there's nothing we can do about it. The fact that we're not unionized makes it hard to do things like boycotting bars. I think that we're kept from organizing, or the idea that organizing is viable, by the idea of being shameful people doing shameful work.

COMMENTARY

Before the explosion of the feminist porn wars, a go-go dancer could read Andrea Dworkin in her dressing room and get something out of it. Soon after this interview the lines of rhetoric would be so tightly drawn that such an interest would be unthinkable. This discussion took place right on the threshold of dramatic change in the discourse on sex. Diane recounts the first New York introduction of go-go dancers in a public lesbian context and reports on the mixture of acceptance and hostility. But by eight years later, go-go dancers would become staples at lesbian bars like The Clit Club in New York City and earlier at The Baybrick Inn in San Francisco. Of course the experiences of go-go dancers in the dominant culture hasn't changed at all.

Torr had her first success as a performance artist with a piece called "*Avant-Garde à Go-Go*" when she brought her act from the Mafia bars of New Jersey to the art bars of New York's East Village, perhaps appealing to the same prurient interest but receiving a very different kind of appreciation. She toured her show in Europe, encountering bottle-throwing audiences in England and Amsterdam, audiences who thought she was a transsexual until she had a baby.

An early eighties performance of hers, "*Boys Will Be Girls Will Be Queens,*" was one of the first performance art pieces to explore female-to-male gender change. Years later, when fashion caught up with her discourse, Torr again made a name for herself holding "Drag King" workshops in which women were taught how to pass as men. After an all-day class in disguise and movement, the new graduates would go on a field trip to a go-go bar and attempt to pass as men. She appears in a video "*Sluts and Goddesses*" by Maria Beatty and remains a dancer, performer, and activist with PONY (Prostitutes of New York).

Recently I read a review in the *New York Times* by Stephen Holden of a performance by Phranc, a folksinger, in which she dresses like and sings songs by Neil Diamond. Holden referred to Phranc's male drag as the "cutting edge" of performance art. It had been almost fifteen years since Torr brought self-conscious female cross-dressing out of the drag clubs and go-go bars and into performance art. But it is in that gap between invention and *New York Times* commodification where credit often is denied the originator.

WHO WANTS TO DRIVE BLUES OUT OF BUSINESS?

Womanews,
November 1982

by Sarah Schulman and Peg Byron

Ninth Avenue from 33rd Street to 49th Street belongs to the men and women who work the streets. Recently Mayor Koch and real estate developers like Manhattan Plaza have started "cleaning up" Times Square. This process includes pushing the prostitutes, drag queens, and transsexual hustlers out of the neighborhood.

On Monday, September 27, a black drag queen got in a fight with a police officer from Midtown South—19th Precinct. On Wednesday the police came to Blues to get even.

Blues, at 264 West 43rd Street, is a bar frequented by black gay men. Many hustlers and drag queens hang out there. As a result, Blues is constantly being hassled. A week before the raid, officials of the State Liquor Authority came to investigate "complaints." This is the same agency that took away the liquor licenses from the Dutchess and Déjà Vu (two lesbian bars) for discrimination against men. A few days before the Blues raid, police came in looking for "a man with a gun." They lined up all the patrons against the wall and searched them without a warrant. But, by Wednesday, the police were not just threatening. The bar was completely wrecked. Patrons were attacked with nightsticks, kicked, and in one case a disabled man was beaten with his own crutches. Men and women in the bar were sent to the hospital. The police also robbed the customers of jewelry and money and cleaned out the cash register. Hours after the raid, one of the officers involved in the brutality returned as the official officer sent to file a report on the event.

According to Blues manager Lew Oliver, the officer mockingly asked, "Did you call me?"

"You're the last one I'd call," Oliver replied.

The victims of the police assault contacted Arthur Bell, gay columnist for the *Village Voice* and front page stories appeared in

both the *Voice* and the *New York Native,* New York's weekly gay paper.
Then, on Friday, October 8, the same police officers returned to
Blues, this time with guns drawn. They kicked one patron in the
groin and boasted about making the *Voice* headlines.

According to Oliver, the police are attempting to drive Blues
out of business by scaring away customers. On the day of this
interview a policeman had been standing outside the bar for three
hours intimidating customers. "The best support the gay community can give to this bar is to come in, buy one drink and say you're
not afraid," Oliver said.

Who wants to drive Blues out of business? In a general climate
of more anti-gay, racist and antisemitic street violence, these tactics
occur with frightening frequency. Gentrification may also play a role
in this case. Although no one would be quoted, many people
interviewed speculated that the *New York Times,* whose offices are
across the street from the bar, may have a role in the harassment.
Two *Times* employees confirmed that Blues is considered "a place to
avoid" by the staff. Additionally, a number of the policemen
working in that precinct also work security for the *Times* as a
second job. The *Times* has not reported on the incident.

The pressure may also be coming from City Hall and its efforts
to build suburban-like shopping malls and luxury housing in the
Times Square area. It may also explain the willingness of borough
president Andrew Stein to come out against the raid. Stein is a
likely candidate to oppose Koch in the next mayoral primary.

COMMENTARY

In many ways this event represents the end of an era. It was one of the last
overt bar raids in New York City before AIDS became the excuse to close down
or harass gay clubs. It also came at the height of the gentrification of the city.
After an entire generation of white flight, middle-class whites from the suburbs
were returning to live in the central city, requiring massive displacement of poor
tenants as condo-conversion and "redevelopment" for the wealthy became
epidemic. It came two years into Reagan's slashing of federal funds for the city,
which, combined with Mayor Koch's massive tax breaks for the rich, made
gentrification one of the primary factors in the explosion of homelessness that
New York experienced in the eighties.

One of the effects of gentrification was to homogenize certain blocks or
neighborhoods as rents skyrocketed out of control. This split the gay community

according to race, class, and gender lines as some white gay men with good incomes became pioneers of gentrification in previously mixed or poor neighborhoods, paving the way for white heterosexuals. Other gay men and lesbians, both white and people of color, who did not have economic power, were often the victims of displacement and the police/landlord harassment that accompanied it.

These events had a strong impact on the gay and lesbian movement because demonstrations, held in reaction to the raid on Blues, turned out a multiracial, mixed-gender response. Inter-racial demonstrations were held from time to time in reaction to racism *in* the gay and lesbian bars. Often black or Latino patrons would be asked for multiple pieces of identification, or in other ways excluded from entry while white patrons were welcomed. After the events at Blues catalyzed a particular, mixe, segment of the community, demonstrations were held against exclusionary admission policies at such clubs as Bacall's, Shescape, and the Ice Palace. Ironically, the exclusion of women from gay men's bars and large dance clubs like the Saint was never a topic for discussion.

Just as a sidebar, although this article was co-written with Peg Byron, her name appeared on the byline as "Molly Malone" because she had just that week been kicked out of *Womanews* for printing pro-S/M material in the newspaper. The official charge was that she didn't take out the garbage regularly. Her supporters called in Joan Nestle of the Lesbian Herstory Archives (one of the community's most respected leaders) to arbitrate and the real charges quickly surfaced. Peg quickly took a job at the *Native*. The clamping down on difference and rigidity around sexuality issues was at its height in feminist circles at this time and forced many women into the world of gay men, which in some ways was the first coming together of the sexes, right on the brink of the explosion of AIDS.

FIFTEEN HOUR CIRCUS
ENDS IN ARRESTS

Womanews,
April 1983

For the thirteenth time, a New York City Gay Rights Bill that would have guaranteed equal protection in housing, jobs, and public accommodation, went down to crushing defeat at the hands of the City Council General Welfare Committee.

Over two hundred speakers testified for fifteen hours as speeches ranged from the boring to the bizarre. All the anti-gay speakers, except for one, represented religious organizations. The Neighborhood Church, the Catholic Church, Knights of Columbus, the Jewish Anti-Abortion League and Catholic War Veterans were among those who called for a range of punishment from sustained illegality to execution. They claimed that gay oppression does not exist, prayed in English and Hebrew and yelled "Praise the Lord."

Support came from gay organizations and from city officials. The National Organization for Women and the Reproductive Rights National Network were the only mixed women's organizations to speak in favor of the bill. They were joined by the United Brotherhood of Teamsters and the Italian-American Organization among other community groups.

The debate frequently became a battle between orthodox anti-gay groups and gay Jews. The visible presence of religious Jews in beards and long coats also provoked a significant amount of anti-Semitism from gay activists. Rabbi William Handler of the Union of Orthodox Rabbis opened the hearing by declaring that "just as we will never accept a murderers' rights bill, we will never accept a gay rights bill." Joseph Papp, artistic director of the Public Theater, testified for the bill saying, "It pains me to see my colleagues in Judaism taking the most backward, repressive positions." In response, an orthodox man yelled out, "You don't eat kosher." One gay Vietnam vet kept yelling, "Go back to Williamsburg." He told me that "it is the Jewish people of New York State who are keeping this bill from being passed." When one Jewish speaker accused gays of murdering children, bestiality, and spreading disease, a prominent moderate gay figure said, "Go back to Israel," to which a member of the Gay Synagogue replied, "Only if you go to Sicily first."

Penny Dachinger, a spokesperson for Congregation Beth Simchat Torah (the Gay Synagogue) told how a Maryland board of rabbis had pronounced her "Jewishly dead" for having contributed to *Nice Jewish Girls: A Lesbian Anthology.* When she said, "Being declared dead is the price I pay for being an out Jewish lesbian," the hall was filled with jeers of "abomination" and "blasphemy." When Jesse Friedman, National Coordinator of the Jewish Moral Committee of the Moral Majority, got up to speak, the audience turned their backs and chanted "Shanda. Shanda." (Yiddish for shame.)

Gay people gave hours of testimony about their experiences with job, housing, and public accommodation discrimination, ridicule, physical and sexual violence, aversion therapy, terror, electric shock therapy, incarceration, psychiatric drugs and other forms of torture, yet the opposition repeatedly insisted that gay oppression does not exist. They also portrayed homosexuals as primarily concerned with cross-generational sex, promiscuity, sado-masochism, orgies, and public sex. They described these acts in vivid detail that made it all sound very appealing to the audience. By the end of the hearing when a speaker claimed, "Gays want to destroy the family, dress in women's clothes and take over our cities," the punch-drunk gay spectators would cheer in agreement.

A lot of emphasis was put on the issue of man/boy love. When Genevieve Klein, a former school teacher, spoke out against gay teachers as "deviates and perverts," Councilwoman Miriam Fried-lander (from the Lower East Side) asked if she had ever spoken out against male heterosexuals teaching in the schools since they are known to molest children. Klein replied that she knew of no sexual attacks on young girls and that homosexuals spread disease. Friedlander asked her if she was willing to deprive heterosexuals of housing because they spread herpes.

Dov Lerner of Jews for a Moral America claimed that gays supported the bill so they could go on the streets and procure boys. When informed that gay rights legislation had passed in forty cities and towns and one state, Wisconsin, without this result, Lerner said, "If gays want rights, let them go to Wisconsin."

The much beloved Parents of Gays was also present. Anne Marie Harris, the mother of two gay children said, "As a mother, I taught my children to love others and treat them fairly. To be violated and degraded as a human being is something I did not foresee in the lives of my children." Maxine Wolfe, of Women for Women, speaking as a lesbian mother and professor at the City

University Graduate School said, "I hope that my daughters will grow up and be able to choose to be lesbians, and I'm glad I can be a lesbian so they can see this as a possibility for their lives." Wolfe said that "depriving your children of the right to be gay is child abuse." Longtime activist Joyce Hunter called for protection for "the thousands of gay and lesbian children."

After midnight the vote was taken as the audience held up pink triangles and chanted "Justice. Justice." Members of Women's Pentagon Action and Women for Women, joined by other lesbians and gay men unfurling a banner, "We Won't Go Away: Lesbian Liberation Now," refused to leave the chamber. Twenty-four men and women were arrested and charged with trespassing.

These hearings were really hard to believe, not only because of the power of sexual repression in this city—but also because of how gay oppression generates strange bedfellows. Most of the speakers represented the more conservative elements of the gay community. Religious groups, gay businessmen, gay professionals, and many gay Democrats spoke. Their general appeal was for "equality through law." Still, there were radical lesbians and gay men who supported the bill. "This is a stepping stone towards freedom to be who I am," said gay activist Ellen Turner. "There are many people supporting the bill who are not for total freedom and really believe that we live in a working democracy and will abide by the law." At one point in the proceedings, Turner and Craig Rodwell, owner of the Oscar Wilde Memorial Bookshop, broke into a chorus of "There's No Business Like Show Business." That about said it.

COMMENTARY

For thirteen years gay people in the Democratic party had attempted to pass a basic gay rights bill through the primary strategy of behind-the-scenes negotiating, support for specific candidates, and building strength within the party. Street organizing and direct actions were rarely used and generally not encouraged. But, by 1983, the "protest from below" was becoming impossible to control and this, combined with increasing AIDS hysteria finally forced the passage in 1986.

As evidenced by the short list of non-gay supporters, gay men and lesbians fought this, and most other battles, alone. Unfortunately not much has changed in this department since 1983. Ironically, one of our only early supporters, Miriam Friedlander, was defeated by a gay, pro-gentrification candidate, Antonio Pagan, who ended up using his seat on the City Council to oppose housing for homeless people with AIDS in his district.

The most significant element of the civil rights debate that is still with us is the power of the religious right in maintaining Jim Crow legal conditions for lesbians and gay men. Once these events are placed clearly in the context of decades-long battles between gays and organized religion, it becomes obvious why gay people have had such a sense of focus and purpose when it comes to standing up to the intimidation tactics of the Church.

Ten years later, in 1993, the Catholic Church led a vicious campaign against a small group of gay and lesbian Irish immigrants who wanted to march in the Saint Patrick's Day Parade. At first the Irish Lesbian and Gay Organization's petition was rejected by the parade's organizers, the Ancient Order of Hibernians. But due, in part, to the support of Mayor David Dinkins, ILGO was permitted to march without a banner and did so with Dinkins's accompaniment. The Mayor and ILGO were pelted with beer cans and garbage and had anti-gay and racial abuse hurled at them by parade watchers.

The following year ILGO was excluded from the parade because they refused to march without their banner. Dinkins was hospitalized during that period and out of the proceedings, so ILGO was resigned to a penned-in area on Fifth Avenue, where, trapped and angry, they watched the exclusionary parade pass them by. By 1993, the third year of battle, the Catholic Church came out so strongly against them that Cardinal O'Connor told Catholics not to march at all if ILGO were to be included by court order. After a series of dramatic losses to the Church by the mayor's office, including the failure of the proposed multicultural school curriculum and the collapse of AIDS prevention in the schools, Dinkins capitulated completely to the Church and the city barred ILGO from marching in the parade.

At this point ILGO—a group led by Ann MaGuire and Marie Honan, both office workers, and Paul O'Dwyer, an attorney—had the mayor, the Catholic Church, and the New York City Police Department standing firmly against their right to march. Not one organization in the straight Irish community would publicly stand up for them, giving the excuse that support of gays and lesbians would hurt U.S. private donations to the cause of Northern Ireland. Finally Bernadette Devlin McAlisky sent a statement of support from Ireland, but even this dramatic step provoked no response from Irish American groups. Completely abandoned and alone, ILGO went to the gay and lesbian community for support in building a counterdemonstration. Then, the city capitulated even further to the Church by issuing a court order forbidding a demonstration—an act of repression almost never seen in New York City politics. It had been used a few years earlier against a black demonstration led by Reverend Al Sharpton for which he served jail time, but was exceedingly rare.

ILGO was put under intense political pressure. Both Mayor Dinkins and Governor Cuomo went so far in their intimidation tactics as to actually call ILGO organizers personally at home asking for the counterdemonstration to be canceled. Straight and gay mayoral aides and gay men with ties to the Democratic Party looking for political appointments, also personally pressured ILGO, claiming that their counterdemonstration would cause the defeat of Dinkins's re-election bid, the failure to pass a bias crime bill and the collapse of domestic partnership rights. ILGO members came under intense scrutiny from the press, appearing on *Sixty Minutes,* in the *New Yorker* and a full profile in the *New York Times,* all this being coordinated from Marie Honan's secretarial job.

The gay and lesbian community proved to be overwhelmingly supportive of ILGO. Fifteen hundred people showed up on Saint Patrick's Day to violate a court order and illegally counterdemonstrate on ILGO's behalf. Over two hundred were arrested including Councilman Tom Duane, Pulitzer Prize winning playwright Tony Kushner, and even Dinkins's own deputy liaison to the gay and lesbian community, Jan Carl Park. Straight politicians, on the other hand, were noticeably absent. Even longterm supporters of our community like Manhattan Borough President Ruth Messinger and Comptroller Liz Holtzman, did not show up to support us.

Ironically, a small group of gay people calling themselves the "C.D. Rebels" opposed ILGO. Positioning themselves as "more radical," the C.D. Rebels wanted ILGO to have a direct confrontation with the parade, a strategy that ILGO rejected for fear of provoking violence and because their goal was to be included in the parade—not cause a riot. During the whole pre-demonstration planning period, the Rebels held secret meetings, harassed ILGO members, and created even more pressure on the gay Irish organizers. When the day of the demo came, the Rebels produced a very tepid alternative action. First they tried to run into the street ahead of ILGO, to get in the front of the parade. Then, as two hundred ILGO supporters were being arrested, they ran up ahead, marched for four blocks with their banner and were arrested too.

Of course, in the history of every political movement, there are always people who make careers out of dividing and opposing other movement groups. It provides a comfortable closet. While ILGO was directly confronting the state, the "Rebels" could comfortably oppose only ILGO. This situation arises over and over again at pivotal moments in the development of political opposition, and it is never clear as to whether the perpetrators are just destructive, self-oppressed individuals, or professional provocateurs, or a combination of both. But what was also at stake in this case was a larger political question. Namely—when gay people make a stand within their own hostile ethnic, religious, or racial community, do they have the right to determine their own positioning and strategy? I believe that they do. And this right must be clearly asserted to assure all gay people a place of self-determination within the larger gay community.

The City was adamant about taking all of us to trial. Some defendants pleaded guilty in exchange for one day of community service cleaning parks, but others felt that they had been excluded from the parade only because they were gay and lesbian and so were determined to fight the case until the end. In pre-trial hearings the ILGO lawyers argued that the City's ban on counterdemonstrations was unconstitutional. The lawyer for the C.D. Rebels argued, among other points, that they should not be charged with criminal contempt because they were not ILGO—a morally questionable defense.

The City pursued us with unusual vehemence, focusing particularly on the favorable media presentation of Ann MaGuire and citing the content of her press interviews even though she was only one of 190 ILGO defendants. At the end of the pre-trial hearing, ILGO lost on all counts, with the court ruling that even if the order was unconstitutional, ILGO was required to obey it until it could be set aside at a later date. As for the C.D. Rebels, the City never even acknowledged their existence. Since all but four of them were not charged with contempt, they were exempted from the trial, and so the case of the People of New York v Ann MaGuire plus proceeded to jury selection.

However, ILGO continued to fight the case politically. One of the defendants, Tony Kushner, began to organize a big-name fundraising/publicity benefit. A defendants' subcommittee began a pressure campaign against Mayor Dinkins, who desperately needed the gay/lesbian vote in the approaching mayoral election. After a number of pickets aimed at Dinkins and a postcard-writing campaign, on November 1 all charges against ILGO were officially dropped. Just in time to begin organizing for the next Saint Patrick's Day Parade.

Looking at this event in its historical context, it seems clear that ILGO, this small collection of working immigrants, were the only body in New York City willing to stand up to the power of the Catholic Church. And the larger gay and lesbian movement was the only community with the guts to support them.

By the way, this account of the 1983 gay rights bill hearing was the first time that I had ever acknowledged AIDS in my reporting. It was the first time that I had seen AIDS used as an excuse to deny people basic civil rights. But, in the spring of 1983, for me, it was still a subplot, not even one mentioned by name.

On the following October 30th, Bernadette Devlin came to New York and appeared on a panel at New York University Law School with Ann MaGuire, Maxine Wolfe, Derrick Bell, and Sean Macklin—an Irish revolutionary living in exile in New York. Devlin took a strong public stand in support of ILGO and stated firmly that progressive Irish people had a responsibility to march with ILGO the following Saint Patrick's Day. Dinkins had lost the mayoralty by a slim margin and Giuliani was a known enemy of Irish Nationalists. The conditions for a broad coalition in support of Irish lesbians and gays seemed better than ever. But looking at this event in its historical context . . .

Gay books back in school

New York Native,
August 1983

Gay and lesbian books have been returned to the shelves of a New York City public school by order of the Board of Education. The books were removed in response to an anti-gay campaign that coincided with the City Council hearings on the gay rights bill last February.

Early this year, Carol Bloom—a tenured teacher and dean of girls at Brandeis High School on the Upper West Side—raised $125 from private donations to purchase gay and lesbian materials for the school library. Titles including *Our Right To Love, Reflections of a Rock Lobster,* and *Gay American History* were finally accepted after a long review process. Bloom, who is a lesbian, wrote an article for the Gay Teachers' Association newsletter explaining how personnel in other schools could make gay literature available to their students.

Two weeks before hearings on the gay rights bill, the *New York Tribune,* which is owned and operated by Sun Myung Moon's Unification Church, ran an article about Bloom's piece. The story was then picked up by the *New York Post* whose headline screamed "High School Given Homosexual Books by Lesbian Dean."

Betty Wein, the reporter who wrote the initial story for the *Tribune,* told the *Native* that she is a resident of the Village but added, "I probably differ with the gay community in that they should be prepared for negative coverage. That's what I call equal rights."

The sudden burst of publicity created a certain amount of tension at Brandeis High. "My principal was getting phone calls and letters and was rattled by all the attention, even though most of the response was pro," Bloom recalled.

The principal, Murray Cohen, proceeded to remove the books from the library for "review." Louise Latty, superintendent of schools for the Borough of Manhattan, decided that the books should not go back into circulation until a process was developed for evaluating private donations to public school libraries. The Board of Education subsequently established a committee to set criteria for library books. Cohen is reported to have claimed to the committee that the gay books in question had never actually been on the shelves.

Bloom approached the New York Civil Liberties Union about legal proceedings to challenge the de facto book banning but she was turned down. According to attorney Art Eisenberg, it would have been impossible to win in court. When the Supreme Court decided against book removal in the landmark Island Trees case (where right wing book removal of progressive novels was challenged in the courts), they differentiated between *removal* of books from library shelves and the simple resistance to book acquisition.

Eisenberg told the *Native*, "Island Trees involved political opposition. Brandeis was a different case. The political motive was not clear." Whether or not homophobia is sufficiently political in the eyes of the NYCLU, the case was ignored by the liberal press including Nat Hentoff, a board member of the NYCLU who writes a lengthy column on the First Amendment for the *Village Voice*.

The tide did change, however, when librarian Alice Ward informed the committee that the books *had* actually been on the shelves. In addition, the Brandeis chapter of the United Federation of Teachers and the central union office both supported Bloom. The UFT representative Laura Goodman also advocated keeping the books available to students. In mid-June, they were put back on the shelves, just in time for summer vacation.

Carol Bloom is tired but happy. "The precedent is now established in New York City schools," she said, "that we have a right to access to gay literature."

COMMENTARY

The battle to provide services to gay and lesbian students in the New York City public school system is a long, complex one with roots that go deeply into the history of city politics. In the 1960s New York City suffered a long and torturous strike by the United Federation of Teachers that pitted ethnic white public school teachers against black and Latino communities in which they worked and against other white leftist public school teachers. The issue was "community control" and it split friendships, families, and neighborhoods in a bitter ideological battle. In the end community school boards were established, with elected members, to insure broader input into the curriculum and structures of public schools—but without financial power. The intention of these programs was to create more progressive input and more community involvement with education.

The original plan allowed all people, not just parents, to run for the boards. Organized religious groups and the UFT have dominated ever since. Thirty years later, community boards elected anti-gay, anti-abortion fundamentalist Christians to positions of power. Some of these board members were even elected as "stealth" candidates (named after the stealth bomber). That is to say they would file petitions for election quietly and not campaign or draw attention in the general community. Instead they would lobby extensively through right-wing organizations and fundamentalist churches whose members would turn out in droves to elect candidates that many other voters didn't even know existed.

The battle that Carol Bloom thought was resolved in 1983 was only the tip of the iceberg. Christian school boards were able, ten years later, to defeat the city's proposed multicultural curriculum which called for a public school learning program emphasizing more than white European male history. It also acknowledged the existence of students with lesbian and gay parents and advocated respect for lesbians and gays in the classroom. But these school boards were so powerful that they were not only able to defeat the programs, but also to force the resignation of Dr. Joseph Fernandez, the progressive and dynamic Chancellor of the New York City schools. The right-wing community representatives were also able to, amazingly, prohibit explicit AIDS education, limit condom distribution, and avoid any health curriculum that advocated sexual practices beyond celibacy.

I HAVE MY DOUBTS ABOUT
THE SENECA PEACE ENCAMPMENT

Womanews,
October 1983

After many discussions with women who have participated in the Seneca Falls Women's Encampment for Peace and Justice (also known as "Peace Camp") outside of an army base in upstate New York, and through visiting Seneca for a few days, I have become convinced that—while campers are thoroughly enjoying themselves and getting a lot out of this experience—the broader political impact may be hovering near zero.

My first hesitancy comes with the whole idea of symbolic actions. After all, the military and the government are real and their impact on most of the people of the world is concrete. So, what are the real benefits to using symbols to oppose them? Also, when symbols are used, like weaving webs around an army base, how can we be sure that people outside the movement will understand them?

I also think that it is time for us to sit down and re-evaluate the way we are using the tactic of civil disobedience. Why are we spending so much time and effort to get into jail when so many other women are trying to get out? At Seneca it felt like arrest was becoming the focus of actions, with less effort going into communication with the outside world. The primary efforts at communication were directed to arresting officers. Can Military Police really be the critical mass most worthy of our attention? I always thought that arrest was a noble sacrifice in political work, *when necessary.* It means that the activist is not willing to stop herself from acting for freedom. The government will have to stop her. Getting arrested in the course of action is one thing, but when getting arrested is the action, then some re-evaluation needs to take place.

The women's peace movement is very popular right now. What does that mean? It is my impression that many women are going into the peace movement out of a commitment to engage in a more "broadly" defined political manner. Unfortunately, men are not getting "broader." Does this cumulatively mean less attention to issues that specifically affect women? What kind of work were the Peace Campers doing before Seneca and who has replaced them?

I guess this last question leads to my BIG POINT, which involves taking a good look at the new American peace movement. It appears to be a rather amorphous grouping around a huge spectrum of political commitments. There are those hoping to convince Reagan not to deploy nuclear arms, those who want to elect a Democrat, those who seek a legislative freeze, those who pray to God for peace, those who seek a transformation of every institution in which we live. In the past, broad, general movements often become co-opted by their most mainstream components. Does feminist participation in this potpourri actually help us reach our goals?

Alice Walker suggests that if saving the world means continuing the domination of white men, maybe the world should end. Is Seneca supposed to serve as a model for alternative living? Are we asking for social transformation through internal subversion instead of structural change? Who was organized by the Seneca Peace Encampment? Can these methods be applied to urban areas? In New York City, housing and hunger are the life and death issues—what about an encampment in Prospect Park?

I hope these questions and more can be openly discussed on the pages of *Womanews*. Let's use this newspaper as an organizing tool.

COMMENTARY

In many ways Seneca was the last real manifestation of the feminist movement as an activist movement of both lesbians and straight women trying creative strategies for social change. A combination of Reaganism, homophobia on the part of straight women, and streamlining of feminism to behind the scenes of the Democratic Party demobilized this kind of activist formation. But Seneca seemed to represent a political softening, a lack of clarity of goals and a confusion of tactics. Looking back, it is easier to see how pre-ACT UP lesbians had increasing difficulty finding efficient, empowering tactics, setting winnable concrete goals, and having a clear idea who was supposed to be affected by our organizing efforts. There was something in the amorphous, generalized nature of Seneca's politics that guaranteed defeat. But it was only through

ACT UP that I understood how to sequence political action. First make a demand that is possible. Then propose it brilliantly. When there is no response hold direct actions until your target is forced, through embarrassment or necessity to respond in some way and then work with them to see the proposal through, whenever possible. Not only can this kind of focus bring you closer to your ultimate goal, but it creates positive and satisfying experiences for fellow activists and motivation for strategizing for political change. I remember the first time I participated in an ACT UP demonstration where protesters sat in at government offices, and I realized that while the early eighties' feminist movement encircled the Pentagon, we never walked in through its front door.

ZAPS OFF WITH FINES
AFTER THREATENING CONGRESS

Womanews,
November 1983

On September 30, after a five day trial, I and five other women known as the Women's Liberation Zap Action Brigade were convicted of "using loud, abusive or threatening language to knowingly and willingly impede the orderly proceedings of Congress with intent to violate the law."

We were charged as the result of an action at the Senate hearings on the Human Life Amendment last April 23, which would have outlawed abortion, IUDs, and certain forms of birth control pills. No witnesses advocating abortion rights were allowed to speak. As one man testified that "the fetus is an astronaut in a uterine spaceship" we stood up in the chamber and chanted, "A Woman's Life Is a Human Life." Because the hearings were prominently featured in the news, our action ended up being the lead story on all three national network news broadcasts.

Our defense attorney Lois Yankowski used the argument that we believed it was necessary for the public to understand that this bill would result in the deaths of women. She also stated that we were the first people prosecuted for political demonstrations at Senate hearings since 1973 including the Imperial Wizard of the Ku Klux Klan who shouted racial obscenities at a subcommittee on racist violence. Yankowski argued that these arrests were a case of government overreaction and that women are not criminals for defending their rights.

The prosecutor, Bruce Peterson, argued that "America is the freest country in the world." He said that all Americans are free to express their views. At sentencing, Peters said that "civil disobedience is an American tradition, but accompanying that tradition is the responsibility to stand up and suffer the consequences."

Before sentencing, five of us addressed the court. We spoke about the necessity for women to control our own lives. We challenged the concept that the law was "fair and objective" and we said that we believed that we had acted appropriately. One of us, Tacie DeJanikus, said that "the action was a service to our country." Two of us, Stephanie Roth and myself, identified ourselves as lesbians. Judge Harriet Taylor responded, "This is the society under which you live and this is the society that will judge you. If you do construct your own system it will be that system that will judge you." But she ignored the maximum possibility of six months imprisonment and instead imposed fines of one hundred dollars each.

In the course of the trial the government submitted photos of the event taken from television videotapes and processed by the FBI. During the jury selection, seven people excused themselves on the grounds that they could not, under any circumstances, bring themselves to vote for conviction. We found it frightening that these progressive people had swallowed the myth of a fair justice system. If even one of them had stayed on the jury there would not have been a conviction.

COMMENTARY

At the time of the Zap action, I was a member of CARASA—the Committee for Abortion Rights and Against Sterilization Abuse—a left women's reproductive rights organization. Lesbian members of CARASA had been in hot water for some time because of our insistence on visibility inside the movement. For many of our homophobic comrades, this action was the last straw. It exhibited a kind of anarchist spirit that violated their sense of order and provided huge, international coverage for direct action as well as for lesbians fighting for abortion rights. The hearings that we disrupted were being televised live and so our demonstration was the lead story on all three national network news programs (before the advent of CNN).

Tensions around lesbian issues and direct action strategies such as this one resulted in about eight of us getting purged out of CARASA which soon fell apart after our removal. But history would show that direct action was the organizing tool of the future and would soon capture the imagination of progressive people in the form of AIDS activism.

The homophobia of women in CARASA was politically stupid and personally devastating. After all, we had worked with them on a daily basis for years and the personal relationships were very important to me. It first started to surface around arguments about tactics. They wanted to constantly apply old left methods of organizing, which felt outdated and irrelevant if your target group included lesbians.

For example, a number of women in CARASA favored workplace organizing as the primary focus of our "outreach." But, in the early 1980s the workplace was the worst place to reach lesbians because there was no job protection for gay people and the vast majority of homosexuals could not be out on the job. Instead we proposed targeting laundromats—the one place where all kinds of women go and actually have time for a discussion or to read distributed materials. This was resoundingly defeated as anarchistic and preposterous.

Another tactical battle came up when the Moral Majority opened a church on Bleecker Street in Greenwich Village. We went out and stickered the storefront with decals reading "A Woman's Life Is a Human Life" (in response to the Human Life Amendment which would have made abortion illegal). That was followed by a demonstration organized by CRASH (a gay left coalition which included the Lesbian Rights Committee of CARASA as well as groups such as Lavender Left, Committee of Gay and Lesbian Socialists, Dykes Against Racism Everywhere, and Black and White Men Together). Very few straight women in CARASA attended the demonstration, and they condemned us for "vandalizing churches." Most revealing of all was when an older woman who had spent a lifetime in the left accused us of "substitutionalism" saying that we were "substituting ourselves for the masses." What she didn't realize was that we saw ourselves as part of the gay community, not some vanguard organization out to organize the "other."

Once the overt homophobia started to overshadow the tactical debates, the attacks were vicious and disgusting. We, who had spent years working for a broad vision of freedom, with a wide range of people, were accused of being lesbian separatists, as though that was an accusation of shame. We were accused of being "man-haters," of "lifestylism," and of being divisive by raising lesbian issues. Stephanie Roth, their devoted and workaholic staffperson was forced to resign because they did not want her, as an out lesbian, to represent the organization.

Not all the straight women in CARASA attacked us in such a hateful way, but many—especially the academics—just sat by and watched, never interceding on our behalf. It was lambs to the slaughter, pretty much. Personally, my expulsion from CARASA was one of the most painful experiences of my political life. It signaled the symbolic end of my activism in a purely women's movement. At the same time, it revealed to me how important my homosexual identity was to me and how far I would go to avoid sacrificing it.

ADRIENNE RICH TRANSFORMED BY NICARAGUAN VISIT

*Gay Community
News,*
November 1983

At a community forum sponsored by *Ikon* magazine, poet Adrienne Rich surprised the audience with her talk about a recent visit to Nicaragua.

Rich spoke about the "cultural chauvinism" of North American feminism which "feeds itself on racism." She acknowledged that American feminism has defined and organized around areas hitherto not defined as political, "but that the movement reflects the manic self-assertion of privilege" that had motivated the U.S. since the advent of the Cold War.

In a recent issue of *off our backs,* Rich wrote that U.S. feminists should not use their politics about abortion as a measure of the status of women in revolutionary Nicaragua. "The priority at this moment is life itself and the protection of the revolution," Rich told the forum's audience.

In the same issue of *off our backs,* Susan Sherman quotes Milo Vargas, Nicaraguan chief counsel, as saying, "We cannot pass a law on abortion without preparing the people. For many Nicaraguan women, the revolution has come to signify the right to be a mother." Sherman then quotes Margaret Randall that "abortion legislation in the context of the present Nicaraguan society would be a perfect issue for the right wing to exploit." She concludes that "most Nicaraguans are Catholic and that permeates every facet of their lives and thoughts."

However, Jennifer Hull, in the same issue, records that "Maria Lillian Torres, director of the Children's Hospital cites unsafe abortion as one of the three major causes of maternal death in Nicaragua." They see one or two women a day with botched abortions. In Managua, one hospital admits ten women a day with illegal abortions. This in a country of only three million people.

This presentation by Rich marks a dramatic departure. As a leading theoretician of the lesbian feminist movement, she has previously analyzed the sexual coercion of women into mother-hood as a central theme of culture. In this speech, however, Rich suspended her gender analysis. Responding to the tragedy of U.S. intervention in Nicaragua, she said that applying our feminist agenda there is an inappropriate, culturally biased act.

However, Hull's illegal abortion statistics from Nicaragua illustrate that women in all cultures do whatever they can to resist unwanted pregnancy. To say that Nicaraguan women are not ready for abortion when they are currently endangering their lives to get abortions ignores reality. Rich wrote in *off our backs* that when rebuilding society, "you begin by stopping torture and killing." A Nicaraguan woman dead from an illegal abortion is just as dead as a woman killed by a U.S.-backed Contra. I don't see a contradiction between support for the revolution and an articulation of what we know about how women really live.

COMMENTARY

I now realize that there was a lot more going on here than a specific political analysis of Nicaragua. Adrienne Rich was perhaps the most respected openly lesbian artist and intellectual at this time. She had had a long and successful career as a poet, but when she bravely came out as a lesbian her work was, for a time, mocked and derided by the same mainstream that had formerly praised her. Her 1982 article "Compulsory Heterosexuality and Lesbian Existence" was perhaps the most influential theoretical article of the lesbian feminist movement. And, despite the revisionist critique of the late eighties that objected to the "essentialism" of her argument, it remains a work so filled with rage and insight that it could hardly be written in today's tempered, vague theoretical atmosphere. Susan Sherman was one of the first poets to write openly about her lesbianism and to read in public as an overtly stated lesbian writer. She also had a long, long history on the left and in anti-imperialist political movements. Here they were trying to speak globally *from* their lesbian perspectives to their primarily lesbian audiences, in other words, to participate fully in the intellectual and political life of the world and not be resigned to a narrow set of acceptable subject matter. Unfortunately, then as now, once an intellectual comes out as a lesbian, the rest of the world ceases to be interested in what she has to say, and so the audience remains narrow, no matter what the scope of the subject. From this vantage point I look back on this event still in political disagreement, but with much more sympathy and understanding as well as appreciation of their willingness to be provocative and take risks.

Low marks for German democracy

Womanews,
March 1984

This January I had the opportunity to visit the German Democratic Republic (GDR) with a delegation of American feminists. Because we were guests of the government we spent most of our days in meetings with low-level officials. At night we tried to meet as many people as we could and piece together an understanding of life in this complicated country.

The GDR was founded thirty-five years ago when the Soviet Army invaded fascist Germany from the east and the U.S. army invaded from the west. So, this is not a country where socialism developed organically, nor was it chosen by the population, but instead it was imposed by military occupation. Out of sixteen million people, two million belong to the Communist Party, and they make up a privileged ruling class. They often have the best apartments, cars, and jobs. For example, in a country where the lowest income (paid to students and some old people) is 300 marks per month, a factory director can earn 4,000 marks per month. To get that kind of job you must have a relationship with the Party, thereby making it a haven for careerists.

Racism? no problem!

There were three black women in our delegation. When we walked together in the streets, Germans stared, pointed, laughed, touched them and took their picture. When we confronted the officials with this experience, we were told "racism does not exist in the GDR." We were also told that black people can't judge racism because they are "hypersensitive."

We went to the campus of Karl Marx University to talk to African students (mostly male), some of the only non-German people in this totally homogeneous country. They lead fairly segregated lives, socializing together and not going off campus very often because of the racism. We went to a toy store looking for images of black people and found a doll, half-human, half-animal, called Piti-Platch, a Sambo-like character on a state-produced television show. We went to a kindergarten asking to see their materials for teaching about racism. After being told four times that "there is no racism in the GDR," the teacher finally dug out a picture from the closet which showed three children against a grey background. One was blonde and blue-eyed, one was Asian, and one was the same color as the background. We learned quickly that the response "no problem" usually meant that there was a big problem.

WOMEN? NO PROBLEM!

The line is, "Equality for women is a reality in the GDR." This is bullshit. Women in the GDR share the same economic and social problems as women in capitalist countries. Officially women have the right to "equal pay for equal work," however they are segregated into the lowest paying jobs. For example, nine out of 380 professors at the university (earning around 3,000 marks a month) are women. But in the bindery of the printing factory (earning around 800 marks a month) 90 percent of the employees are women. In the printshop of the same factory (where workers earn 1200 marks) 4 percent are women. There is a law prohibiting women from jobs in which they must carry over twenty pounds. Coincidentally, these jobs are the best paid.

In addition to their lack of economic power, East German women are victimized by an all-encompassing pro-natalism. After World War II, 70 percent of the German population was female. A Rosie-the-Riveter type program was instituted to bring women into the industrial labor force. By 1971, women's attitudes had changed so dramatically that they were demanding divorces in high numbers and refusing to have more than one child. The government began a program of increased pressure to procreate and accompanied it with financial incentives.

For example, when a couple marries they can borrow 5,000 marks from the state. If they have three children they don't have to pay it back. This pro-family policy, of course, functions off the backs of women, of whom 90 percent work and 85 percent are mothers. Although there is no child care for two thirds of the women who want it, what does exist ends with the working day, leaving women with the burden of a second unpaid job. In the GDR, like under capitalism, the home is an unpaid workplace for women. Furthermore, many women don't want to leave their children in centers where they will be raised by the state.

It was on the topic of reproductive rights that many of the GDR's contradictions became clear. There is health care for everyone for a nominal fee, but there is only one kind of health care. Women have a gynecological exam every two years, but it lasts five-to-ten minutes. The pill is the major form of birth control; the diaphragm and cervical cap are virtually unknown and impossible to obtain. When we asked about the relationship between the pill and disease we were told that the GDR has conducted research "proving" that there is no such relationship. Sterilization is only permitted after three Cesarians "because the woman might divorce, remarry, and want more children." Abortion is free, but it is only available up to twelve weeks, minors need parental permission—and each woman is given a little speech before the procedure encouraging her to have the child.

HOMOSEXUALS? NO PROBLEM!

The official theory on homosexuality is that it is caused by maldevelopment in the embryonic stage when one's gender endorphines develop like those of the opposite gender. While specific and ridiculous, this "theory" allows gay people an identity if they will accept themselves as biologically deviant.

It was very hard to find and talk to gay people in the GDR. One contact was already in prison when we arrived. Another made an appointment to meet us and never showed up. We did go to a gay bar in East Berlin which was a depressing dive on Friedrichstrasse with a waitress who forced us to buy drinks we didn't want. We were constantly told by every official we asked (and we asked everyone) that for homosexuals in the GDR there was . . . "No Problem."

PERSONAL FREEDOM? NO PROBLEM!

A visitor to the GDR immediately senses the lack of personal freedom. Personal expression is repressed on every level, from art to organizing to street life to travel. On the street and in public life there is little color except for large paintings of Marx and Lenin on tractors or leading workers. You do not generally hear loud laughing or noises. People would walk up to us and say, "This is a terrible country. We are not free here," and then walk away.

One result of this oppression is that East Germans, like most Americans, do not have access to ideas. They are denied access to the history of ideas and as a result the opposition is very vague. However, one striking difference between East Germans and Americans is that East German people really believe in and want socialism. They want the ideology that they have been promised, not the distorted reality that they live. So, the different levels of political opposition fall generally within the framework of elements of socialism.

The most popular belief about how to achieve change is based in the hope of working within the Party. These people claim that the stagnation comes from "errors" by Party leaders, not explicit policy. Lacking a critique of power dynamics, they have enormous faith in the state. The second group is based in the Protestant church which is currently the only alternative to the state. It is here that the few homosexual groups meet, and it is also the base of the *unofficial* peace movement. The *official* peace movement is controlled by the government. Everywhere there are government-placed slogans calling for peace. But "peace" to the state means unilateral disarmament by the United States. To the people "peace" is more likely to mean freedom since the government justifies its internal repression with the American threat. It is only the *unofficial* peace movement (which some officials claim does not exist) that opposes all weapons. Their leaders, like Ulrike Poppel of Women For Peace, are often in prison and the government goes back and forth between denying their existence and claiming they are tools of the West. We told them that our government claims we are tools of the East, which they could clearly see was not the case.

The least organized opposition was the hardest to find out about. They are called "A-Socials" by the state. "A-Social" is a category, left over from the Nazi era, which was applied to lesbians, prostitutes, and other deviants who were forced to wear black triangles in concentration camps. Everyone I asked had a different definition of an A-Social. Some said they were people who didn't want to work (a crime in the GDR) or who live communally, and who committed acts of vandalism. Others said they were alcoholics, homeless by choice, and children of criminals. We never actually met an A-Social, but two long haired young men drinking wine did come up to us in Leipzig and say "GDR is shit."

COMMENTARY 1

In the early eighties my friend Bettina Berch, then a professor of Economics at Barnard College, had the opportunity to meet and interview Christa Wolf, the famous East German novelist. Through Wolf's contacts and a developing relationship with the New York based GDR/U.S. Friendship Organization, Bettina arranged for the first delegation of U.S. feminists to visit the German Democratic Republic. The delegation consisted entirely of Jews, blacks, and lesbians plus one elderly straight, white member of the Communist Party USA who was receiving her trip to "socialist" Germany as a reward for her years of service to the party. Ironically, by the time we got there Wolf was in disfavor because, we suspected, of the publication of her novel *Cassandra*, a feminist work viewed with great suspicion by East German authorities and was unable to meet with us. It was a difficult and challenging visit.

The *Freundschaft* (The Friendship Organization) which I now assume was Stasi (the GDR's secret police) organized most of our days, accompanied by a translator Karin, also assumed to be Stasi, and a shady older man named Eric who had previously lived in Rhodesia and refused to allow his picture to be taken.

On the first day, the *Freundshaft* arranged for us to visit Ravensbruck, the women's concentration camp. It was my first day ever in a German country. My grandmother had two sisters and two brothers killed by the Nazis and I was raised with extremely anti-German sentiment. A women's concentration camp would not necessarily be my first choice as a tourist site. But, tentatively, we all boarded the van and went off.

I had always been taught that World War II was a war against the Jews, but that was, I realized, only because I grew up with the victims. For the oppressors, who have never met the victims, it was quite a different experience. And this telling differed dramatically from West to East. Even though the East was the same Germany that perpetuated the extermination policies as the West, its leaders, like the GDR's dictator Eric Honecker, had been virulent anti-fascists and many had been imprisoned by the Nazis. After the war, the GDR history goes, as former resisters ruled the GDR, former Nazis ruled West Germany. The GDR positioned itself as the historical opponent of the fascists of the West. And so, their version of World War II was that it was a war between fascists and communists. This was an interpretation that I had never heard of before arriving in Ravensbruck. There, the walls were lined with photos of women who had been exterminated at the camp. They had Jewish faces. They had Jewish names. But under each woman's photo was the word "communist." The fact that they were Jewish was completely erased in the telling.

We objected strenuously to this interpretation and expressed our reactions to our East German hosts. On our VISA applications, I had listed the YIVO Institute for Jewish Research as one of my affiliate organizations because I was, at that time, a student in their Yiddish language and history program. For this reason, I believe, I was singled out the next day to meet with an elderly Jewish couple for a little talk. They told me that they had been members of the KPD (the German Communist Party) before the war. They had worked vigorously against Hitler and had been in concentration camps but had survived. They then came to live in the GDR. The couple was adamant in insisting that they were communists first and had no need of a Jewish identity. They were internationalists and did not need to differentiate themselves from their fellow citizens in the GDR. Yet, later that afternoon, they took me to their comfortable, well-stocked house (an immediate sign of a privileged position), and I found that their bookshelves were crammed with writings by Jewish intellectuals including the complete works of Issac Bashevis Singer. So much for assimilation.

Our delegation was tirelessly challenging in our interactions with officials and we constantly asked about the conditions of lesbians' lives in the GDR. Clearly we were embarrassing and annoying our interpreter Karin, with this insistence and finally, out of desperation, the *Freundshaft* organized a special trip. We went by van to Karl Marx Stadt (now Chemnitz) and were brought to the medical offices of Dr. Schnabel, who was introduced as "the Kinsey of the East." Later we were to learn that he had written the official socialist sex book for Cuba. Dr. Schnabel was a stereotypical mad scientist type. He told us he viewed homosexuality as just one variation within the scope of human sexuality. At that time he was particularly interested in transsexuals and was traveling around the world to study them.

We were led into his study and there we were introduced to two demure young women who Dr. Schnabel told us were "two official lesbians." So we sat, stiffly, in the office—us, Dr. Schnabel, the interpreter, members of the Freundschaft, and the official lesbians. So, of course, whatever questions we asked, the answer was "Kein Problem," "No Problem." Everything was fine, they insisted. They had no problems. OK, so, at the end of the pseudo-discussion, I passed around my notebook for the women to give me their addresses. One of them wrote "Be careful."

After two weeks of interpreting our relentless feminist onslaught, Karin began to get used to us. The last night in the GDR, we all presented her with the various books we had brought over, and she seemed generally transformed—not only by our ideas—but also by interacting with people who were ethnically and racially different from herself in a very homogeneous nation. After dinner she asked for the number of my hotel room and said she had something very important to tell me. While I waited and waited she never appeared. About a month later, home in New York, I received an anonymous scrawled postcard from the GDR saying that we had changed the sender's life. I always assumed it was from her.

COMMENTARY 2

I returned to Germany, in an official capacity, on two more occasions. First, a few months after the "unification," Michael Callen, Robert Hilferty, and I were invited by filmmaker Rosa Von Praunheim to tour the western part of the country. Rosa was opening his new films "Silence=Death" and "Positive" and wanted us to try to bring AIDS activism and ACT UP to Germany.

What we found was a very high level of denial on the part of gay men. There was little interest in AIDS and little understanding of what disaster that lack of interest could produce. For the three of us, this was absolutely tragic because they had the information and the opportunity to avoid the kind of devastation that we live with every day in America. And yet, even with this possibility, they were unable to take action to protect their own futures.

The key point of resistance was the use of condoms. Even when confronted with Michael, one of the people with AIDS who has lived the longest after diagnosis, and Robert, whose lover had died of AIDS, we faced seas of objection in almost every city. The most memorable comment was "What about the right to commit suicide?" At first we dismissed this question because it seemed so absurd. Obviously anyone who had experienced AIDS first-hand could not take such a cavalier approach. But when it came up city after city we realized that we had to come up with an answer. So, Robert usually responded "Why would you want to infect someone else?" and the answer inevitably was, "Everyone is responsible for themselves."

The second most strenuous level of objection came with regard to the relationship between West Germans and their government. Many people told us that there was no need for an AIDS activist movement in Germany because the government provides health insurance. This level of passivity was truly frightening. Immediately we started asking questions and found out that AIDS services, although funded, were totally inadequate; that the pharmaceutical companies were setting the agendas for treatment; that there was no patient input into what treatments were to be made available etc., etc., etc.

In the end we did manage to start some ACT UP chapters and a few had already been in place. Even though some of these chapters are still functioning as of the summer of 1993, ACT UP never really caught on in Germany. Some people ascribe this to the lack of a tradition of civil rights movements in Germany, where service organizations like the AIDS Hilfe are a lot more successful than activist groups. It may also have to do with the high standard of living for West Germans and the aftereffects of all that comfort. But these issues came up again during my next visit to Germany, in the spring of 1993, to promote the German editions of my novels.

COMMENTARY 3

The Hamburg-based Marxist press Argument Verlag developed a feminist imprint called Ariadne, specializing in crime novels but also including some general interest feminist literature. They brought me to Germany for a book tour which, ironically, began the day after the Maastrict vote insuring the unification of Europe under the domination of a Germany that was quickly spiraling to the right. During my short stay, the asylum law (guaranteeing haven to political refugees) was repealed by the Parliament, the abortion law was repealed, and a Turkish family was firebombed to death. All of this within twenty-one days is a good indication of the rapidity of Germany's plummet to the right.

Unfortunately for me, the state of gay and lesbian life, although economically and legally comfortable, was functioning on an invisible parallel track reminiscent of some of the pre-AIDS conditions in the United States. So, men and women were completely separate, and straight people paid virtually no attention to lesbian books. As a result I was forced into the "women only" sphere of separatism. Even though I did make an express "author's wish" that gay and lesbian organizations cooperate in co-organizing my readings, in some cases the desire for separatism was so powerful that even this request was impossible. In city after city I had to argue the merits of a mixed world. Some women claimed that if even one man was in the room there were women who would not be able to talk freely—an absurd and condescending rationale, in my opinion. In those women-only readings, I had to justify over and over again why I write about AIDS and gay men. In some cities the readings were organized by gay men and they seemed unable to get lesbians to attend. Only a few places, such as Bielefeld, were able to successfully cooperate. But most shocking of all was the complete lack of discussion about current events in Germany. For example, the new abortion restrictions were met with a demonstration of two hundred women. This lack of organizing, combined with a strange desire for purity (separatism) and virtual disinterest about AIDS on the part of most women and many men, seemed to bode badly for the future. "How are you going to organize against the Nazis if your community is closed?" I would ask. But there was no answer.

Most interestingly, I returned to Leipzig after ten years and read at the newly opened women's bookstore. The former GDR is now a source of as much of the neo-Nazi action as the West. This new fascism appears to be the only authentic people's movement in Germany. It is the protest from below, from the disaffected working class. Yet, from my most superficial impressions, the lesbians in the East seemed much more aware and politically engaged than their sisters in the West.

Only about ten people could fit in the store, but in that audience were lesbians, straight women, and two transsexuals in the midst of going through their changes. This was the only place where the audience asked globally politicized questions and where there was a clear realization about the rise of fascism. Of course, there was also a profound nostalgia for the old, repressive GDR. Especially in the face of the West's attempt to discredit and erase anything that had occurred there during its forty years of existence. The West German and U.S. media had been conducting prominent campaigns claiming that all respected GDR artists were government collaborators and therefore should be forgotten and discredited. Of course, the fact that almost all of the most popular American writers are also complicit with our government was never raised as a point of comparison.

"Yes, it's true," said Catherine, a beautiful lesbian from Leipzig working as an openly gay representative in the city government. "In the past we couldn't have meeting places or publications. But when we did meet it was always filled with feeling and unity. That sense is gone now." Had she traveled out of the GDR yet? Only three days in a West German city. I wondered what she would say five years from now after having seen lesbian life in Amsterdam or London or San Francisco. It was a strange moment of transition for Germany. These women were losing their economic benefits rapidly to the West, but they still hadn't realized what possibilities lay in their future. Meanwhile their Western compatriots passively tumble to the right.

ENTRY FEE DISPUTED AT BLACK LESBIAN BAR

Gay Community
News,
January 1985

Garbo's, a lesbian bar at 225 West Broadway in Manhattan, was temporarily closed the week of December 8 when the lesbian management team got involved in a dispute with their male business partners over admission prices. According to one customer who asked not to be identified, the men insisted on raising the entry fee from five to seven dollars. In response, the managers Sandy Quiros and Minnie Rivera requested that the entire staff resign and asked customers not to frequent the club.

Garbo's primarily served young black lesbians from New Jersey and the boroughs, many of whom followed the Rivera/Quiros team from Network, also a lesbian bar. Network closed over a year ago under similarly unclear circumstances. According to Alicia, a customer who asked to be identified by her first name, black lesbians gathered at Garbo's because bars like the Cubbyhole and the Dutchess, which are primarily white, have no dance floor, while Shescape (the largest women's bar in Manhattan) reportedly has a quota system for black customers. Black women have reported arriving at Shescape with Latina friends and being turned away after their friends were admitted. Black customers came to Garbo's from around the tri-state area and were "faithful customers," Alicia said, in spite of the admission price and high cost of drinks.

Another black regular who asked to remain anonymous told GCN that Garbo's had not been doing well for the last few months, with the exception of Friday nights which were "black nights." Saturday nights, which she called "white nights," were attracting a smaller crowd.

In the past many lesbian bars have been accused of maintaining quotas for women of color. Some years ago, Bacall's on Fifth Avenue was closed by lesbian demonstrators who successfully boycotted the bar's discriminatory admission system. The Dutchess was also the subject of a boycott several years ago when bouncers reportedly asked black women for identification and let white women enter freely. This boycott was interrupted, however, when the State Liquor Authority closed down the bar for discrimination against men while ignoring its racist practices.

More recently bars have been accused of attempting to restrict black and Latina women to specific off-nights by regulating music.

All lesbian bars in New York City are owned by business interests outside the lesbian community, with extensive participation by organized crime suspected.

COMMENTARY

The lesbian bar scene in Manhattan has changed dramatically since those days. In the West Village, the Dutchess was "renovated," underwent a number of name changes, and re-opened as Pandora's Box, a black lesbian bar, and finally closed for good. After Sandra Bernhard and Madonna told David Letterman that they'd been to the Cubbyhole, that place took on a hipper veneer, but the bars remained basically racially segregated.

The East Village scene was transformed by the advent of Deb and Jenny's Girl Bar, a traveling lesbian night set primarily in gay men's clubs or in groovy East Village spots—most notoriously Deb Parker's GIRLWORLD at the World (now an evangelical church). Lesbians, gay men, and drag queens (and kings) mixed at the Pyramid (also known as the Queeramid), but no place had a greater impact on lesbian social life than Jocelyn Taylor and Julie Tollentino's Clit Club, the first truly interracial lesbian dance club, which has operated for years one night a week in a gay men's West Side Highway fuck bar. Both Taylor and Tollentino had a broad sweep of cultural influence. Taylor was also a member of House Of Color, a lesbian and gay people of color video collective, and curated the D.C.T.V. Lesbian and Gay Video Festival. Tollentino, a dancer, achieved anonymous international stardom by appearing with her lover Allistair as the two "lesbian skinheads" who menaced Madonna with a knife in the Platinum One's SEX book, which appeared to great fanfare in 1992.

In addition to interracial socializing which resonated throughout the community, another significant difference stimulated by the Clit Club is that the bars are no longer as hostile to activists as they once were. I remember trying to sell *Womanews* at the Dutchess and having the bouncer threaten to punch my "teeth in." Now bars are much more likely to encourage activist groups to do benefits and distribute materials for fundraisers, making it more possible to narrow the historic gap between bar dykes and movement dykes.

84

Feds Stop Anti-Violence Grants to Women's Groups
Cite Lesbian Rights as Anti-Family

New York Native,
July 1985

Attorney General Edwin Meese has stopped a $625,000 grant from the Justice Department to the National Coalition Against Domestic Violence. The grant was held up after members of the Free Congress Foundation, a right-wing "think" tank, charged that the coalition supports lesbian rights.

Although the request was initially unanimously approved by the Attorney General's Task Force on Domestic Violence, Meese imposed a stay after receiving a letter from Congressman Mark Siljander of Michigan and twenty-three other members of Congress calling the Coalition a "pro-lesbian, pro-abortion, anti-family, anti-Reagan, radical feminist group."

According to Patrick Fagen, director of the Child and Family Protection Institute of the Free Congress Foundation, the Coalition "has a very different view on marriage and sexuality than those of the traditional Judeo-Christian values. The feminist agenda puts the woman paramount in a selfish way."

Meese's action has drawn criticism from groups that do not usually support progressive causes. Maureen Reagan, the president's daughter and a member of the official U.S. delegation to the Nairobi Women's Conference has attacked Meese in the national press.

"There are people in the United States and throughout the world who take the idea that domestic violence comes with a marriage license," Reagan said. "Beating up people, murdering people, does not come with a marriage license. It never has and it never will."

In 1982, Suzanne Pharr, of the Little Rock, Arkansas Women's Project, co-founded the Lesbian Task Force of the National Coalition Against Domestic Violence. She currently co-chairs the task force with Nan Stoops of Santa Monica, California. "When our grant was at the Justice Department," she said, "it was somehow leaked to the Heritage Foundation (a right-wing think tank based in Washington, D.C.). This was a grant asking for money for media work, information and referral, developing protocols for police, and mental health professionals. The Lesbian Task Force was included because we have been working very hard on lesbian battering. Under this grant we would expect to write protocols on battered lesbians. A lot of social change organizations are looking to the coalition to see how we stand up to their pressure, whether we are going to be courageous or not."

COMMENTARY

Reagan had begun cutting service programs and funding to women's groups from his first moment in office. One of the initial range of cuts was the elimination of the CETA program, a federal government subsidy permitting community-based groups to hire staff. Because the women's movement had allowed itself, during the Democratic regimes, to become partially dependent on government funding, a number of institutions, like health care centers and community job training programs, were unable to survive without government support. Defunding social services to women and children was one of the most devastating tactics of the Reagan/Bush era.

Some activists learned their lesson about dependence funding, but others went on to rely on progressive foundations. Unfortunately, these too proved unreliable as they changed funding agendas from year to year or suffered budget cuts themselves and eliminated grants, causing disarray in the supported organizations.

The only viable alternative turned out to be grass-roots fundraising where, through dances or parties or other community-based events at a five-to-ten dollar price per head, activist groups could finance their activities. Besides financial independence, there are other advantages to community-based fundraising. It forces groups to keep the community informed about their work and to involve the community in their ongoing activities. It is also a very efficient measure of how much the community values or rejects an activist project. Anyway, socializing together forges bonds that demonstrations don't always achieve. Finally, there will always be women who are willing to come to a party and give ten dollars but who will never attend an action, and grass-roots fundraising gives organizations the opportunity to involve them as well.

In this case, the Reagan administration was ferreting out any advocates for women or for lesbians working within governmental agencies. Suzanne Pharr lost this battle but she kept writing and organizing. In 1993 she emerged as one of the most visible organizers in leadership in the battle against Proposition 9, the anti-gay ballot measure that appeared in the state of Oregon at the end of the Bush era. Proposition 9 was one of the first of a persistent onslaught of anti-gay ballot measures organized by right-wing groups such as the Oregon Citizens Alliance. Pharr and others were able to get national attention on the Oregon proposition. There were enormous fights within the No-on-Nine movement about how openly gay the campaign should be. Some elements of the national community argued that we should present ourselves exactly as we are. Others wanted a more muted, assimilationist approach. This conflict over strategy may have contributed to the fact that Proposition 9 was defeated by a frighteningly small margin. And within a few months, other local anti-gay ballot measures would pass in the state of Oregon.

AIDS REPORTED IN THE SOVIET UNION

New York Native,
September 1985

According to a story filed from the Soviet Union by United Press International, Soviet doctors have admitted that an undisclosed number of AIDS cases have been diagnosed there. The doctors are reportedly searching for a cure.

Although the Soviet Union does not admit to the presence of homosexuals or drug addicts among its population, official press reports have blamed the spread of the disease on these groups. They have also warned against sexual contact with foreign visitors including a forty member homosexual contingent from the Netherlands to the International Youth Festival in Moscow this summer.

One doctor, Leonid Filarov, chief of the Odzhinkidze Sanatorium in the Black Sea resort of Sochi, said that some doctors believe AIDS results from "mixed marriages." According to Dr. Filarov, "Mixed marriages can create genetic mutations, and it is possible AIDS could also be a result of these marriages."

An annoyed woman at the office of the *Daily World,* the New York newspaper of the Communist Party, USA, told the *Native* that she had "no information" and referred us to the official Soviet news agency, Tass. A representative there said that three or four articles on AIDS had been published in the Soviet Union, but that he had "no information." He did remember, however, that a "leading Soviet spokesman" believed that AIDS was the result of mixed marriages, but he could not recall which races the doctor had referred to.

NEW YORK
A MASS OF INDIVIDUALLY BEAUTIFUL FACES

*Gay Community
News Travel
Supplement,*
September 1985

Let's say that for some bizarre reason you decide to spend your August vacation in New York City. Let's say you don't have much money and you're looking for fun. Well, the first thing to remember is that while many New Yorkers do leave the city in the summer, there are endlessly fascinating throngs who remain. I hope this article will help you find them without too much sweat. Also, remember, New York is changing rapidly. Bring your camera.

The first stop for every dyke is the Dutchess. Yes, that historic lesbian bar at the corner of Sheridan Square and Christopher Street is now reopened under the name the Grove Club. It still looks like the old Dutchess, though, with overpriced drinks, tacky interior, and cute waitresses. The major change is that there is no more black paint on the windows. We're liberated now, remember? One of the funniest things to do at the Dutchess is to watch people come back to the newly re-opened place for the first time in two years. They smile, squeal, and tell old stories—and everyone runs to the bathroom to see if it is still flooded like it used to be. Then you can watch the sixteen year olds in black spandex make out on the dance floor and listen to the woman breaking up with her girlfriend over the pay phone. It's nice to know that some things never change.

Okay, so now that you've made a friend at the Dutchess, you need something romantic and fun to do without having to spend any money. Just ask her if she wants to go for a walk and start off down Christopher Street. You can watch all the gay people holding hands and kissing and looking so cute. Pass the River Hotel along the waterfront, find a place on the pier, and look out over the Hudson River under the New Jersey sky. Then, if you get bored you can watch the men have sex, or kill some time trying to get into the men's bars. Just tell them you only want to dance and there's no room at the Dutchess. If you're lucky, they'll laugh but you won't get in. This, however, can work to your advantage because it will bring you and your new friend closer together and give you some stories to tell the friends back in Boston where lesbians and gay men get along so well.

Now it is time to head over to Washington Square Park where you can buy pot for five dollars. Don't buy anything else, however. You might even walk past Folk City and look at the photos of Bob Dylan and Judy Collins when they were poor too. Don't be surprised by what you see in the park. It's hot, dark, and full of American contradictions. A black, gay comedian tells racist, anti-gay jokes to a crowd of laughing tourists. Break dancers gossip and squabble, spending more time negotiating than dancing. A country western band discovers that all anybody really wants to hear is Grateful Dead songs. This all goes on between the Rastas selling, buying, and playing soccer. Kids, newer than New Wave, with frisbees and guitars sing John Cougar songs for people who don't know who John Cougar is. Suburban white people looking for nickel bags stand next to suburban white people who've never heard of nickel bags. Straight couples on dates pass Puerto Rican faggots in midrift tops having dramatic jealous scenes and fabulous reunions. Inevitably the cops will come and disrupt everything, travelling in packs of three. Just make sure they don't catch you smoking that joint.

The next day you wake up in her apartment and notice that it gets incredibly hot very early. Linger over an iced coffee until the bookstores open at noon. Then you can browse in air conditioning for hours. There's A Different Light, the overtly gay bookstore, and Three Lives, the subtly gay bookstore. Pick out what you want and then go over to Oscar Wilde's on Christopher and Gay Streets and buy it there. They need the business. Be sure to gossip a little bit with the people behind the counter. Then you'll really feel like a New York queer.

Okay, you're a tourist. So, even though I tell you it is too hot, you decide you have to go to Soho and Tribeca. But the garbage smells awful and you've got a headache and nothing in Soho is interesting anyway. So, stop by Leroy's Coffee Shop where me and my friend Robin Epstein waitress. It's on West Broadway, two blocks south of Canal. We'll make you a nice egg cream and give you better advice. We'll probably suggest you get on the F train and go to Brighton Beach—it's great there. There's a boardwalk with a lot of old Jewish people and new Russian people and Mrs. Stahl's

Knishes where you can buy a borscht whip or a cherry-lime rickey. The stores' signs are written in Russian and there's a whole ocean in front for you. Just walk a few blocks down the boardwalk and you're in Coney Island which is really a trip.

You could say it still looks the way it always looked: crowds of poor people, thousands of screaming children, and an increasingly declining amusement park. Only now the people are Caribbean and Greek and Eastern European and East Asian and Latino. They sell *cerveza fria* and uncooked crabs freshly caught from the filthy ocean water. There are disco radios and every kind of beautiful way a human can look.

Suddenly you don't mind the heat and the dirt and all you see is the mass of individually beautiful faces. And you think to yourself, "How wonderful and magical this strange city is." On the way back to Manhattan on the F train you become determined to change your life and move to New York. You even buy a *New York Times* to search the want ads. But the only possible apartment is a closet in Staten Island for $600. And the only job is selling Tofutti for minimum wage. So, on your way to Penn Station, you wonder how any of these crazy people can possibly live in this city and you settle down in the train to head home.

A.c.l.u. FOUNDS GAY PROJECT

New York Native,
September 1985

The American Civil Liberties Union has begun a fundraising process to support a national Lesbian and Gay Rights Project.

According to executive director Ira Glasser, the organization has raised $15,000, which is one third of what is needed to hire a full-time attorney and officially begin the project's activities. Glasser says that the ACLU has been primarily soliciting contributions from individuals because they "don't want to compete with existing gay organizations that already receive grant money." Glasser conceded, however, that the money gathering had proceeded less quickly than anticipated.

The project grew out of the meetings of the Ad Hoc Task Force to Challenge Sodomy Laws (founded in 1983) which included the ACLU, Lambda Legal Defense and Education Fund, Lesbian Rights Project, Gay and Lesbian Advocates and Defenders, Texas Human Rights Foundation, National Committee for Sexual and Civil Liberties, and National Gay Rights Advocates. Eradicating existing sodomy statutes is the first priority of the project. Sodomy laws are used as a legal justification for police harassment and form a legal basis for housing, employment, and child-custody discrimination. Even when not enforced, "their mere existence defines gay relationships as a crime," says Glasser. The project's agenda also includes such constitutional issues as the right to "advocate" homosexuality in the classroom. Glasser said that the project's formation is based on the principle that "as long as civil rights for gays remains a gay people's issue alone, it will be too easy for gays to be isolated in their struggle for equality."

AIDSPAC ESTABLISHED BY DC GROUP

New York Native,
September 1985

The Human Rights Campaign Fund Board of Directors has announced the formation of an AIDS Campaign Trust (ACT) to elect members of the U.S. House of Representatives and Senate who favor increased AIDS funding on a federal level. ACT will operate as an arm of the campaign fund, a national political action committee which advocates for gay civil rights legislation.

According to fund executive director Vic Basile, "The AIDS crisis is worsening and has become a political issue, even though it should be a public health issue." In the past the fund has raised money for candidates supportive of a large range of gay-related issues. However, it felt it was necessary to begin a second project to focus solely on AIDS funding. "There is a body of politicians," Basile said, "who aren't going to put their names on a gay civil rights bill. But some of them could be encouraged to be supportive on the public health issue. Given the nature of the crisis, they need to be encouraged."

Is AIDS the only issue determining financial support for a candidate? "For ACT, it will be," confirmed Basile. For example, ACT will support Tony Coehlo, an incumbent Congressman from California. Although he is not a sponsor of the gay rights bill, Coehlo has been "very helpful on AIDS funding issues and there ought to be a way to acknowledge his support."

ACT plans to do heavy fundraising, including direct mail and benefit events. They will try to identify "new money" through individual donors who have not yet contributed to gay causes. According to board co-chair Duke Comegys, "Only the federal government can stop AIDS. And we're going to see that they do it. Elected officials understand campaign contributions."

COMMENTARY

Fifteen years into the post-Stonewall gay rights movement, mainstream groups like the ACLU finally started to participate. As the mainstream began basic recognition of gay issues, established gay groups were themselves transforming to begin to address AIDS. Five years into the epidemic it became increasingly clear that the public would not accept AIDS as a health crisis, but was determined to view it as representative of sexual and political threats to cultural values posed by gay people.

Shocked by the widespread brutality rained on the gay community in the face of AIDS, our organizations tried a wide variety of tactics to neutralize this political football. At the same time, gay organizations and early AIDS lobbying groups tried to separate the disease from the gay community in order to encourage government action and public support. In many ways, this separation tactic was the last-gasp strategy of assimilationist politics, although an understandable one. The original name for AIDS was GRID (Gay Related Immune Deficiency). Its first mention in the *New York Times* was an article proclaiming that a "rare cancer" had been found in a small number of homosexual men. So, from the beginning, gay men and AIDS were linked in the public mind. The attempt to disconnect them was strategically comprehensible in the short run, because the organizers were well aware of the full range to which gay people are despised in this country. Yet, in many ways this strategy ultimately backfired, especially later when it made the gay community promise over and over again that a middle-class heterosexual epidemic was just around the corner. When the epidemic did not appear, straight people once again lost interest in the virus.

Gay Men's Health Crisis had been operating for a few years, so had the People With AIDS Coalition, but they were not yet fully perceived as major representative organizations for the lesbian and gay community.

LIP-SYNCHING AT SHESCAPE

New York Native,
September 1985

Shescape is definitely where it's happening if you are a lesbian with a lot of energy. Women of every color and age dressed in their best dance to loud disco music under flashing lights, lounge in their Provincetown and Riis Park t-shirts, and exchange sultry glances over the crowded bar where Budweiser sells for $2.50. Managers Laurie and Joni keep an eye on the throngs of women who make it past the male bouncer on the street and the woman checking through purses for bottles or guns. The place is large enough to host marble steps and conceal discreet joint smoking. As you work your way through the boogeying hordes, women seductively slip their hands around your curves just to pass by. On Wednesday, admission is free all night, with free food at 8:00, and the place is usually packed by 9. You might know half the people there and never run into them because Wednesday night is lip-synch night and full to the rafters.

The contestants meet in the women's bathroom, using one stall to change into their costumes while a long line of bar goers wait to get into the other one. A woman with the name "Lulu" tattooed on her shoulder and a black handkerchief dangling from her left pocket waited with a glassy stare while a tall Latina in a blue crepe gown dusted glitter onto her lover's shoulders. By the time the show started, the audience was rowdy and roaring.

Acting as master of ceremonies, Joni, in printed Bermuda shorts, seemed somehow like a substitute teacher on her first day in a public school. "Girls, girls, please be quiet," she pleaded. "I'm getting angry now. I know you're going to hate this but you girls have been grabbing a little too much. If you want to give dollars or flowers to the performers, please wait until after the show. Girls— shut up! I'm getting pissed."

But the girls just laughed.

The three run-off contestants were introduced by the names of their chosen icons and each one took her job very seriously.

Lip-synching is one of those fields that reveals the performer's fantasy life immediately. Chaka Khan, Pat Benatar, and Colonel Abrahms obviously spent hours alone in front of their mirrors dancing their hearts out, dreaming of celebrity.

Maggy Smith, decked out in wig, gown, and glitter, exhibited the exuberence of a Chaka Khan performance. Maritza Gonzalez chose to present a brutally sexy Pat Benatar, eliciting a chorus of hoots and cheers whenever she wiggled her behind. Finally, Sheila Parham, a powerlifter, gave a sweaty, emotional performance as Colonel Abrahms singing "Unity" which inspired the audience to break the ban on gifts and start stuffing dollar bills into her gym shorts.

Pat Benatar took home the $200 prize while the others took home a moment in the spotlight. A lot of people were also taken home that night from Shescape while this overwhelmed reporter went back to the quiet provincialism of the Grove Club where nothing is happening and a Budweiser also costs $2.50.

STRAIGHT ADS HURT GAY FIRM

New York Native,
October 1985

Christopher Street Financial (CSF) is an openly gay financial planning firm, founded in 1981 with offices at 80 Wall Street. They serve a primarily gay clientele and are oriented towards a gay market. After years of advertising in the gay media, CSF attempted to expand their services by promoting themselves in mainstream publications.

According to president Robert Casteletto, CSF decided that their first step would be to advertise in a *New York Times* financial planning supplement. The copy read "Gay Money, Straight Advice." The ad was sent to the Times Advertising Acceptability Committee which requested that the word "lover" in the text of the ad be changed to "partner." CSF agreed.

The next step was the submission of a similar ad to the *Wall Street Journal*. The *Journal* rejected the ad on the grounds that its content was discriminatory on the basis of "lifestyle." According to Casteletto, CSF has a non-discriminatory policy, but, "It is hard to find straight people who are willing to be identified with a gay company."

A subsequent ad appearing in *New York Magazine* resulted in "virtually only crank calls." "People would call asking if you have to have AIDS to do business with us," Casteletto said. CSF had to hire an additional employee to handle these calls.

As a result, Christopher Street Financial has decided to only advertise in the gay press. "We'll be at every gay event," Casteletto said, "and that is it."

COMMENTARY

Despite the smarmy behavior of the mainstream press, there is also another interesting historical moment buried in this story. Christopher Street Financial was being accused of discrimination against straight people because straight people were too prejudiced to invest in a gay firm. Over a year before, the Dutchess Club had been shut down for discrimination against men.

Ironically the upper-crust financial planners and the working-class lesbian bar patrons were being subjected to the same kind of twisted rhetoric. Each was accused of "reverse discrimination" against more powerful dominant culture groups. These cynical manipulations were the seeds of what, five years later, would explode into the famous "p.c." debates—a media-created non-issue in which dominant institutions accused oppressed people of "discrimination" or bias while shifting all attention away from their own ongoing power and privileges.

Saving Our Space on the Lower East Side
An Interview with Marguerita Lopez

Womanews,
October 1985

> I've spent the last four years trying to save my apartment from spec-
> ulators. Then one day I opened my window and the neighborhood
> was gone.
>
> —Lower East Side Resident

I was sitting on my stoop on Ninth Street and First Avenue when a
friend stopped by.

"I just saw something incredible," she said. "Marguerita Lopez
chained herself to a girder during an anti-gentrification demo."

Marguerita, a member of the Lower East Side Community
Board and an out lesbian, was kind enough to agree to an
interview, conducted from the apartment she shares with her lover
in a low income project in the neighborhood she loves.

SARAH   *What is the role of lesbians and gay men in gentrification?*

MARGUERITA   Like every struggle, you will find blacks, Hispanics,
Asians, and gays who are part of the rich people. I
hear accusations but I don't think that gay men are
a force for gentrification. On the contrary, gay people
in this community are a part of the fighting back.
You hear a lot in this country that gay men have
money, but I know a lot of gay men personally and
none of *them* have money.

SARAH   *Artists have always lived in this neighborhood, and yet all
these horrible new art galleries are objects of extreme hatred.*

MARGUERITA   Art is the most beautiful expression of the human
being, but capitalism discovered that art can produce
a lot of money, and art was commercialized into an

item of luxury and status. Recently a lot of bodegas, old stores, have been displaced by galleries. It's not that the neighborhood is against artists, but the galleries bring art to the neighborhood that the community cannot understand. The only people who go into these places are from outside. I'd never seen a mink coat before in my life until I passed a gallery on 10th Street and Avenue B and a woman got out of a Mercedes Benz.

Community artists, on the other hand, are very respected. If you go to Charras on 9th Street, people respect the building and the artists who work there. But in the galleries you never see a black or Hispanic or low income artist. I cannot define art as something used by the oppressor. I cannot.

SARAH   *You have made your stand as an out lesbian in the housing movement. How can feminists participate?*

MARGUERITA   The feminist and lesbian movements have been making a big mistake for a long time. They isolate themselves. They hold their activities in the basement of a building. I define myself as a feminist and I know that our issue is a real difficult one to fight. We have to be part of every movement that is going on. I know it can hurt a lot, but no matter how much they can hurt us, we have to get out of the basement and join the movement. Not just marching, either. Marching together is easy, especially when everybody separates themselves with banners. I'm talking about real work together. Does the feminist movement know that this neighborhood is full of single women with children and that they are the last to get housing? The housing movement is vital for women. Look, a person can be scared for a few minutes or they can be scared for their whole life. Each person has to ask themselves *which do you prefer ?*

COMMENTARY

I look back on the piece with complex emotions. The period described here was one of rapidly growing parasitism. Middle and upper-class whites rampaged through previously mixed neighborhoods buying up rental property, displacing families and poor people into homelessness while promoting overpriced condo-conversion. During the height of gallery-mania, basic service stores were closing rapidly to be replaced by expensive boutiques, expensive restaurants, and endless, endless galleries.

Because the city provided tax breaks for private development, because of the lack of ethics on the part of realtors, renters, and homeowners alike, and because the city has virtually stopped constructing low income housing, there are now over 100,000 homeless people on the streets of New York. In the East Village, the neighborhood Marguerita discusses, the art market bottomed out. A handful of artists got very rich, some of them were gay men. The upper-class, white clientele that they attracted to the neighborhood bought overpriced co-ops and condominiums. But gentrification was never able to defeat crack addiction and in many ways, the spread of crack, combined with the stock market crash of 1987, broke the white stranglehold on the community, even though the damage was irreparable.

Today, pet shops, T.V. repair shops, and barber shops are re-opening. Rents have gone down 40 percent although they're still four times what they should be. Yuppies got tired of paying $1,100 a month to step over drug addicts and homeless people on the way to work. Many became absentee landlords, subletting their apartments at lower than maximum rents. The drug traffic is out of control and the large numbers of homeless people still have nowhere to go.

It is interesting to look back on Marguerita's comments because the eighties' gallery boom has only been described, historically, from the point of view of the invaders, but the perspective of gay and lesbian people like her—who are not the glamorous and powerful, but just residents of the community—rarely gets acknowledged. As for the majority of artists who have always lived in the East Village, they're still there. And most of them are still working on a volunteer basis, making lifetime commitments to work that will never be sold and may never really be seen. But that community and its story really requires its own book.

HEALTH OR HOMOPHOBIA?
RESPONSES TO THE BATHHOUSE GUIDELINES

New York Native,
November 1985

As the drama of the state's imposition of guidelines for gay bath-houses unfolds, the *Native* asked a variety of community figures and officials for their reactions.

MARVIN BOGNER—ASSISTANT COMMISSIONER OF PUBLIC INFORMATION, NEW YORK CITY BOARD OF HEALTH

NATIVE   *Does your office favor the closure of the bathhouses?*

BOGNER   State guidelines have been adopted and we are going to follow them.

NATIVE   *Do you support the monitoring of sexual activities?*

BOGNER   We are going to follow the state's guidelines.

NATIVE   *Do you think these guidelines could be used to outlaw sodomy on medical grounds?*

BOGNER   I can't answer that.

VIRGINIA APUZZO—FORMER EXECUTIVE DIRECTOR, NATIONAL GAY TASK FORCE

APUZZO   I've asked Tom Stoddard of the ACLU to petition the legal network around the country to get a white paper on the legal implications of this action and see whether, in fact, we're correct in our concern. If that is indeed the case, then I feel it is imperative that the governor avail himself of these implications.

NATIVE   *Do you support the monitoring of sexual activity in the baths?*

APUZZO   No.

NATIVE   *Do you support the closure of the baths?*

APUZZO   I wish they could go out of business on their own.

NATIVE   *Could these guidelines be used to reinstate sodomy laws?*

APUZZO   That is precisely the link we've been worried about which has precipitated the need for this white paper. Whether or not that concern is as accurate as it appears to be, we have to hold off until we get the best thinking of all the legal sources across the country. The only thing I'm deferring judgment on is the legal implications of this for sodomy statutes and litigation.

NANCY ROTH—GAY RIGHTS NATIONAL LOBBY

ROTH   Bathhouses don't spread AIDS, people spread AIDS. By focusing our attention on the bathhouses, we are diverting our attention from positive things we can do to reduce the spread of AIDS. By focusing energy on closing the baths, which is not a terribly effective health measure, we are diverting energy from education. I think the reality is that people are going to behave the way they want to behave—in baths, hotel rooms, and the privacy of their own homes. Our focus must be about educating people to lower risk behaviors. Other measures are simply not effective.

NATIVE   *Can this be used to outlaw sodomy?*

ROTH   Certainly AIDS is used as an argument in those situations. Clearly there's a distinction that needs to be made. We run a real risk that those kinds of arguments will be made.

NATIVE   *What is behind these guidelines?*

ROTH   My sense is that there is a tremendously widespread sentiment, even within the gay and lesbian community, that bathhouses are not good places. Unfortunately, bathhouses are not an appropriate target.

NATIVE   *What do you think would be a more appropriate measure?*

ROTH   To pour money into public education about what AIDS is and is not, what the symptoms are, how it is spread, and what kinds of behaviors are less risky.

Time and energy need to be spent on thinking about how to make behavioral changes socially acceptable.

RON NAJMAN—MEDIA DIRECTOR, NATIONAL GAY TASK FORCE

NAJMAN Probably some government intervention was welcome seeing there was a great deal of sentiment within the gay and lesbian community. For example, the Coalition for Sexual Responsibility tried to get the recalcitrant bathhouse owners to institute safe sex guidelines. The patience of the local community had worn thin. However, we remain opposed to outright closure and we're glad that's not the policy of Albany or the Koch administration. What we are most disturbed about right now is the language of this regulation per se. That's the slippery slope towards sodomy laws.

NATIVE *Do you oppose monitoring sexual activity in the baths?*

NAJMAN I think that we would have to see what the enforcement procedure would be.

NATIVE *What enforcement procedure would be acceptable?*

NAJMAN We wouldn't want to comment on those until something is worked out between the representatives in the community and the state and local authorities.

NATIVE *Does the proposal endanger the civil rights of gay people?*

NAJMAN I think it does. It's troublesome. It appears to target private behavior rather than regulating business in order to discourage high-risk activity. These regulations suggest an unequal application of the law. While they are now talking about gay establishments per se, they're not just talking about anal intercourse, but about fellatio. It is clearly being geared to sexual acts between gay men. That is made most obvious by the fact that they haven't included vaginal intercourse. Even though that may be a rare means of transmission, most of the medical community believes that it is a means of transmission. That's discriminatory—not necessarily in intent, but in fact. They may well be doing a sharp disservice to society at large by not reminding heterosexuals that they are at risk. It is clear that whatever one says about this and whatever one's motivations are and how good they are, there is also a publicity effect. This is going to heighten certain concerns. It is something of a mystery to us why they are not reminding heterosexuals that they are also at risk. Those are secondary concerns, but they exist.

MICHAEL CALLEN—COALITION FOR SEXUAL RESPONSIBILITY

CALLEN   I've been incorrectly perceived as a leader of the bathhouse closure group. My position has always been that the status quo in these places is unacceptable during an epidemic. Prior to the efforts of the Coalition for Sexual Responsibility, it was possible to go into any number of bathhouses and backroom bars and not have any acknowledgement that there was a health crisis. The Coalition came to an agreement on not regulating behavior. Instead, we recommend monitoring for structural, educational, and hygienic regulations. We wanted bathhouse and backroom bar owners to put up posters, to do active as opposed to passive education, to hand each patron—upon admission—a brochure and a condom. We wanted the lights turned up to reduce anonymity and to encourage people to talk about health issues and safe sex practices. We got them to agree to permit community groups to come in and do education on their premises. We asked them to keep the places clean, remove glory holes, bathtubs, and slings. And we did inspect for compliance with these regulations.

The underlying principle is that two consenting adults have the right, in private, to engage in behavior which the majority of medical experts may well feel is not in their best interests. It's a very unattractive liberal position. I sometimes compare it to the right of Nazis to march in Skokie. Basically, consenting adults in private have a right to kill themselves if that's what they want to do.

I believe people ought to have that right, but before people make these momentous life and death decisions, they must make them in an informed manner, so that they're not making these decisions out of ignorance. I want to make sure there is no way that somebody from out-of-town or who didn't read the gay press, would not know about safe sex. I'm critical of the gay community's feeble and tardy and not frank efforts at education, and I want very much to make it the obligation of these businesses, which are profiting from this epidemic, to be responsible.

The State Health Commissioner Dr. Axelrod told me that he felt that our recommendations were unenforceable, and I told him that what he's done is unenforceable. He told me that he is willing to testify in any court of law that he opposes the recriminalization of sodomy. He is responsible for protecting public health. It is his opinion that bath-houses are public. He is talking about regulating a business over which he has authority. But you know the history of our community and the government has been very troublesome. We must remain ever vigilant.

NANCY LANGER——LAMBDA LEGAL DEFENSE AND EDUCATION FUND

LANGER   We strongly favor the guidelines proposed by the Coalition for Sexual Responsibility, which would ensure certain hygienic and structural changes in the bathhouses. We also support the Governor's AIDS Advisory Council's recommendation that bathhouses be subject to state regulation to ensure that education is ongoing at these establishments. However, we have strong reservations about the regulations proposed by the governor. We worry about the slippery slope and we fear that the language is particularly bad and might fuel the fire of recriminalization of sodomy in New York State, as the AIDS situation has fueled the fires in, for example, Texas, to return that state's sodomy laws to the books. We're worried that, in many locales, the AIDS crisis is being used as pseudo-scientific rationale to justify archaic sodomy laws. We would like for this not to happen in New York State.

LORI BEHRMAN—PUBLIC INFORMATION DIRECTOR, GAY MEN'S HEALTH CRISIS

NATIVE   *What is GMHC's reaction to the guidelines?*

BEHRMAN   Well, they're not being enforced yet. The guidelines are that any place which allows "high risk" sex will be closed. We feel that focusing on the bathhouses alone takes away from the broader issue of education. Bathhouses themselves do not cause AIDS, behavior does. These activities would probably still take place if the bathhouses were closed. They would take place in locations that we would not be able to get to, to educate the patrons. You have to remember that a very small percentage of people still go to the bathhouses.

NATIVE   *Do you oppose closing the baths?*

BEHRMAN   I don't think it's a question of opposed or not opposed. I think it's taking away from the issue of education.

NATIVE   *What is your position on monitoring sexual behavior?*

BEHRMAN   We feel there should be some regulation as the Coalition for Sexual Responsibility has been trying to do. For the most part we have had good co-operation from the bathhouses. We have set up tables in the bathhouses to educate people on healthy sex, to distribute literature and counsel people who want information.

107

NATIVE   *Could the guidelines evolve into sodomy laws?*

BEHRMAN   I don't know. I can't comment on that. Certainly, we feel that the focus should be on other issues, not the bathhouses.

ANDY HUMM——COALITION FOR LESBIAN AND GAY RIGHTS

HUMM   By focusing on the baths, the governor is misleading people that if we would just clear up that problem, we would solve the AIDS crisis. I worked on the Coalition for Sexual Responsibility, which worked on getting the baths to provide information, condoms, things like that. If a bathhouse refuses to do that, I think the community should boycott it, but I don't think the governor should close it.

   The main problem I have with Cuomo's whole approach is that it's so incomplete. He's talking about all these restrictions on gay behavior, but he doesn't refer to straight behavior. He didn't once mention the fact that we need to pass a comprehensive gay rights bill. In other words, if you're going to solve this crisis, you need to embrace gay people as responsible citizens. The state would legalize relationships between gay people. There are gay people who would like to do that. I'm not putting any special value on that, but certainly it seems that if they want to, the state would have a certain interest in encouraging it at this point. Obviously more stable relationships are less likely to involve a transfer of whatever it is that causes AIDS.

   I am opposed to government closure. I think that the gay people who sue bathhouses have to be better consumers. If you just close them, that segment of the population will find a way to have sex, without benefit of any place where they can be educated. If they can limit behavior in a commercial establishment, they can limit behavior in other establishments. Does that include hotels? Or rented apartments?

Dr. Joseph Sonnabend—Co-founder, AIDS Medical Foundation

NATIVE   *What do you think about the new regulations?*

SONNABEND   I think they're dreadful. Regulations are not a sub-stitute for education. I feel they're a retrogressive move.

NATIVE   *What do you feel is behind it?*

SONNABEND   I have no idea. It's said to be a political thing to show that there's some kind of response to the con-stituency that seems to wish to keep children with AIDS out of the schools—to please them maybe.

NATIVE   *Are you opposed to the monitoring of sexual activity?*

SONNABEND   Of course.

NATIVE   *Could this be used to outlaw sodomy?*

SONNABEND   Of course.

NATIVE   *What do you think would be appropriate action?*

SONNABEND   Appropriate action would be to increase educational efforts. There is no substitute for education.

Jeff Levi—Political Director, National Gay Task Force

LEVI   I'll be real honest with you. I have very little desire to speak to the *Native* and I think you can understand why. I have no desire to cooperate with you.

Although Mayor Koch and Dr. Mathilde Krim, Chair of the AIDS Medical Foundation, both spoke to the *New York Times* on the sub-ject of guidelines, neither returned the *Native*'s calls.

COMMENTARY

1985 was a pivotal moment in the public perception of AIDS. For years, gay people had been trying to get the attention of the government and the straight media, hoping for responsive funding and compassion. But as soon as the dominant culture noticed AIDS, they started to distort its meaning and use this visibility to isolate and punish people who were infected. In other words, 1985 proved that heterosexual awareness equaled AIDS hysteria.

That year wholesale stigma and persecution of the infected exploded. Parents boycotted schools with HIV-positive students and in some cases firebombed their homes. Suggestions of quarantine began to circulate. People with AIDS faced severe housing and job discrimination as the press fueled new unfounded fears and paranoia on a daily basis.

In the midst of this cold-hearted panic, Mario Cuomo, the governor of New York, handed down "guidelines" designed to shut down the gay bathhouses and sex clubs. As City Hall reporter for the *New York Native,* I covered a number of different aspects of the bathhouse closings. One of the most historically revealing was this survey of prominent gay leaders and city officials. Some of these organizations are no longer in existence. Many of these people are out of the spotlight of gay politics.

But, most important, I think, is the utter confusion and lack of clear vision articulated by much of the leadership. It is a stark look at a symbolic moment —perhaps the first full realization by the old guard that the government was going to scapegoat the gay community and that no amount of behind-the-scenes manipulation was going to be able to stop them. Their fear that the state could and would use AIDS to outlaw homosexual sex is accurately revealing of the vulnerability and isolation that gay people felt at that moment.

Buried in the subtext of many of the statements is a hint that some people from the gay community itself were involved in bringing in the state to take action regarding the baths—although it also is implied that those people thought they could use state intervention to pressure bathhouses to comply with guidelines and that they did not intend to force closure.

Most telling of all is the fact that, despite the high degree of panic exhibited by the leadership, not a single person called for street activism or a grass-roots movement to respond to the government's action.

KOCH READY TO CLOSE
MORE BATHHOUSES

New York Native,
December 1985

Does Mayor Koch intend to close more bathhouses?

"I hope so," he said at a December 16th press conference at City Hall. "We are monitoring institutions which we believe are allowing unsafe health practices to continue."

Claiming that New York provides more to "AIDS victims" than any other city or state including San Francisco, Koch announced new insurance and health service proposals. Most of these, however, were made in the form of a request to Governor Cuomo, placing the burden for action on Albany.

Koch's proposal included a request for a higher rate of reimbursement for AIDS patients. While average treatment rates hover at about $500 per day, AIDS patients require from $800–$1,000. He also requested that the state monitor abuse by insurance companies attempting to deny coverage to persons with AIDS on a wide variety of grounds. Most frequently, AIDS can be classified as a "pre-existing condition." He suggested that nursing homes which refuse AIDS cases be punished by the state and recommended that the governor impose regulations forbidding funeral homes from refusing the bodies of people who have died of AIDS, an action currently protected by law.

Early on in the press conference, a reporter cited repeated instances of mistreatment and abuse of AIDS patients either inside hospitals or by virtue of being denied adequate placement. Koch replied that he received personal mail on a wide variety of subjects but that "no one has written me a personal letter saying that this exists." He added that if he did find out that such a phenomenon exists he would take action.

According to Katy Taylor of the Commission for Human Rights, since 1983 there have been two hundred complaints of discrimination against persons with AIDS "in every case imaginable including employment, housing, public accommodation, insurance, and violence." These have been accompanied by what Taylor calls "a huge number of complaints" of discrimination based on sexual orientation. She says that this indicates the impact of AIDS hysteria on people with AIDS as well as the rest of the lesbian and gay population. In comparison to other issues addressed by the Commission, AIDS discrimination was the third largest category following race and sex. "Many of the problems that people with AIDS face have a discrimination element," Taylor said.

The Koch administration acknowledged that the rate of increase of AIDS is higher among intravenous drug users than gay men, except for cases in which these categories overlap. According to Dr. David Sencer, the outgoing Health Commissioner, who also spoke at the press conference, "the gay population in New York knows what needs to be done and in large part has changed their habits." But the Koch administration has been unable or unwilling to come up with a plan to educate the drug user population about the communicability of AIDS and AIDS prevention. At present, according to Sencer, the best the city can offer is to work through counselors in drug rehabilitation programs. "You don't solve an epidemic by meeting," Sencer said. "But we are trying to continually meet to convince drug counselors that they need to speak frankly with their clients about sexuality."

Koch rejected the idea of trying to stop drug use saying it was too prevalent. "A shooting gallery," said Koch, "is where two or more people are shooting up. Otherwise it's an apartment. The only way you're going to stop it is by keeping marijuana, cocaine and heroin from coming into the country." "What are you going to do with a guy who likes drugs but doesn't want treatment?" asked Koch. He then answered, "He doesn't want AIDS of course. Then he should stop taking heroin."

While AIDS rates of increase are declining, Sencer anticipates that the number of cases will double in two years. The city expects to spend between $42 and $56 million on AIDS in 1986. To date there have been 5,300 diagnosed cases.

COMMENTARY

Koch was widely believed to be gay himself, and in his early political career he was supported by gay and lesbian organizations. But, his behavior during the AIDS crisis was one of buffoonery and deadly contempt. The argument that gay bathhouses were ideal places to spread information about safe sex was a logical one, but ill-suited to the sexual hypocrisy of the city administration. In the late eighties, gay male sex clubs and backroom bars started to quietly re-open. By 1990 they were in blatant operation provoking more media hype and threats of bar closures. Interestingly, it was a gay writer, Daryl Yates Rist, who brought the television crews into the Crow Bar, an East Village club with a back room. Five years earlier, Rist had written a front page story in the *Nation* magazine (the *Nation*'s first ever front page piece on any aspect of gay or lesbian life) *condemning* ACT UP for focusing on AIDS to the exclusion of other gay issues. People often play the same roles through a variety of historical moments.

Anyway, the second time around, the "public health" issue was handled by the new health commissioner Margaret Hamburg whose office worked closely with the gay bars to negotiate a second series of guidelines including condom availability and informal monitoring that kept the state out of the bars.

Implicit in Koch's comments (and in the press hysteria years later), was the twisted demand to gay men concerning safe sex. Safe sex was invented by gay men. Michael Callen and Dr. Joseph Sonnabend claim authorship. It was publicized by gay men through networks and service organizations and graphic design and street activism, all born in and supported by the lesbian and gay community. In fact, virtually all constructive responses to the AIDS crisis have originated at some point in the gay and lesbian community with no help or else outright obstruction from the government.

The dominant culture has provided no social context for gay men or for straight women to negotiate condoms. Gay sexuality and female sexuality is still viciously repressed, condoms are still not advertised on television, explicit safe sex information is not readily and publicly available. The culture has made no commitment to selling safe sex the way it sells Coca-Cola. Yet, they expect gay men, living in this hostile environment, to perfectly utilize safe sex without any human disruption. When they're not perfect, they're immediately vilified. The tabloid print and T.V. press is more than willing to demonize gay men for having sex in a context where condom use may not be strictly adhered to, yet there is no public outcry against straight men and either their refusal to use condoms or their continued brutality against gay men in the AIDS context.

One of ACT-UP's most creative actions was developed by Maxine Wolfe and organized under the auspices of the Women's Caucus, when activists wanted to design an action that would give straight women support for asking men to use condoms. They decided to go somewhere where straight men gathered, deciding on Shea Stadium for the Mets game. Three hundred ACT UPers attended the ball game with huge banners advertising safe sex in baseball terminology. Signs proclaiming "No Glove No Love" and "Don't Balk at Safe Sex" were waved from the bleachers during significant plays on the field. And thousands of condoms were handed out to Mets fans as they entered the stadium. Of course, these kinds of direct, creative campaigns are the responsibility of the government, not lesbian and gay AIDS activists.

COMMITTEE RESOLVES TO CLOSE BATHS
MALONEY JOINS ANTI-GAY SELLOUT
GAY ACTIVIST ARRESTED

New York Native,
December 1985

While Mayor Koch was away in Japan, the City Council Health Committee voted unanimously in favor of Resolution 1985, calling for the closure of bathhouses and other public establishments where "certain high-risk sexual practices" occur. Although the resolution cites both "homosexual and heterosexual" establishments, it specifies only oral and anal sex and does not mention vaginal intercourse. Joining the vote was Councilmember Carolyn Maloney, a sponsor of the Gay Rights Bill (Intro 990).

On November 15 the U.S. Public Health Service announced that there is no need to restrict food handlers or health workers with AIDS. Yet the City Council Health Committee chose to proceed with hearings on Intro 1027, which called for a prohibition on the attendance of all public school children, teachers, and personnel who test positive for HTLV-III antibodies. It was sponsored by Jerry Crispino, chair of the committee, and Noach Dear, virulent anti-gay campaigner.

The resolutions were supported by a coalition of black, Orthodox Jewish, Puerto Rican, and Italian council members, many of whom have vigorously opposed the passage of a gay rights bill.

The hearings began on Friday with testimony from Congressman Ted Weiss (D-NY). "Many of my constituents are suffering directly or indirectly from this health emergency," said Weiss. "Thousands of Americans have been victimized, not only by this disease, but by societal and government reticence" to provide services. Weiss called the new school-related council proposals "reckless and irresponsible" and claimed they would violate "individuals' rights to privacy." He cited a statement from the Centers for Disease Control in Atlanta saying that they do not recommend HTLV-III testing. The statement also opposed the denial of employment to those who test positive. Weiss is currently sponsoring legislation which would establish a $60 million stand-by fund to help cities and states pay for health care and social services during the health crisis. A second Weiss bill would expedite Medicaid benefits for AIDS patients. Under current laws, they must wait two years and may die before eligibility is approved.

The heated racial and religious issues surrounding the bill were highlighted during the testimony of Jerry Nadler, a sponsor of the legislation to ban discrimination by insurance companies against people who test positive. When Nadler, who is Jewish, introduced city health department statistics that 51 percent of NYC AIDS victims are black and Hispanic, Councilmember Victor Robles, who is Hispanic, accused Nadler of distorting his information. Black councilmember Archie Spigner, condemned "a certain weekly" (the *Native*) for articles about the development of AIDS among minority communities. Councilmember Patricia Wooten, of East New York and Brownsville, also attacked Nadler for introducing these statistics saying she was "offended" by discussions of AIDS among blacks and Hispanics. She accused Nadler of having "a hidden agenda." Robles, Spigner, and Wooten also supported the public school legislation.

Cecil Butler, a Baptist minister and frequent demonstrator in front of Saint Mark's Baths, testified for the restrictions. "There is an arrogant community within the gay community," he said. "They will not allow you, as a city, to protect its citizens. The gay community doesn't want you to know that there is a smokescreen to cover up the goings-on. They have pedophiles marching in their gay parades; they have sado-masochists." Butler also said that the *Native* was used by men with AIDS to find sex partners. Councilmember Wooten complimented him on his testimony.

Dr. Sigmund Friedman, an Orthodox Jewish physician, attacked Nadler, claiming that if a drop of blood from a person with AIDS got on a salad and someone ate that salad, they would get AIDS. Councilmember Miriam Friedlander, who is also Jewish and a sponsor of the Gay Rights Bill, objected. She admonished Friedman for "whipping up hysteria." Friedlander said, "We know personally the effects of hysteria against Jewish people."

While community leader David Rothenberg told the Committee to stop "scapegoating in the guise of providing medical security," the gay community was making their own statement outside City Hall. A crowd of about fifty high-spirited gay men and lesbians arrived in front of City Hall for a noon demonstration called by the Coalition for Lesbian and Gay Rights. They were protesting the bills and the

115

refusal of the Council to bring the Gay Rights Bill to a vote. The crowd was very enthusiastic, perhaps as the result of a town meeting the night before in which 700 gay men and lesbians listened to speakers at Duane Methodist Church encouraging activism against the rising tide of homophobia. At one point, David Summers, spokesperson for People With AIDS, climbed the steps of City Hall and was accosted by a policeman who refused him entry, despite the fact that Summers was scheduled to testify. The incident coincided with the appearance of Paul Cameron, the noted homophobe, who was also scheduled to testify. When the demonstrators recognized Cameron and saw Summers's encounter with police, a fracas ensued in which Summers was handcuffed, arrested, and taken to a room inside City Hall.

The demonstrators became very angry and pressed the front steps of the building calling for his release. "If David doesn't come out we're going in," a number of them said. A police line took position in front of the demonstrators, stopping them from entering the building. Through the efforts of Councilmembers Ruth Messinger, Carole Greitzer, and activist David Rothenberg with attorney Jim Levin, Summers was released and re-emerged to address the crowd. They then followed him peacefully into the hearing room. Summers was subsequently issued a summons for disorderly conduct.

The hearing resumed with eloquent testimony from Richard Dunne, Executive Director of Gay Men's Health Crisis. "The burden of AIDS is not only the burden of death," Dunne said, "but the burden of contending with fear. It is the gay community that has provided the muscle, the resolve and the dollars to educate the general public." At this point Councilmember Maloney underlined the fact that GMHC had only received their first funds from the city the day before.

Assemblyman Denny Farrell, speaking against the legislation, compared community refusal of AIDS hospices to rejections of shelters for the homeless. He also endorsed the concept of one-time-only needles, to be distributed to IV drug users to limit the spread of AIDS.

Other witnesses included David Wertheimer, director of the Gay and Lesbian Anti-Violence Project, who commented on a "distressing pattern of incidents of harassment and violence that appear to be directly related to public fears of AIDS and violent acts by individuals engaging in those practices into locations where they will be more open to homophobic assault." But Wertheimer added, "The city's response to AIDS thus far has been an outstanding example of public stewardship."

When the hearing resumed on Monday, November 18, witnesses followed the announcement that State Health Commissioner David Axelrod had revealed his intention for the state to enter hotel rooms where oral and anal sex were taking place, in order to put an end to those activities. The Mayor was still in Japan. Health Commissioner Dr. David Sencer opened the proceedings by stating that he was "unable to discuss" either of the bills before the Committee. He then proceeded to read a sixteen-page list of all the things the Mayor's office claimed to have provided during the health crisis.

"We still do not have any proof that AIDS is transmitted by female to male sexual intercourse," he said. "We do not know that men have been infected by sexual intercourse with women." Sencer did not address the impact of this information on crackdowns on prostitutes accused of spreading AIDS. Nor did he mention male to female infection. Again, Councilmember Robles raised the issue of statistics on minorities with AIDS. Sencer gave them as follows: 58 percent bisexual or homosexual men, 6 percent bisexual or homosexual IV drug users, 1.4 percent sexual partners of drug users, 1 percent no risk group, 1 percent transfusion associated, 3 percent from countries with high rates of AIDS, 2 percent died before being interviewed, 28 percent heterosexual male and all female IV drug users. Racially this breaks down to 48 percent white, 30 percent black, 21 percent Hispanic and 1 percent Asian and Native American. He noted that the list was compiled from municipal and voluntary as well as private care hospitals, so that minorities would not be represented out of proportion. Sencer added that, in his opinion, "There is no risk at all of getting infected by a blood transfusion," due to extensive HTLV-III screening. When asked his personal opinion of the governor's guidelines, Sencer stated, "I do not feel that this would contribute to the control of AIDS, but when this became a state regulation, I, of course, agreed with it." Sencer added that, to his knowledge, there are currently four children with AIDS in the school system.

Finally Intro 1027, to keep people who test positive for HTLV-III out of the public school system, was defeated unanimously although five of the no votes were delivered grudgingly. Only Maloney made an urgent statement contending, "This legislation would violate individual rights to privacy." The second resolution, to close the baths, was passed unanimously, despite Chairman Crispino's constant interruptions of the vote to give reports on the Jets game. Maloney, explaining her vote, said on the floor, that she had proposed five amendments. Three were added specifying the words "heterosexual and homosexual" and targeting establishments used as "venues for multiple sexual contacts." Then she voted yes. Her vote was greeted by calls of "outrageous" and "sell-out" from the audience. Speaking later, Maloney said she took credit for killing the first bill. "Once I put forth these amendments and they accepted them, I couldn't go in there and vote no. I watered it down."

Andy Humm, spokesperson for the Coalition for Lesbian and Gay Rights, who has worked extensively with Maloney for a Gay Rights Bill, called her vote "an absolute disgrace." Humm added that "the council's resolution will be used when the Georgia sodomy law comes before the Supreme Court. They will be able to say that even New York City passed a resolution of this nature."

After the vote was taken, most of the politicians, legislative aides, and press left. A quiet, sparse collection of gay people sat and listened to David Summers, who was finally allowed to testify for the record. Summers was the only open person with AIDS who testified during the entire hearing. "I will fight with my last breath, this witch-hunt under the guise of protecting the public. With courage and compassion we may one day see the end of AIDS," said Summers. And then he went up to each remaining Councilmember and, one by one, shook their hands.

COMMENTARY

Buried in this story are a number of important moments in the development of AIDS politics. I believe this marks the first AIDS-related arrest. David Summers was a cabaret singer and an openly gay actor who appeared in such early gay plays as "The Faggot" by Al Carmines at his Judson Memorial Church. Summers continued to perform openly as a person with AIDS and was one of the earliest organizers of the People With AIDS empowerment movement. Ironically, in AIDS politics, he who lives longest, declares history. And so the courageous pioneering efforts of men like Summers, Michael Hirsch, and Max Navarre often go unheralded. But there was AIDS activism before ACT UP.

The homophobia of the black and Latino members of the Council is absolutely staggering. Contained in this event is a crystal clear example of how black and Hispanic leaders let their homophobia keep them from seeing the threat of the crisis to their own districts. It also reveals their absolute refusal to acknowledge the existence of black and Latino gay men.

David Summers and Richard Dunne died of AIDS, Carolyn Maloney was elected to Congress. Only one heterosexual establishment, Plato's Retreat, was temporarily closed under this ordinance. In fact, the bathhouse closings were clearly more motivated by political rather than health reasons. Only the most visible, predominantly white, establishments like the Saint Mark's Baths (still abandoned) and the Mineshaft were shut. The Mount Morris Baths in Harlem remain open to this day. The issue Dr. Sencer raised about the lack of evidence for female to male transmission has still not been resolved. We will see how the manipulation of these fears, even without sound statistical evidence, came to be a sub-theme in the social pathology of AIDS hysteria.

BECOMING AN ANGRY MOB
IN THE BEST SENSE
LESBIANS RESPOND TO AIDS HYSTERIA

New York Native,
December 1985

We're in this together now. Not only are lesbians losing friends and relatives to AIDS, but they are feeling the effects of the new homophobia accompanying AIDS hysteria. Individual gay men and lesbians have often been great friends. Socially, gay men and lesbians have a historically tenuous relationship. Grossly unequal in terms of money and power, lesbians have watched gay men develop their social legitimacy and financial resources. In the meantime there has never been a lesbian play on Broadway, a lesbian newspaper with a paid staff, or an exclusively lesbian bar that wasn't Mafia controlled, overcrowded, and frequently closed down. When women have experienced economic or physical brutality, gay men as a group never really cared. They've had men's money, men's arrogance, and men's self-absorption.

Suddenly there was AIDS. Society turned against gay men, proving that all the assimilation and upward mobility in the world did not erase homophobia. Now the gay community is seeing daily attacks from the state and the media and a need to formulate a political response is becoming apparent. Socially, as much as emotionally, the AIDS crisis is a disaster for lesbians. Not only is the hysteria hurting us but the gay response is being formulated in a way that brings out the stark contrasts between lesbian and gay politics.

According to Maxine Wolfe, a professor at the City University Graduate Center, "The majority of people don't make distinctions between lesbians or gays. In their minds, we're queer. I think it's a mistake to assume that if and when a cure is found, everything is going to be fun again. What's being unleashed on us has little to do with the communicability of this disease. When you get down to it, the guidelines could be used to close anything. We need to be out there despite the homophobia, to resist the moves to deny lesbian and gay existence."

120

Like many lesbian activists, Wolfe is concerned about the quality of the gay community's response to the political crisis.

"I think part of it is that the disaster in the community is consuming people with the deaths of those around them and their own potential deaths. That's one group of people. Another group has put themselves in with the Democratic Party and thinks that somewhere behind the scenes this is all going to be taken care of if everyone plays nice. I also think that there are a lot of people who want to disassociate themselves from *those people* who engage in the baths or backroom bars. There are also some radical gay men who still believe that sexual liberation is okay, though it is hard not to get guilt tripped at a time like this."

Abby Tallmer is a former employee of the AIDS Medical Foundation and the author of one of the first articles on women with AIDS. She, too, has seen more hostility directed towards lesbians. "Women as well as men report increased street harassment due to the hysteria," she said. But it is the response of the gay community to the closing of the Mineshaft that Tallmer points to as significant of larger problems within the community.

"It was no coincidence that the Mineshaft was the first club closed under these regulations," she said. "In any community under attack, the most marginal subsets are the first to go. S/M people are among the politically marginal, and, for some, embarrassing members of the gay community. This move is an attempt by the city and the state to engage in divide-and-conquer tactics. In other words, they knew that no gay leaders would rally to the Mineshaft's defense, afraid that their names would appear next to the words 'S/M AIDS DEN' on the front page of our daily newspapers. I find it quite distressing that the government's reasoning seems to have been right. Most of our spokespeople are content to write off the Mineshaft's closure, implicitly accepting the assumption that because S/M was practiced there, it was more of a risk for AIDS than any other club in New York, which is ridiculous. It is also distressing to see virtually no one willing to defend the ethic of the Mineshaft and the baths, the importance of the pursuit of sexual pleasure as an end in itself. As a woman I've learned a tremendous amount from gay men and gay male culture in this regard. And I think these ideas still hold, regardless of the health crisis which prohibits us from acting all of them out."

Jewelle Gomez, a writer and critic, spoke at the November 14 Gay and Lesbian Anti-Defamation League Town Meeting. Gomez told the *Native* that "closing baths or bars is the first sign of political repression. Whether we think bars and baths are wonderful or not, they're not going to stop with the baths. We can't pretend that and still be self-respecting." When it was pointed out that none of the major gay organizations has made statements or taken action corresponding to her point of view, Gomez answered, "That's probably why I don't belong to any of them." She described the difference in approach between lesbians and gay men as being based in self-image in relation to society. "Gay men see themselves," she said, "in spite of being gay, as part of the structure. They are not totally *other* the way that lesbians feel they are."

Not all lesbians are so disappointed by the community's response. Sandy Feinbloom, Assistant Director of Clinical Services at the Gay Men's Health Crisis, speaking as an individual, told the *Native*, "The handling by the government tried to be responsive to the messages they heard from the gay community." Yet, she opposed the closing of the bathhouses. "I would rather know where people are doing high risk activities so you can have an opportunity to reach and counsel them."

She briefly discussed the effects of AIDS hysteria on the lesbian community. "There are certain people, who, when they hear *homosexual* don't distinguish between gay men and lesbians. We saw that early on in Los Angeles when blood was refused because it was donated by a lesbian organization. They clearly were not making distinctions about the risk group. Many lesbians fear that they are at risk, medically, since they occasionally sleep with men. A number of lesbians have been artificially inseminated by gay male donors, and they are also concerned. So, there is a hysterical reaction from the world at large and some from the community itself."

Joan Nestle, a writer and co-founder of the Lesbian Herstory Archives is one of the most respected leaders of the lesbian community. Her work is known by women throughout the U.S. and in Europe. Joan is a veteran of the pre-Stonewall gay community and was involved in the great sex debates in which the feminist movement divided over issues of pornography and sado-masochism.

When the S/M issue was raised among lesbians, some leather women claimed that when things heated up, they would be the first to be attacked. Many observers, including this reporter, scoffed at those statements, dismissing them as melodramatic posturing. Yet, with the closure of the Mineshaft, they have, in a sense, been

122

proved correct. According to Nestle, "We got lulled into a circle of respectability. I don't believe people really thought there would be police campaigns again, like in the fifties—that there would be circles of safety and if you were on the outside you would be the most vulnerable. It wasn't taken seriously that the state would become the aggressor again, as it had been. No matter how you feel about the bars, the fact that there wasn't an immediate street demonstration after the closing of the Mineshaft—well, compare it to the sixties when there would have been. These are sexualized territories that we have fought to win, no matter how we feel about what goes on in them. Every lesbian and gay man is going to have to ask themselves who they are willing to scapegoat. The answer always is that, in the long run, it can be any one of us, no matter how unthreatening or how clean we think our sexual act is."

Nestle attributes the lack of demonstrations to "a state of shock, and—I think a state of shame. Are we willing to fight for sexual territory that we are being told is death? When I saw the television and I saw policemen standing in front of the bar, it came home to me that this was a fifties image. Even though this act was not one to protect lives, there was a collective numbness that prevented us from responding."

Nestle expressed a belief that a grass-roots movement would develop from these events. "The recent meeting of the Gay and Lesbian Alliance Against Defamation (GLAAD) was not sponsored by the National Gay Task Force. This was an ad-hoc group of people who pooled their experiences and said *we know what's happening and it can't go on.* That's where the real leadership in this battle is going to come from. It had to continue into the streets. At the City Hall demonstration David Summers got arrested. He's not from the group that loves to get arrested either. There's really a chance for street responses like we used to have, by an angry mob. I think we have the potential to be an angry mob and I say that in the best sense of the word."

COMMENTARY

Although lesbians are constantly portrayed in the straight and gay media as prudish and anti-sex, clearly grass-roots lesbian activists were a lot more willing to go on record as opposing the closing of the baths than a good percentage of the gay male leadership. After ten years of the feminist movement while most gay men were apolitical, lesbians had a more sophisticated analysis of the state and a clearer impetus towards direct action. Although gay men had access to significantly more resources and power than lesbians, they were just realizing that the state did not care whether they lived or died. This process of revelation was an obstacle that lesbians did not have to overcome, having been clear on their exclusion from the beginning. What some lesbians were never able to overcome was their resentment towards gay men for the years of self-absorption and the pre-AIDS goal of trying to access the same power as straight men. But others did not hold grudges, or were willing to work hard to build a more enlightened and effective community. Some of the women speaking here—especially Wolfe and Abby Tallmer, were among the first lesbians to take part in the emerging AIDS activist movement. Jewelle Gomez's comment about not belonging to any of the existing gay and lesbian organizations was indicative of the general protest from below that was soon to transform gay politics. The statements and actions by David Summers and by these lesbian activists came months before Larry Kramer's speech sparking the creation of ACT UP in February 1986.

WHEN WE WERE VERY YOUNG
A WALKING TOUR THROUGH RADICAL JEWISH WOMEN'S HISTORY ON THE LOWER EAST SIDE 1879–1919

from
The Tribe of Dina
(Sinister Wisdom
1986/Beacon
Press 1987)
edited by Melonie
Kaye/Kantrowitz
and Irena Klepfisc

When I investigated the history of my own neighborhood, I discovered that radical Jewish women like myself had carried on many of the same political activities in the same buildings that my friends and I live and organize in today. It was an enormous relief to find out that despite society's insistence that my kind are freaks of nature, we are actually historically consistent.

1. FOURTEENTH STREET AND BROADWAY—UNION SQUARE

Our walking tour begins at Union Square, for decades the site of demonstrations for progressive causes from the Rosenbergs to abortion rights. Here, radical Jewish women joined with the larger American left. Isidore Wisotsky, an anarchist leader, recalls:

> We gathered to make revolution and stayed to talk. And how we talked—anarchism, atheism, against the military, for birth control, against injustice, for socialism and for the rights of workers to organize. . . . The right to speak at Union Square was more precious than the bread we sweated to earn. Many in the crowd were immigrants, but not all. The square also attracted every kind of radical from Greenwich Village, as well as the dilettanti and just plain spectators and rubbernecks. Almost any issue could draw a crowd of 20,000 or more. Our slogans were simple and to the point—"War Is Murder," "The Eight-Hour Day Today," and "Capitalism Is the Cause of All Evil."

2. 208 EAST THIRTEENTH STREET

Anarchist and feminist Emma Goldman lived here on the top floor from 1904–1914. Born in Kovno, Poland in 1869, she moved to St. Petersburg at age thirteen. In her autobiography *Living My Life*, she acknowledges the influence of women revolutionary leaders in Russia, especially Sophia Perovskaya, who was executed for the assassination of Czar Alexander II, and Vera Figner, imprisoned for twenty years for the same act.

After threatening to throw herself into the Neva River if she could not emigrate to America with her sister, Emma reached Rochester, NY, married and divorced, and moved to NYC by the time she was twenty. Within one year she was elected to the board of the Anarchist Congress. When Alexander Berkman, her lover and comrade, was imprisoned for fourteen years for an assassination attempt, Emma very briefly tried to earn a living at prostitution and studied midwifery. She continued to defend Berkman's name within the left, even jumping on stage to lash one of his detractors with a bullwhip.

When President McKinley was assassinated by the anarchist Leon Czolgosz, Emma was arrested and held for a month. As government repression of anarchists intensified, she assumed the name E.G. Smith and worked as a nurse, seamstress, masseuse, manager, and agent for a Russian acting company. Alix Kates Shulman writes:

> Combative by nature, she always presented the most provocative topics in the most dangerous places, thus feeding her legend. She talked up free love to puritans, atheism to churchmen, revolution to reformers. She denounced the ballot to suffragists, patriotism to soldiers.

Emma was imprisoned in 1896 and sentenced to seven months on Blackwell Island for inciting riot at a Union Square demonstration organized by Eugene Debs in support of railway strikes. Thereafter, she was arrested so often that she always took a book to public meetings so that she would have something to read if she ended up in jail.

A free thinker who would be considered radical by progressive movements today, Emma lectured in English and Yiddish on unions, feminism, collective living, co-operation, and birth control. The latter topic sent her to prison several times. An advocate for tolerance for homosexuals at a time when there was no visible gay rights movement in the U.S., Emma was "the first and only woman, indeed the first and only American to take up the defense of homosexual love before the general public," said Magnus Hirschfeld, the German gay leader.

A tireless organizer, agitator, and publisher of two anarchist papers—the *Blast* and *Mother Earth News*—Emma was called "The Most Dangerous Woman in America" by the FBI, and her deportation hearings were presided over by J. Edgar Hoover. In 1919 she was deported for opposing U.S. military conscription during World War I, and in 1921 she went to the Soviet Union, where she accused Lenin and Trotsky of "the new despotism." Allowed to return to the U.S. she published *My Disillusionment With Russia* and *My Further Disillusionment With Russia,* which earned her the enmity of the left.

When Berkman committed suicide, Emma joined the anarchists of Spain, who then controlled Barcelona. She lived the rest of her life on thirty dollars a month with no passport, dying in Canada in 1940. "What I believe," Emma wrote, "is a process rather than a finality. Finalities are for Gods and governments, not for human intellect."

3. TWELFTH STREET AND SECOND AVENUE—CAFÉ ROYALE

Across the street from Maurice Schwartz's Yiddishe Arts Theater was the Café Royale, hang-out of writers, actors, philosophers, and kibbitzers. It was also frequented by a new generation of radical, single Jewish women, who drank tea from samovars in the classical Russian style—among them Communist organizers Miriam Zahn and Rose Wartis of the Dress and Cloak Makers' Union, journalist Meta Stein Lilienthal, and Annie Netter, an activist in the Knights of Labor who roomed with Emma Goldman.

4. 193 FIRST AVENUE

One block down from the Royale lived Lena Myers, a Polish refugee from Cracow. In 1896, at age twenty-eight, she committed suicide by drinking carbolic acid. She had been sending her family money earned from prostitution. Two weeks before, Lena got a letter from her mother written in Hebrew thanking her for the money and asking, "Lena, why don't you get married? Do you want to be an old maid?"

5. SECOND AVENUE AND NINTH STREET—CAFÉ MONOPOLE

Now a Ukrainian restaurant, Café Monopole was a meeting place for activists, actors, and community residents. According to one journalist describing Jewish café life:

> Where the cigarette smoke is the thickest and denunciation of current forms of government the loudest, there you find women! . . . To none would gentle words sound more strange than to the women of the radical coffee parlor . . . pallid, tired, thin-lipped, flat-chested and angular, wearing men's hats and shoes, without a hint of color or finery.

Although unattractive to that reporter, radical Jewish women were involved in a whirlwind of vibrant and creative activities, among them women's liberation. For example, Manya Mirsky, Katya, Rose Goldberg, and others managed to publish birth control information in Yiddish, although Emma Goldman had already been imprisoned for attempting the same. They found a printer willing to take the risk if he got cash first and if the literature was removed as soon as it was printed. They distributed ten thousand copies from baby carriages in Harlem, the East Side, the Bronx, and Brownsville.

Other women were trying to preserve their experience on paper. Anzia Yezierska was one of a few Jewish women writing in English about life on the Lower East Side. Then, as now, most working-class women writers' work was never published, so Yezierska's accomplishments are even more extraordinary. Born in the early 1880s in Plinsk, a shtetl in Russo-Poland, she emigrated in 1892. She married at seventeen, had the marriage annulled a few months later, remarried almost immediately, and divorced three years later, leaving her daughter to be raised by her husband. Historian Alice Kessler-Harris describes her as "fiercely independent":

> Traditional notions of marriage discomfited her, yet she sought out male companions and lovers. Contemptuous of the ordinary and impatient with the unimaginative, she could not conform to social convention for its own sake.

In 1915, she published her first story—"The Free Vacation House" in *Forum*, and four years later won the Edward O'Brien Best Short Story of the Year Award for "The Fat of the Land." In 1920, Hollywood film mogul Sam Goldwyn bought her book *Hungry Hearts* for $10,000. Moving to Los Angeles, she found she could not write when away from the Lower East Side and returned to NYC. Her fascinating autobiography, *Red Ribbon on a White Horse* (1950), tells of moving from Jewish poverty, of confronting anti-Semitism among the rich and famous, of being marketed as a rags-to-riches "Cinderella of the Slums." She also describes her experiences in the WPA Writers' Project with other artists like Richard Wright and exposes the exploitative aspects of the Depression recovery programs.

In the 1920s possibly influenced by her love affair with WASP educator John Dewey, Yezierska became interested in the mysticism of Gurdjieff, Krishnamurti, and Bahai. Her books include *Salome of the Tenements* (1922) a roman à clef about the East Side, *Children of Loneliness* (1923), and *The Bread Givers* (1925), the story of a Jewish woman determined to become a writer against the wishes of her religious father. Yezierska died in 1970.

6. ASTOR PLACE—COOPER UNION

Named for multimillionaire Cornelius Astor, this was the site of a strike organized by Jewish and Italian immigrant women workers which affected the history of union organizing in this country. NYC was the center of the American "needle trades," producing half of the country's ready-to-wear clothing. By 1909, there were 600 garment factories and workshops involving over 30,000 workers, three quarters of whom were women between sixteen and twenty-five. Workers had to pay for utilities and equipment in the factories, and garment producers charged them twenty percent over cost for electricity, needles, and electric belts. They worked with flammable materials, had to pay for their lockers and chairs, and were heavily fined for their mistakes.

Small strikes were first initiated against the Leiserson shop and the Triangle Shirtwaist Factory in September 1909 by the 100 members of the original union, Local 25, which had four dollars in the treasury. Strike benefits were three dollars a week for those with dependents and $1.50 for individuals. Both factories hired scabs to break the strike and prostitutes to taunt the picketers. Certain firms specialized in hiring out strikebreakers on a per diem basis and eventually the union also resorted to violence. According to Jenna Joselit, historian of Jewish crime:

> Unions relied on their own membership, particularly those who were endowed with brawn, to do the dirty work of physical intimidation. Eventually, though, professional gangsters replaced the volunteers.

A primary organizer at Leiserson's was sixteen-year-old Clara Lemlich. Born in Gorodok, on the Austrian-Ukraine border, she emigrated to New York in 1903, after the pogrom and massacre of Jews at Kishinev. Clara was one of the seven women and six men who founded Waistmakers' Local 25 of the ILGWU in 1906. During the eleven-week independent strike at Leiserson's, Clara was arrested seventeen times and had six ribs broken.

In November, thousands of workers attended a meeting at Cooper Union, where leaders like Samuel Gompers spoke for hours until Lemlich took the floor saying, in Yiddish, "I'm tired of listening to speakers. . . . I offer a resolution that a general strike be declared—now." The resolution passed. Twenty thousand shirt-waistmakers, mostly women and two-thirds Jewish, went on strike. The five-hundred-member Teachers' Association, headed by Henrietta Rodman, raised funds for it. The Women's Trade Union League (WTUL) picket line was the first volunteer picket group formed outside the union's. Anne Morgan, daughter of J.P., provided bail. Seven hundred twenty-three women were arrested in the first month. The *New York Sun* reported that:

> The girls, headed by teenager Clara Lemlich, described by union organizers as "a pint of trouble for the bosses," began singing Italian and Russian working-class songs as they paced in twos before the factory door. Of a sudden, around the corner came a dozen tough looking customers for whom the union label "gorilla" seemed well chosen. "Stand fast girls," called Clara, and then the thugs rushed the line, knocking Clara to her knees, striking at the pickets, opening the way for a group of frightened scabs to slip through. . . . The thugs ran off as the cops pushed Clara and two other badly beaten girls into the wagon.

Picketers brought to the Jefferson Market Courthouse on Ninth Street and Sixth Avenue were either processed or released or sent to the workhouse by judges who berated them with statements like, "You are on strike against God and Nature, whose firm law is that man shall earn his bread by the sweat of his brow." In her *Diary of a Shirtwaist Striker*, Theresa Malkiel wrote about being arrested on a picket line:

> I'm pretty dazed. I've just come back from that living hell called Night Court. I'm sure nobody could help cursing the world that we're living in after spending a few hours in that place. Our girls were all fined from ten to twenty-five dollars a piece. I, being convicted a second time, was fined twenty-five dollars and the judge warned me to keep out of his way or he'll send me to the workhouse next time. I listened to him and said "Yes, sir" but he needn't think that I'll give up the strike on that account.

Anne Morgan rented Carnegie Hall for a meeting to protest police violence. The "convicts" sat on the stage wearing sashes that said, "I am not a criminal." By March, 354 of the 400 struck shops had signed contracts with the Ladies' Waistmakers' Union of New York. Workers won the right to a closed shop, fifty-two-hour work week and pay raises. Local 25 grew to 10,000 members.

Blacklisted after the strike, Clara Lemlich had to work under assumed names. She was later elected to the executive board of the WTUL and eventually became a paid organizer and speaker for the Suffrage Party. A charter member of the U.S. Communist Party, she worked in shops until 1954.

7. GREENE AND WASHINGTON STREETS

The largest shirtwaist factory in NYC employed 800 to 900 workers, mostly women. Pauline Newman, who came to America in 1901 from Lithuania, started working in the Triangle Factory as a child:

> We started work at seven thirty in the morning and during the busy season we worked until nine in the evening. They didn't pay you any overtime and they didn't give you anything for supper money. . . . Of course there were child labor laws on the books, but no one bothered to enforce them. The employers were always tipped off if there was going to be an inspection. "Quick," they'd say, "into the boxes." Then some shirts were piled on top of us and when the inspector came—no children! The employers didn't recognize anyone working for them as a human being. You were not allowed to sing. My pay was $1.50 a week no matter how many hours I worked. You got up at five thirty, took the horse car, then the electric trolley to Greene Street.

In 1911, the factory burst into flames. Because doors and windows were locked to prevent theft, 146 Jewish and Italian women died within eighteen minutes. Many jumped out of windows. A giant funeral of 120,000 marchers and 400,000 spectators took place on April 5th. Through drenching rain, a crowd of shop and factory women marched from uptown. A second division of mourners, led by an empty hearse, proceeded silently through the East Side. According to one newspaper:

> It was not until the marchers reached Washington Square that the women gave vent to their sorrow. It was one long drawn out heart

piercing cry, the mingling of thousands of voices, a sort of human
thunder in the elemental storm—a cry that was perhaps the most
impressive expression of human grief ever heard in this city.

The WTUL held a mass memorial meeting on May 2 at the
Metropolitan Opera House, rented by Anne Morgan, where Rose
Schneiderman delivered her speech in a whisper:

> This is not the first time girls have been burned alive in the city. Every
> week I must learn of the untimely death of one of my sister workers.
> Every year thousands of us are maimed. Too much blood has been
> spilled. It is up to the working people to save themselves. The only way
> they can save themselves is by a strong working-class movement.

After the fire, the owners Harris and Blanck were acquitted of
any wrongdoing and opened a second factory which the Building
Department closed as non-fireproof. As in the Triangle, sewing
machines blocked the fire escapes. In another factory on 16th Street,
Blanck was charged with chaining the doors during work hours and
fined twenty dollars. Three years after the fire, twenty-three suits
against them were settled at seventy-five dollars per life lost.

8. EIGHTH STREET AND AVENUE B—CHRISTADORA HOUSE

Looming over the park is probably the largest abandoned building
in Manhattan, slated for development into luxury condominiums.
Founded in 1897 as a Christian Community Center called
Christadora House, it held many services for the Jewish
community, including English and stenography classes, and provided space for those agitating for women's suffrage. According to
historian Elinor Lerner, in the 1915 and 1917 NYC referenda on
women's right to vote, "the largest, strongest and most consistent
support came from the Jewish community. Of the top 100 pro-
Suffrage election districts in 1917, at least seventy-eight were
Jewish neighborhoods."

The National Progressive Women's Suffrage Union, whose
main support included Jewish garment workers, pioneered grass-
roots strategies for suffrage. Lerner reports:

> It was the first suffrage group in the city to hold open air meetings,
> attempt a foot parade, and approach the working class at such public
> places as ball games, beaches, and amusement parks. They also

distributed leaflets and demonstrated outside of factories and formed alliances with workers on union and labor issues.

One group, the Wage Earners' League, included women from the Henry Street Settlement House and organizers like Clara Lemlich. They canvassed and held mass meetings and rallies, including a joint rally with black women.

Although Jewish leaders like Rose Schneiderman and Lillian Wald were active in suffrage and the Socialist Party even opened a suffrage committee headquarters, Lerner points out that the upper-class Christian suffrage movement never recognized Jewish support. In fact, some leaders actually blamed immigrants for defeats. In a letter to the *New York Times,* Lillian Wald wrote that immigrant voters were more receptive than the American-born. But the movement continued to view foreign-born voters as a monolith without differentiating between Jews and those groups like the Irish who were largely anti-suffrage. After the 1917 referendum victory, the suffragists played down the aid they got from radicals, especially pacifists and revolutionaries. They obscured Jewish support because many Jews, together with the Socialist Party, opposed U.S. intervention into World War I.

9. 624 EAST FIFTH STREET—HEBREW TECHNICAL SCHOOL

Seventy-three percent of unmarried Jewish women were in the labor force at the turn of the century. The Hebrew Technical School, founded in 1879 by the Hebrew Free School Association, was one of the Jewish institutions that trained girls in what the administrators viewed as proper and marketable skills. The school served about 125 fifteen-year-old girls who had graduated from public grammar schools. According to the United Hebrew Charities Annual Report of 1883:

> The primary object in forming our school was to afford girls . . . an opportunity to become skilled workwomen and to render themselves comparatively independent. The second object was to assist these girls in acquiring such knowledge of cooking, housekeeping, and of sewing as a requisite for every woman to possess, and which they cannot, as a rule, properly obtain at home.
>
> Teach a girl to read, to write, and to think and you make of her a clerk. Teach her to read, write, think, and sew and she is a clerk and a seamstress as the occasion may require. Teach her all the foregoing with cooking added and she becomes a clerk, seamstress, and housewife.

10. 64 EAST FOURTH STREET—THE LABOR LYCEUM

On June 3, 1900 eleven delegates from seven unions in four cities, with a combined membership of 2,000, met at the Labor Lyceum to form the ILGWU. For the first twenty years its membership was primarily made up of young Jewish women. Alice Kessler-Harris notes:

> Their rapid organization and faithful tenure was responsible for at least one quarter of the increased number of unionized women [in the second decade of the twentieth century]. And yet they were unskilled and semi-skilled workers, employed in small scattered shops, the-oretically among the least organizable. These women, having unionized at their own initiative, formed the backbone of the ILGWU, which had originally sought to organize the skilled male cutters in the trade. The commitment of some women was such that when arrested on picket lines, they offered to spend the night in jail in order to save the union bail costs before returning to the line in the morning.

Pauline Newman, a member of the WTUL, was one of the first ILGWU organizers and participated in the 1909 shirtwaist strike. Looking back at age 86 she said:

> I stopped working at the Triangle Factory during the strike of 1909 and I didn't go back. We didn't gain very much at the end of the strike. I think the hours were reduced. The best thing that the strike did was to lay a foundation on which to build a union. . . . Even when things were terrible I always had faith. Only, now I'm a little discouraged sometimes when I see the workers spending their time watching television-trash. We fought so hard for those hours and they waste them. We used to read Tolstoy, Dickens, Shelley by candlelight, and they watch the Hollywood Squares. Well, they're free to do what they want. That's what we fought for.

A friend of Rose Schneiderman's, Newman always advocated for women in the unions, despite the sexism of male organizers. Frequently women organized a local only to be rejected by the male controlled parent union. In 1910 Newman organized women candy makers in Philadelphia, but the International Bakery and Confectionery Workers Union delayed issuing them a charter for so long that the organization eventually fell apart. Newman agitated within the ILGWU against sexism, arguing for more women in leadership positions. "Girls are apt to have more confidence in a woman than in a man."

In 1913, Pauline became Executive Secretary of the Joint Board of Sanitary Control, the bargaining unit between garment labor and management. A long time member of the Socialist Party, she was its nominee for Secretary of State in 1918, and in 1919 she was made director of the Unity Health Center, which provided union members with health care.

11. FIRST STREET AND SECOND AVENUE—WOMEN'S TRADE UNION LEAGUE

This was the East Side office of WTUL, an organization of upper-class Christian women committed to organizing across class and ethnic lines. Founded in 1888, it sought legislation to regulate women's hours in factories, fought clothing and cigar sweatshops, and forced the appointment of women factory inspectors. In 1903 members adopted the slogan "An Eight Hour Day—A Living Wage—To Guard the Home," and began cultivating leadership from among working women. According to historian Nancy Dye, League members:

> believed that women of all classes, working together, could organize women into trade unions and persuade the labor movement to integrate women into its ranks.

The June 1911 *League Bulletin* noted:

> The League's representation in the suffrage parade was small. The lack of industrial representation was a source of regret. Enfranchisement will strengthen the position of working women, and it is the workers who can make the legislators realize, more than any other group, that the demand for the entranchisement of women is a real and vital demand.

The next year they again encouraged their membership to participate in a multiclass parade, emphasizing that the contingents would include women riders on horseback, actresses, architects, waitresses, cashiers, and men sympathizers bringing up the rear.

The League provided money, publicity, and strategic support to women who wanted to unionize. Photos of affluent society women Anne Morgan and Alva Belmont being arrested on the 1909 shirtwaist picket line brought publicity and financial support to the strike.

While the League was theoretically committed to cross-class organizing, anti-Semitism prevailed:

> Leaders scheduled a citywide conference of working women, on Yom Kippur, despite Jewish members' protests. Only one League ally . . .

studied Yiddish. Some allies held stereotypical conceptions of immigrant women. Jewish women were often described as "dark-eyed," "studious," and "revolutionary" in League literature.

Many women affiliated with the League were lesbians and formed lesbian networks. Pauline Newman and her lover had a lifelong lesbian relationship and adopted a child together. Mary Dreir lived for years with Frances Keller and then with organizer Lenora O'Reilly, providing her with a house and life income. Helen Marot lived all her adult life with organizer Caroline Pratt. When Lillian Wald, lesbian founder of the Henry Street Settlement, spearheaded the formation of a child labor committee in 1902, Marot was employed as its chief inspector. In 1905 the League received an anonymous grant to employ Rose Schneiderman as the first full-time working-class Jewish organizer. The donor was later revealed to be Irene Lewisohn, a wealthy German Jew who was part of Lillian Wald's lesbian community.

The broader society was, to an extent, aware of these women's lesbian relationships as documented in the 1913 novel *Comrade Yetta*. A roman à clef about the East Side, it featured Mabel Train, a thinly disguised head of the WTUL who was "always accompanied by her roommate Eleanor Mead." Mead was:

> feared and hated by all of Mabel's admirers. It was impossible to call on Miss Train, it was necessary to call on both of them. Without any open discourtesy, with a well-bred effort to hide her jealousy, Eleanor made the courting of her friend a hideous ordeal.

It has taken over sixty-five years for historians to acknowledge what the community knew all along, that lesbians were at the center of radical organizing on the East Side and that their relationships influenced radical politics and strategy.

Rose Schneiderman was a good choice for lesbian sponsorship because she worked as a lifelong advocate for women. She was born in Poland in 1882 and emigrated in 1890. After her father's death, United Hebrew Charities placed her in the Hebrew Sheltering Guardian Society. She worked sixty-four hours a week in a department store for $2.16 an hour and then got a job as a cap liner, for which she had to purchase her own sewing machine. In 1903, anarchist Bessie Braut, her co-worker, influenced Schneiderman and two others to form a local in the United Cloth Hat and Cap Makers' Union. They got the required twenty-three members and Schneiderman became secretary.

At twenty-one she organized her first action. On Saturday, when employees worked half a day, the men got paid as they left, but the women had to return at four. They protested and won. A year later, she was elected to the executive board of the United Cloth Hat and Cap Makers union, the first woman to hold such a position in the trade union movement. When her union struck for thirteen weeks, the strike fund paid all married males six dollars a week, but women were not eligible for any money.

Sexism within the trade union movement was very high. "The left wing male leaders paid lip service to equality for women but in practice excluded them from positions of importance," Schneiderman said.

After being hired by the WTUL, she concentrated on improving the status of women within the trade union movement. The Irene Lewisohn grant of forty-one dollars a month enabled her to quit factory work, attend the socialist Rand School on 15th Street and organize.

In 1917, she became the chair of the industrial section of the Women's Suffrage Party and, three years later, the first Jewish woman to run for U.S. Senate on the Farmer-Labor ticket. Although she had only four years of formal education, she was on the Board of Directors of Brookwood Labor College of Bryn Mawr and Hudson Shore Summer Schools for Working Women. She served as president of the WTUL from 1926 until 1950 when the organization dissolved. In 1933, FDR appointed her as the only woman on the labor advisory Board of the National Recovery Act and from 1937–43 she served as secretary of the New York State Department of Labor. When she died in 1972 she had a photo of Mary Drier on the mirror in the Jewish Home and Hospital for the Aged.

12. ALLEN STREET

Black, white, and Latina prostitutes still work on Allen Street, which has been a center of prostitution for the East Side since before the turn of the century. But then, according to an unpublished paper by April Shour:

> The pimp was Jewish, the woman was Jewish, the tenement was Jewish and all in a Jewish neighborhood. The prostitute lived with her community and her clientele and boss were also members of that community.

Reformers complained about the integration of prostitutes into Jewish neighborhood life. Robert Deforest and Lawrence Veillir wrote in 1903 that:

> Frequently these women engage one family in the tenement to do their laundry work, another to do their cooking, and still further financial arrangements are made with the housekeepers. The patronage which they distribute is thus utilized to make friends and to purchase the silence of those who might otherwise object to their presence. The children of respectable families are often sent to the prostitutes on various errands, and because of the gifts made to the children, these women became important personages in the house and their affairs, the subject of frequent conversation.

The three blocks from Houston to Delancey were full of brothels, dance halls, and other places where prostitutes worked, many owned by church corporations and wealthy New York families. Men found Italian girls as young as ten in the fifty-cent brothels on nearby Elisabeth Street, or they could solicit women who worked under the elevated tracks, careful to avoid the cinders and hot oil that fell from passing trains.

Jews have always been reluctant to acknowledge the existence of prostitution in our history, preferring the cleaned up myths about our past. The authors of *Jewish Women in America* explain:

> Prostitution among Jewish women in America, no longer the rarity it was in the old country, caused the community great despair. Parents were known to sit shiva for those who became prostitutes.

Jewish prostitutes were a firm part of Jewish life in America, just as Christian prostitutes were of Christian life. Of women incarcerated in Bedford Hills prison early in the century, Jews (who made up almost twenty percent of the population of New York City) comprised eighteen percent of imprisoned prostitutes. In a 1912 study of 647 prostitutes, Bedford Hills supervisor Katherine Davis found that most of the Jewish prisoners were American-born of immigrant parents, living with their families, and contributing most of their money to the family nest egg. So families knew they were prostitutes.

Money, of course, was their motive. Davis reported that most women in prison said they earned between five and nine dollars a week before turning to prostitution and from forty-six to seventy-two dollars a week after. This was at a time when high paid male workers earned under twenty-five dollars a week. Prostitutes were among the highest paid members of the Jewish community and their money must have contributed substantially to the upward mobility of their families.

13. ELDRIDGE AND RIVINGTON—UNIVERSITY SETTLEMENT HOUSE

Founded as the Neighborhood Guild in 1886 at 147 Forsythe Street, and moved to its current home in 1903, this settlement provided services, classes, vacation space, meeting rooms, libraries and other programs to improve the quality of daily life on the East Side. It even ran a cooperative dairy and distributed fresh cut flowers.

In 1905, Rosa Harriet Pastor, a young English language columnist for the Yiddish newspaper *Die Tageblatt* (*The Daily Page*) interviewed the director of the University Settlement, millionaire socialist James Graham Stokes, a non-Jew. As in the Cinderella tale *Salome of the Tenements*, written by Anzia Yezierska and based on Pastor's life, they married and Rosa Stokes became a leader of the Jewish left.

She was born in Poland in 1879 and started working at age four. Her family emigrated to England where her mother led a strike in London's East End. Pastor wrote poetry in Yiddish, helped translate the work of Morris Rosenfeld into English and in 1914, started writing a lovelorn column at *Die Tageblatt* for fifteen dollars a week. When her marriage deteriorated—her increasing sympathy for the Communist cause was one of the reasons for her divorce—she wrote a friend that Stokes had accused her of becoming "unladylike and hazardous" and "utterly crazy." In 1918 she was convicted under the Espionage Act and sentenced to two years for criticizing the U.S. government during World War I. The verdict was later reversed.

Pastor ran for Borough President of Manhattan on the Communist Party ticket in 1921. In 1922, she was a delegate to the 4th Congress of the Communist International in Moscow and began to write for *Pravda* and *The Workers* (later *The Daily Worker*). She was active in the labor and birth control movements. After her divorce in 1925, she experienced extreme poverty and married Jerome Isaac Romaine, editor of the communist magazine *Political Affairs*. In 1929, she was severely beaten by the police during a demonstration in support of the people of Haiti. She died of cancer in 1933.

At her trial, Pastor spoke of her rags-to-riches-to-rags life.

> For ten years I worked and produced things necessary and useful for
> the people of this country and for all those years I was half starved.
> . . . I worked at doing useful work and never had enough. But the
> moment I left the useful producing class, and did not have to do any
> productive work in order to exist—I had all the vacations I wanted, all
> the clothes I wanted. I had all the leisure I wanted—everything I
> wanted was mine without my having to do any labor in return for all I
> had received.

Yezierska described her Pastor-inspired heroine as a "blazing
comet," an "electric radiance," and a "tragedy queen."

14. THE BOWERY

Currently filled with the homeless, drug addicted, and emotionally
ill, the Bowery was once filled with theaters and factories. At 48
Bowery was the Thalia Theater where the great Bertha Kalish ("the
Sappho of the Yiddish theater") performed. Like the rest of the East
Side it was also an area where women organized. In 1904, 125 girls
ages fourteen to sixteen walked out of the Cohen Paper Box Factory
when their wages of three dollars per 1,000 cigarette boxes were
cut by ten percent. Support came from benefit concerts, from the
Forwards, the United Hebrew Trades, and WTUL.

In the shops women faced sexual harassment from bosses
and other workers. According to historian Charlotte Baum:

> They suffered their humiliation and fear in private for one did not
> complain publicly about such matters. Anyway, sexual payoffs for the
> privilege of holding a job were expected and a common enough
> practice in cases of advancement within the shop.
>
> The religious culture of Eastern Europe demanded sexual abstinence
> before marriage, but regarded women as sexual beings capable of
> enticing men away from their religious pursuits. Indeed the culture insured
> that the sexes lived very separate existences. With the loosening of
> religious taboos in the workplace, the old restraints gave way to what
> many considered the Americanization of sexual attitudes. . . . While
> many women may have tried to come to terms with the sexual conditions
> prevailing in the shops, once they were unionized and union grievance
> committees set up, charges of sexual abuse were among the major
> complaints made by female workers to union officials.

Despite women's contributions to the trade union movement,
and their domination of certain industries like the garment

industry, trade unions virtually ignored women's issues. Some labor leaders even wanted to push women out of work to provide jobs to men. In 1879 the president of the International Cigar Makers said, "We cannot drive the females out of the trade, but we can restrict this daily quota of labor through factory laws."

The 1890 Cloak Operators and Contractors' union strike settlement specified that, "No part of this agreement shall refer or apply to females," although eighty-five percent of the workers were women. In 1913, the ILGWU agreed to the following settlement:

Terms of Employment and Shop Standards
Wages—the following shall be the minimum rates for week workers:

1. Full fledged cutters	(men only)	$27.50
2. Drapers	(women only)	$15.00
3. Joiners	(women only)	$13.00
4. Sample Makers	(women only)	$15.00
5. Examiners	(women only)	$11.50
6. Finishers	(women only)	$9.50
7. Ironers	(women)	$14.00
8. Ironers	(men)	$17.00

By union agreement women were slotted into the lower paying jobs, sometimes earning half what men earned, and usually earning less for the same work. Unions also made conscious efforts to exclude women from organizing. They used such well-known tactics as holding meetings in a saloon, scheduling them at late hours, and ridiculing women who dared to speak.

15. GRAND AND LUDLOW——PS 75, HOME OF THE WOMEN'S LITERARY CLUB

Of the many radical women on the East Side, women writers appear to have lived especially conflicted lives. Many wrote only in Yiddish, and those who wrote in English had no way to make connections or break into men's networks. When one did manage to publish a book, it was often destroyed by male critics. Very few works by these women have been collected or translated.

Born in Alexat, a shtetl near Kaunas, in 1879, Yente Serdatzky started publishing in 1905 in Warsaw with the journal *Der Veg* (*Path*) edited by I.L. Peretz, the famous Yiddish writer. She came to New York in 1907 and wrote from the *Freie Arbeiter Stimme* (*The Free Voice of Labor*) an anarchist newspaper so open to women writers that

Jacob Gladstein, a well known Yiddish poet, allegedly submitted work under a woman's name. Because of hostile criticism, Serdatzky stopped writing in 1920 and became a shopkeeper.

Esther Luria was born in Warsaw in 1877 and came to New York in 1912. She wrote for the Yiddish socialist press like the *Forwards, Tsukunft (The Future)*, and the ILGWU Yiddish paper. Living in terrible poverty, she died alone in the Bronx in the 1920s.

Fradel Shtock, born in 1890 in Galicia, wrote for the *Freie Arbeiter Stimme*. A café literary figure, in 1916 she began to publish short stories in the *Forwards* and *Tug (Day)*. Her two books, one in Yiddish and one in English, received negative notices. She was institutionalized for mental illness in the 1920s.

Celia Dropkin, an avant-garde writer and painter, and the mother of five children, wrote for the socialist and anarchist press. She was also part of the "In Zikh" literary circle. These non-aligned radicals who called themselves "introspectivists," according to historian Adrienne Cooper-Gordon, "wrote experimentally for a very small readership, behaving as though they were in the mainstream of American political debate, when in fact, they were invisible."

Anna Rappaport was born in 1867 and came to the U.S. from Kaunas in 1876. She made her writing debut in *Die Arbeiter Zeitung (Workers' Times)* with the poem, "A Bild Fun Hungers Noyt in 1893" (A Picture of the Hardship of Hunger in 1893). Anna, whose poetry captured the living and working conditions of poor women, stopped writing in Yiddish in 1919 when she became a columnist for the socialist English language paper *The Call*.

Norma Fain Pratt has compiled a list of 53 Yiddish women writers whose work, most of which remains to be translated, appeared in the U.S. in the first part of the century.

Pessie Bach	Ida Badanes
Sara Barkan	Fraydel Belov
Dora Birek	Minnie Bordo-Rivkin
Liba Burstin	Friedl Charney
Hasye Cooperman	Celia Dropkin
Sarah Fell-Yellin	Rivke Gallin
Sonia Gerbert	Rayzel Glass-Fenster
Eda Glasser	Bella Goldworth
Silva Guterman	Rosa Gutman
Frume Halpern	Bessie Hirshfield Pomerantz
Leah Hofman	Rachel Holtman
Malcha Kahan	Pesi Kahana

Miriam Karpilove	Esther Katz
Leah Kaufman	Bertha Kling
Berta Kudly	Malke Lee
Sarah-Leah Liebert	Shafra-Estehr Levy
Malka Locker	Esther Luria
Anna Margolin	Esther Miller
Kadia Molodowsky	Rosa Nevadovski
Rosa Newman-Wallinsky	Anna Rappaport
Chane Safran	Yente Serdatsky
Esther Shumaitcher	Sarah Smith
Fradel Stock	Deborah Tarant
Malka Heifetz Tussman	Chana Vaitzel
Rashelle Veprinski	Shifre Weiss
Hinde Zaretsky	Miriam Shoner Zunser

16. HESTER AND LUDLOW—THE LABORER'S MARKET

Hester Street, also called Khazer (Pig) Market, was full of craftsmen and pushcarts selling every conceivable item. It was the site of the Mothers' Riot of 1906. When officials vaccinated pupils in school without explaining their purpose, mothers feared their children were being murdered and converged by the thousands on the school. When the principal locked the doors, women grabbed fruit and vegetables off carts and hurled them at the building. Because of their experiences, the mothers believed the murder of their children was a real possibility.

17. 7 ORCHARD STREET

A letter came to the *Forwards* on August 1, 1902 from this address:

> I am looking for my husband David Silecki, the butcher from Prusani. He is thirty-five years old, blonde, of mediocre height with a round fat face. Whoever knows about him should contact Zuckerman.

Thousands of husbands deserted their families once they got to America. A Jewish National Desertion Bureau published photos of deserters in Jewish newspapers across the nation and in Canada, while United Hebrew Charities gave cash relief to deserted women. But they found that many women refused to testify against their husbands once they were apprehended. As a result UHC decided that no deserted wife would be assisted unless she agreed to prosecute. Fourteen of the prostitutes incarcerated at Bedford Hills began in prostitution after they had been deserted.

Large numbers of women had to place their children in institutions In 1913, twenty percent of institutionalized children were from deserted homes. Eighty-five percent of the children in the New York Hebrew Infant Asylum had one living parent. Since Asylum officials wished to Americanize their charges, they prohibited contact between children and mothers. German Jewish directors limited visits of the Eastern European Jewish parents to four days a year, separated siblings, and prohibited food and gifts. They censored mail and often banned Yiddish. As a result, discharged children, who could not speak the same language or eat the same food as their parents, became attached to the Asylum. Sixty-one percent attended High Holy Day services there after their discharge. Girls were often released earlier than boys because by the age of nine they were deemed ready to care for the children still at home. Girls who grew up in orphanages generally worked in domestic service, not clerical or retail jobs like other Jewish girls.

18. MONROE STREET BETWEEN PIKE AND MARKET

The *New York Times*, May 24, 1902:

> It will not do . . . to have a swarm of ignorant and infuriated women going about any part of the city with petroleum destroying goods and trying to set fire to the shops of those against whom they are angry.

In 1902, Jewish retail butchers struck the wholesalers, many of them German Jews, charging them with inflating prices. The strike was settled after two days, but the decreases were not passed on to shoppers. Mrs. Fanny Levi, wife of a cloakmaker and the mother of six children under the age of thirteen, and Sarah Edelson, owner of a restaurant on Monroe and Pike, organized a boycott by thousands of women on the Lower East Side. The strike spread from block to block in one half hour. Twenty thousand people massed in front of New Irving Hall, and on the first day seventy women and fifteen men were arrested for disorderly conduct.

On the second day, with pickets at every butcher shop, 100 people were arrested and money was raised for bail funds. According to the *Tribune*:

> The main disturbance was caused by the women. Armed with sticks, vocabularies, and well sharpened nails, they made life miserable for the policemen.

They also clashed with butchers and dragged meat out of shops to set on fire with kerosene.

That Shabes, using the traditional tactic of interrupting the Torah reading when a matter of justice was at stake, women entered shuls and requested support from the rabbis and men to continue the boycott. When a member complained that women should not speak from the altar, a Mrs. Silver responded coolly that the Torah would "pardon" her.

The next day most butcher shops were closed. The boycott had spread to Williamsburg where meat was burned in the streets. That night 500 attended a meeting of the Ladies Anti-Beef Trust Association which decided to seek support from Christian women and to consolidate in Harlem, East New York, and the Bronx. In Brooklyn 400 women patrolled the streets to control the shops. But when rivalry exploded between Mrs. Edelson and Carolyn Schatzberg, male communal leaders, presided over by David Blaustein of the Educational Alliance took over from the women to "bring order to the great struggle for cheap meat." Joseph Barondess urged the women "to be quiet and leave the fighting to the men." The men founded the Allied Conference for Cheap Kosher Meat with a ten-member steering committee including only three women.

The average woman in the boycott, according to historian Paula Hyman, was thirty-nine years old, had 4.3 children, and had been in America about eleven years. Most husbands were employed in the garment industry. Hyman writes:

> Thus the women formed not an elite in their community, but a true grassroots leadership. . . . The initial boycott committee composed of nineteen women numbered nine neighbors from Monroe Street, four from Cherry Street, and six from the adjacent blocks. The neighborhood, a form of female network, thus provided the locus of the community for the boycott: all were giving up meat together, celebrating dairy shabbosim together and contributing together to the boycott fund.

The *New York Times* of August 14, 1902 reported:

> They are very ignorant. . . . They do not understand the duties or the rights of Americans. They have no inbred or acquired respect for law and order as the basis of the life of the society into which they have come. Resistance to authority does not seem to them necessarily wrong, only risky. The restraint it can have on their passions is very small.

Perhaps the reporter got this idea from observing the response of one boycotter when questioned before a judge:

> —"Did you throw meat on the streets?" Rosa Peskin was asked.
> —"Certainly," she replied. "I should have looked it in the teeth?"

The strike ended with a price rollback, and the networks were used to build rent strikes for the next six years.

19. 265 HENRY STREET—HENRY STREET SETTLEMENT

The Henry Street Settlement House still stands at this spot and still serves the immigrant population of the Lower East Side. Where they previously offered sewing, English, Americanization, and literature courses, they now have Hispanic playwriting workshops and African dance. Founded by Lillian Wald, it was originally the Nurses' Settlement. It had eleven full time staff members by 1898 and twenty-seven by 1906. Wald persuaded the Board of Education to put nurses in schools, opposed child labor, agitated for more playgrounds, joined with suffragists, supported the 1909 shirtwaist strike, and was a pacifist during World War I. She was also president of the American Union Against Militarism, the parent organization of the American Civil Liberties Union and campaigned for services for battered women and children.

Lesbian feminist historian Blanche Wiesen Cook writes that Wald's "basic support group consisted of long term residents of Henry Street . . . (who) worked, lived and vacationed together for fifty years." Cook writes that "Wald lived in a homosocial world that was also erotic. Her primary emotional needs and desires were fulfilled by women. She was woman-supported and woman-allied."

Irene Lewisohn donated the Neighborhood Playhouse on Grand Street (now the Henry Street Playhouse) to the settlement in 1915. The Lewisohn sisters traveled and corresponded with Lillian. One letter from Irene to Lillian is unmistakably amorous:

> I have some memories that are holier by far than temples or graves or blossoms. A fireside romance and moonlight night are among the treasures carefully guarded. . . . As an offering for such inspiration, I am making a special vow to be and to do. . . . Much of my heart to you.

Wald supported the Russian Revolution, prohibition, and pacifism and visited Russia in 1924 at the government's invitation. She supported the League of Nations and founded the National Child Labor Committee, working in public service until her death in 1940.

Of course, social work as a tool for change has always been a controversial issue among radical women. Emma Goldman scoffed:

> Teaching the poor to eat with a fork is all very well . . . but what good does it do if they have not the food? Let them first become the masters of life, they will then know how to eat and how to live. . . . Sincere as settlement workers were, they were doing more harm than good.

20. 175 EAST BROADWAY—THE *FORWARDS* BUILDING

This building housed the progressive Jewish daily founded by Abe Cahan, the Workman's Circle, the United Hebrew Trades, and the Folksbeine Theater.

The *Forwards* was the most popular Yiddish newspaper in the U.S. Socialist editor Abe Cahan promoted a wide range of Jewish activities ranging from labor unions to printing selections from the most prominent Yiddish fiction writers. At its height, the paper had eleven local and regional editions with a circulation of 200,000.

Many community and union meetings were held here. At least one event here challenged the union hierarchy. The leadership of most unions stayed male while the rank and file was mostly female. In 1912, the ILGWU started a system of protocols, agreements with management mandating arbitrators instead of strikes. Predictably arbitrators did not agitate with the same spirit as workers. In 1916 women from the rank and file led a revolt. According to *Solidarity*, February 26, 1916:

> A meeting of shop chairmen at No. 175 East Broadway ended last night in a general fight. Women became hysterical. Miss Ida Grabinski, who has been named chairman of one of the dozen committees of women in the new "equal voice" movement, said . . .

"the officers of the union boss us worse than the bosses. . . . Now they tell us to work. The next minute they withdraw that order. The women workers comprise more than sixty-five percent of the union members throughout the country. Why shouldn't we have something to say about what concerns us most?"

COURT BATTLES CONTINUE
IN LESBIAN VISITATION CASE

New York Native,
January 1986

Two Minnesota lesbians continue to be embroiled in a battle over the rights of lesbians to care for their ill or disabled lovers, in a case that could have wider implications for AIDS patients.

Karen Thompson and Sharon Kowalski of Saint Cloud, Minnesota began their relationship six years ago. Although they bought a house together and took out life insurance policies on each other, they were, for the most part, in the closet to all but their closest friends.

In 1983, Kowalski, a 28-year-old faculty member at St. Cloud State University, was critically injured in an accident with a drunken driver, which resulted in her suffering serious brain stem injury. Today she is a quadriplegic. During Kowalski's initial eight month hospitalization, Thompson was intimately involved in her daily care and recovery.

When Kowalski's parents began questioning and limiting Thompson's visiting hours, a psychologist recommended that Thompson be open with Kowalski's parents about her relationship with their daughter, so that they could understand her intense concern. The parents completely rejected their daughter's lesbianism and accused Thompson of being "sick," "crazy," and of sexually abusing Sharon. Cut off from her lover, Thompson filed for guardianship by the court with the provision that she be allowed "equal access" to visitation and medical staff consultations.

Since that time the family has moved Kowalski farther and farther from Saint Cloud, requiring that Thompson drive as much as seven hours to be with her. While Kowalski rarely responds to others, she is very responsive with Thompson. Court affidavits filed by Kowalski's doctors have stated that "Karen is the key to Sharon's recovery."

Both Thompson and the Minnesota ACLU have contested Kowalski's parents' guardianship. In the meantime Thompson has filed under the Patients' Bill of Rights that Kowalski has the right to see any visitor she wishes. In response, the Minnesota State Appellate Court decided in September that, while the appeal of guardianship is pending, Thompson and Kowalski do not have the right to see each other on the grounds that Kowalski is incompetent to make her own decisions. Thompson has demonstrated that Kowalski can communicate with a typewriter, but the nursing home in which she is confined has no physical therapy facilities.

Meanwhile, Thompson has paid $11,000 in legal fees and still owes over $30,000 to lawyers.

COMMENTARY

This case became the focus of national organizing for a number of years until a high court finally ruled in favor of Thompson and Kowalski. Thompson worked tirelessly to publicize the case by delivering stump speeches and making appearances all over the United States. This was quite a role reversal for a woman who, at the time of the accident, had been completely closeted and had voted for Ronald Reagan, twice.

As sickness, disability, and death became a regular part of gay life, the guardianship issues raised by this case resonated broadly in the gay and lesbian community. It was both a symptom of and a motive for increased interest in domestic partnership rights. For example, ACT UP's action on Free Sharon Kowalski Day was to go to City Hall and have same sex couples register for marriage.

Domestic partnership had been an issue lingering in the background of gay politics for many years. Gay liberationists often opposed it, refusing to assimilate the same unworkable institutions that define heterosexual life. But the larger society was so adverse to the concept of gay marriage that its supporters seemed to be the most extreme, impractical wing. However, the advent of AIDS activism, with large numbers of homosexuals getting arrested and doing disruptive street actions, made the request for domestic partnership seem reasonable and, in fact, more *normal*. Simultaneously, the AIDS crisis also sharpened the critique of increasingly possible domestic partnership, as opponents pointed out that if gay people were divided into privatized family units like straight people are, we never would have responded to the AIDS crisis in the broad and rich way that we have. This is evidenced by the lack of mutual support between straight people in crisis. They do not see themselves as a specific community but rather as objective and neutral.

Another reason that the Kowalski case resonated with the gay and lesbian community was an unspoken one—the battle with our own families to retain basic civil rights. Of course almost all gays and lesbians have, at some point or another, been treated shabbily by their families because of their homosexuality. And it is not unusual for a gay person to have their family punish them or obstruct their basic civil rights.

The AIDS crisis underlined this even further as lovers had to battle constantly with families who had legal but no emotionally legitimate access. Even though familial mistreatment is an integral part of most gay people's lives, and is a subject for much conversation between us, it has not yet entered the public discourse, and was not the focus of the Kowalski campaign. Perhaps it is still too painful to bring to the surface.

JOY OF GAY SEX REMOVED FROM BROOKLYN LIBRARIES

New York Native,
February 1986

The Joy of Gay Sex, a manual of homosexuality, has been removed from the Brooklyn Public Library System because it describes sexual practices, such as anal intercourse, that are considered "high risk" for AIDS transmission. The move has provoked a wide range of opinions from within the gay community.

According to Ellen Rudley, spokesperson for the Brooklyn Public Library, the decision revolved around a simple ordering problem. "The library ordered what we assumed to be a revised up-to-date edition of *The Joy of Gay Sex,*" she said. "However, a reprint of the 1977 edition was sent, which contains outdated information. We understand that the publisher is working on a revised edition. . . . The original reprint remains available in the central library at Grand Army Plaza," she said. *The Joy of Sex,* a heterosexual sex manual in the same format, which also describes oral and anal sex, has remained, untampered.

Rudley's statement raises questions about future publications that may describe sexual activities of gay men. According to an article in *New York Newsday,* a memo was released within the library system on November 25, 1985 ordering branches to "discard and destroy" all recently purchased copies of the book. The article quoted a worker at the Brooklyn main branch saying that there were no copies of the book, old or new, anywhere in the sixty branch Brooklyn system. Last summer, library director Kenneth Duchac came under fire from gays for withdrawing a library brochure listing books of interest to gay men and lesbians. Although the list was later theoretically restored under pressure from the gay community, a spot check by the *Native* revealed that it is overwhelmingly unavailable, even in the Manhattan system. Dr. Charles Silverstein, co-author of *The Joy of Gay Sex* with Edmund White, said, "It is shocking to hear that an important public library destroys books. This book has been banned in many places.

There's a big battle in Manitoba. The British have burned hundreds of copies. One expects that from governments, not libraries." Silverstein says the issue is "one of the professional integrity of the director of the Brooklyn Public Library, who is unable to withstand the pressure of the groups who don't want these books to be seen. The real issue is not AIDS but homosexuality."

The book's publisher, Simon and Schuster, was unable to comment. Their publicity director told the *Native* that they have never before had a book suppressed in this manner and had no mechanism for responding to it publicly.

Lee Hudson, Mayor Koch's liaison to the lesbian and gay community, differs with Silverstein. She says that removing the book "is not an instance of discrimination against our community. This is not taking gay books off the shelves. Our community's message about AIDS education is very strong and we are waiting to see how this information will influence the next edition."

COMMENTARY

So much of the battle over gay and lesbian representation takes place at the level of book removal and availability because, with a few exceptions, gay and lesbian imagery has been excluded from every other genre of public information. Television, movies, and recorded music do not include significant gay and lesbian presence, so books, bookstores, and libraries have become our primary mode of communication.

There was a painfully obvious double standard by which the Brooklyn Public Library justified its repression of gay male sexual imagery. Work about heterosexual sex was not subjected to censorship based on pregnancy, AIDS, rape, or sexually transmitted diseases. It is just more evidence of how gay sexuality is viewed as inherently inappropriate, and institutions are willing to eliminate it on the slightest excuse.

One interesting subplot to this story was the appearance of Lee Hudson, the mayor's liaison to the gay and lesbian community. This is a position that was originated during the Koch administration and now exists in many states and cities across the country. Hudson's response to book removal is pretty pathetic and unfortunately typical of many administrators in the liaison position. Instead of serving as advocates for their community, these liaisons most often become apologists for the administration and work in their role to contain and bureaucratize gay and lesbian political response.

153

DESERT HEARTS

*Gay Community
News,*
April 1986

The plush screening room at the Gulf and Western Building was filled with tan lesbians in designer clothes talking about the Bahamas while reclining in leather armchairs. Yes girls, this is big time now. No more crappy prints of scotch-taped celluloid. No more lesbians killing themselves, running off with men, ending lonely and despondent. For the first time in the history of the world we have a lesbian feature film made with lesbian money for a lesbian audience. Great, right? Well, yes and no. *Desert Hearts* will make you laugh, it will make you cry, and it will make you yawn. But you can't have everything.

First, the good news. This project was put together with the willpower and determination of Donna Deitch, a documentary filmmaker. After reading Jane Rule's *Desert of the Heart* and obtaining the rights, she spent nearly seven years raising funds from coast to coast. Women like Lily Tomlin, Stockard Channing, and Gloria Steinem lent their names to fundraising efforts. And because of these women's commitment, we now have a lesbian film that will play in commercial houses.

The problem is that the movie is slow and predictable. Oh, there are really fun moments and good supporting performances by actors like Gwen Welles. But, aside from a lot of pretty positive imagery, there's not much bite to this film. Of course I am saying this from the safety and security of the NYC lesbian community. I think the film will mean a lot to U.S. dykes who are looking for a public statement legitimizing their lives. But artistically, somehow it is a bit bland.

Patricia Charbonneau is physically perfect as the lesbian romantic lead. She has all those qualities that girls like. She's pretty, tomboyish, rugged, has a nice body and deep eyes. It is great to watch her in that silver lamé cowgirl outfit. Unfortunately she doesn't have much of an emotional range as an actress. By the way,

Charbonneau's press bio mentions that she is married and was pregnant during the filming. I guess she wants to work again. Helen Shaver, as the pursued woman, is flat and the two of them have little chemistry on film.

Deitch has chosen to avoid the fast-paced, breakneck editing of most Hollywood films. That gives the characters time to get to know each other and for scenes to develop. But there is a lot of dead space and too much emoting going on. This initially vulnerable touch becomes dreary as the film progresses.

Alright, here's the real deal. It's corny. Some of it is so corny that it's downright embarrassing. It is a corny love story with very little tension. All along you know that they're going to do it and you know it is going to be pretty and explicit and after a whole bunch of diversions, "it" finally does happen.

But, I know and you know that you're going to see it and something about the experience will feel exciting. Because even though *Desert Hearts* is not the greatest film ever made, it is going to be important to a lot of people. It might even make a difference in their lives. So, just get ready to enjoy yourself and giggle and groan, then get up and go see *Desert Hearts*. Later you'll want to say that you were there.

COMMENTARY

Desert Hearts did become a VCR classic in lesbian livingrooms across America. But, it did not lead the way for the integration of lesbian subject matter into commercial feature films. In fact, no other commercial feature film with primary lesbian subject matter besides John Sayles's *Lianna* has appeared in broad theatrical distribution to date.

Television has produced some overtly lesbian characters, at least for a few episodes. This, of course, is due to more and more T.V. writers being out behind the scenes. But the kind of money necessary for feature film production where lesbianism is the objective, authoritative voice of the film is still in closeted hands, and while more and more projects get optioned, none, so far, have made it into your neighborhood theater.

As for Donna Deitch, she went on to direct the television version of Gloria Naylor's novel *The Women of Brewster Place*, produced by Oprah Winfrey. Although not publicly out as a lesbian, Naylor in her novel gives an insider's view of a black lesbian couple whose passionate relationship is torn apart by their conflicts over how out to be. Unfortunately, the television version was a

155

bit restrained since the two women loved, argued, and made up, but never touched or kissed. While Naylor's book conveyed their dilemma with great authenticity, it resorted, in the end, to the anachronistic punishment of the lesbian by having her brutally raped as the climax of the novel.

Two of the best known openly lesbian filmmakers got married to men and released commercial feature films around the same time. One of the few openly lesbian producers, Christine Vachon, developed only gay male films including Todd Haynes's *Poison* and *Safe,* Tom Kalin's *Swoon* and *Postcards from America* based on the work of David Wojnarowicz. In an interview in *Out* magazine with film critic B. Ruby Rich, Vachon said that she would be interested in producing a lesbian feature, but had not been able to find a quality script. Openly lesbian director Jennie Livingston made a documentary film, *Paris Is Burning* about gay black and Latino men. So the lesbian feature boom that seemed imminent in 1986 still feels a long way off, lagging far behind gay film progress in financing and in the discarding of stigma.

As before *Desert Hearts,* lesbian film production takes place in experimental, personal, and independent film with limited distribution. Film and video makers willing to work with openly lesbian content like Su Friedrich, Cecilia Dougherty, Sadie Benning, Cheryl Dunye, Michelle Parkerson, Andrea Weiss, and Greta Schiller, among others, still seem miles away from the local neighborhood drive-in.

Heal thyself

New York Native,
June 1986

Louise Hay, director of the Love Yourself, Heal Yourself Center in Santa Monica, California, brought her message of alternative healing for AIDS to full and enthusiastic New York crowds. The Metropolitan Duane Methodist Church in Greenwich Village was packed to the rafters for three sweltering nights in May to hear Hay, a New Age preacher with a growing west coast following.

> We come to this planet many, many times. And before we come we choose our sex, we choose our color, and we choose our parents. The ultimate freedom is responsibility.

In a bleached blonde permanent, hot pink shirt, and pale pink blazer, Hay could have been a Bible belt evangelist preaching the word of Christ. But her message was healing through an eclectic philosophy with a New Age individualistic slant.

"You have contributed to creating whatever has gone on in your life. Therefore you have the power to turn your life around and live it differently," Hay told the crowds.

In a 1980s play on the Reichian theme that repression contributes to disease, Hay attributes AIDS and cancer to an emotional blockage of grief within an individual. Unlike Reich, however, she has almost no social analysis. Although she does include nutrition in her program and speaks out against processed foods, she doesn't acknowledge, for example, industrial pollution's impact on cancer or our immune systems. Hay's targets are diet, image, and most of all, attitude.

> Some would rather die than change their diets—and do because they are caught in a prison of self-righteous resentment.

The first step in Hay's healing process is to "stop criticizing yourself, for criticism shrivels the soul and praise, acceptance, and

157

love open it up." Next to her on the altar were three huge vases of flowers and a worn-out teddy bear. Hay uses the stuffed toys in her treatment and encouraged all participants in her $125 weekend workshops to bring one with them. According to Hay, teddy bears are a symbol of unconditional love, as well as a memento of childhood, an issue important to Hay's visualization exercises. "I encourage people to get teddy bears," she said, "and if they have one, bring it out of the closet."

Another of her exercises involves mirror work, where individuals have to confront their own images. Hay particularly encourages people with AIDS to confront and accept their lesions and the diseased parts of their bodies. "When you really don't know what to do, look yourself in the eye and say 'I love you.'"

In a presentation reminiscent of a traveling revival, Hay includes selected personal information. Her own life was "wonderful" she says, until the age of eighteen months when her parents divorced. Her mother's new husband was physically abusive, and Hay was raped by a neighbor at the age of five. She discovered the Church of Religious Science, became a practitioner, and then branched out into her own line of faith.

"About eight years ago," she said. "I created cancer." After the diagnosis, Hay became determined to "change the mental thought pattern" that she believes causes that disease. She attributed cancer and AIDS to resentment and self-hatred. Without chemotherapy, radiation, or surgery, she overcame her cancer.

> No matter how short our life is, we come in at the middle of the movie. It's very helpful to know that everything is in perfect order. Everything.

What are the attitudinal issues specific to AIDS? According to Hay, "Gay people have all the problems everyone else does, plus other people's condemnation which is a heavy burden to carry. Add to that a lot of sexual guilt." "While the community may be gay," she adds, "there is a lot of pain in it and a lot of self-hatred." Self-love is Hay's crucial factor in the difference between health and illness.

As Hay points out repeatedly, the medical establishment and science have little to offer a person with AIDS. "They're looking for a poison that will kill the virus and not kill you," she says. However, Hay does not promise miracles. "There are a few people—not a lot but a few—who are healed," she told the New York audience. What

Hay does promise is improved quality of life and, in some cases, prolonging of life.

Hay then called upon members of the audience to testify. Some were part of her road show, like the healthy-looking sunburnt man who declared that because of Hay he is well and accepting "everybody as they are." He was followed by a spontaneous burst of affection and approval from audience members.

The stand outside was doing thriving business selling some of her popular books such as *You Can Heal Your Life, Love Your Disease*, and *I Love My Body*. There were also customers snatching up cassette tapes and filling out order forms for audio tapes, albums, posters, cards, and videotapes.

Hay supporters would insist that her philosophy can go beyond AIDS, beyond disease in general. Indeed, as I walked out the door I heard her tell the audience, "What did you do when you heard about Chernobyl? Did you send hatred and anger or did you send out love and healing energy?"

For some people that may be just enough.

COMMENTARY

Hay turned out to be just one in a long line of individuals offering "cures." Of course no one can deny the incredible importance of attitude in prolonging the lives of people with AIDS. What seems, in retrospect, more important than any particular mode of treatment is that the person following it made his or her own decisions and took control of his or her own treatment. From AZT to AL721 to Dextrane Sulfate to Alpha Interferon to blood freezing, ozone therapy, vitamin therapy, aspirin, macrobiotics, urine, shark cartilage, and various miracle cures in faraway countries, people with AIDS have been willing to take enormous risks and put their faith in obscure and esoteric treatments. What was particularly heinous about Hay's approach, though, was her emphasis on blame, considering the susceptibility of gay people to shame. I remember feeling that there was something so all-American about Hay. Something that perhaps reminded several of the men in that room of their mothers back in the Midwest who had abandoned them for being gay. Her normalcy represented some way of getting that attention and approval that had been withheld for so long. The great irony behind all of this is the basic concept of "cure." There is no cure, but everybody is looking for one. The answer will not be a single pill or one simple act or gesture that will make your Kaposi's Sarcoma go away. It will be a combination of treatments, different for each person, requiring precise management over long periods of time. But instead, people with AIDS keep being encouraged by the media to chase that one pill, that one method that will provide the cure that cannot exist. Perhaps that is why the Burroughs-Wellcome Company was able to turn AZT—a drug whose efficacy is still in doubt—into the largest profit making pharmaceutical in the history of the industry. It fit the fake model of the one and only cure.

JEAN GENET

New York Native,
June 1986

Many people in this world have an intense one-way relationship with a famous person. His death can be a jolt because he lived and died but never sat across from you at the table. You never held his hand. In *his* life, you were no one. There is a particularly bitter taste around the death of such a person, especially if he was not fully appreciated in his own lifetime.

Jean Genet (1910–April 15, 1986) was this person for me. I am not a great scholar. I can shed no new light on his novels and plays. All I can retell is who he was to me.

When I was a teenager in the early seventies, the current piece of popular literature for girls was Sylvia Plath's *The Bell Jar.* It was an attractive book because it described propriety with the kind of bland disgust that fifteen-year-old girls like me experienced regularly. There was nothing more nauseating than the prospect of doing the right thing. These were the days before Patti Smith and the sexiness of female nihilism. I was a lesbian. I was smart and instinctively I reveled in the underside of myself. This first manifested itself as depression. Later I became a writer.

Genet's novel *Funeral Rites* was handed to me in the hallway of my high school by an older girl named Barbara Pollack.

"Here, you're a romantic," she said.

I still have that edition, with a beautiful black-and-white photo of Genet standing, looking so angelic, one starched button undone, his head too large, his initials carefully embroidered on the bottom right side of his torso. *Funeral Rites* (French edition—*Pompes Funebres*, Gallimard, 1953. English edition—Grove Press, 1969) was the first love story I ever believed. It showed that you can love someone so much you can become them. You can love them so much that you can kill them. It eroticized the asshole, and it taught me to look at the freaks of this world with a sexual passion that made their slightest gestures somehow important and not merely metaphors.

I gave copies to my friends and lovers. I read Genet's other novels *Our Lady of the Flowers* (originally written on toilet paper in prison, confiscated, destroyed, and written again), *The Thief's Journal, Miracle of the Rose, Querelle*. Later, when I was fortunate enough to see Paris, I sat at Les Deux Magots cafe because Genet had sat here. In college I wrote papers about his books for professors who had never read any.

This April I was in the country writing a novel. With each book I write, there is a book I read, slowly—a page at a time—to help me find the tone I'm looking for. The book I chose this time was *Funeral Rites,* dragging out that old copy. In the middle of this, he died.

The *New York Times* obituary was written by a theater critic who barely touched on the novels. He mentioned in the first paragraph that Genet lived in a "cell-like," "pristine" hotel room, with only enough belongings to fit into one suitcase. Oh yes, we are expected to sigh, the tragedy of a man who spent so much of his life in prison.

Jean Genet, I have always believed in you and your vision of love. For better or for worse I write the way I do because your characters were the first ever to thrill me. My life has been richer because you lived yours. Rest in peace.

THIRD WORLD GAYS IMPORTANT PRESENCE
AT ANTI-APARTHEID MARCH

New York Native,
June 1986

On June 14th, 90,000 people poured into New York's Central Park to mark the tenth anniversary of the Soweto uprising in South Africa and to renew efforts to challenge apartheid in South Africa and the United States. This march included a visible gay and lesbian presence, and two separate contingents joined the event. One, sponsored by the Mobilization for Survival and the Coalition for Lesbian and Gay Rights, gathered at 48th Street. The second, composed of the National Coalition of Black Lesbians and Gays, the Lesbian Herstory Archives, the Wild Wimmin Archives, Asian Lesbians of the East Coast, and Men of All Colors Together (MACT) gathered initially at 125th Street at the base of the Harlem State Office Building.

The concept of building a gay anti-apartheid contingent in Harlem, originated when MACT (the NY chapter of Black and White Men Together) was approached by the National Anti-Apartheid Organizing Committee. According to Liddel Jackson of MACT, "They wanted a third world input and a high level of gay and lesbian visibility with a significant third world presence. MACT suggested that the lesbian and gay contingent start from Harlem."

The coordinators thought it was a good idea but didn't have any gay contacts in that community. "We started screaming," said Jackson, "that lesbians and gays aren't just a midtown community. As a third world group it behooved us to make certain we marched from the Harlem State Office Building in coalition with Black and third world people." But the planning committee claimed it would be "impossible" to organize a lesbian and gay contingent in Harlem. Intrinsic to this statement, Jackson charged, was the assumption that the gay community is white and should be defined by proximity to white neighborhoods.

The Harlem contingent was a rousing success, with a good feeling of support and friendliness between men and women. "It's been a good experience for MACT," Jackson said, "because although an alternative route is difficult, with organizing it can work."

Does Jackson think that the Gay Pride March should start at 125th Street?

"It would take a re-conditioning of the predominantly white gay structure to realize that lesbians and gays do come in all colors. And it would take re-educating the people of upper Manhattan. But, if that were done it would mean a great accomplishment for the gay movement."

Says Myra Bain of Wild Wimmin Archives. "Sounds great. I mean we have gone downtown all this time. Now they can come uptown."

COMMENTARY

Ironically, the one thing that forced the white gay leadership to recognize the black gay leadership was the election of David Dinkins to the mayoralty of New York City. Even though Dinkins followed through on very few of his promises and repeatedly betrayed gay people and people with AIDS, he did appoint openly lesbian and gay black and Latino administrators to positions of notoriety and power in the city government. Dr. Marjorie Hill, a black psychologist, was the lesbian and gay liaison; Billy Jones, Dennis DeLeon, and others forced the white homocrats to re-adjust their racial exclusion when dealing with City Hall. Unfortunately some of these appointees were as bureaucratic as their white predecessors.

But activists like Liddel Jackson did not end up with government jobs, nor did he re-position himself within the white movement. Instead Jackson went on the parallel track of political organizing. When safe sex education projects failed to appropriately address gay men of color and white-owned sex clubs asked for three pieces of ID, Jackson opened Jacks of Color, a safe sex club for black, Latino, and Asian gay men. When gay and lesbian magazines like *Outweek*, *QW, NYQ,* and *Out,* opened and closed with predominantly white staffs, Jackson went on to co-found *Colorlife,* a newsprint magazine for gay, lesbian, and bisexual people of color.

Is LESBIAN CULTURE ONLY FOR BEGINNERS?

New York Native,
July 1986

I've just finished reading Fred Starr's engrossing book *Red and Hot: The Fate of Jazz in the Soviet Union* (Putnam, 1985). Starr described how the postrevolutionary Soviet government perceived of jazz as a threat to their vision of a new society. The authorities claimed jazz was "anarchistic," "individualistic," and "sexual." The Stalinists even went so far as to ban the saxophone. When it became clear that the population simply wouldn't let their desire for "dhaz" die, the government tried to manufacture their own version by forming "proletarian folk music" organizations. These promoted muzak-like big band sounds combined with ethnic Russian music. Still, the Soviet people responded to jazz's wild and hot free form, and continued to emulate the improvisational dance steps and lifestyle we associate with "American classical music." Today, jazz continues to grow and be played throughout the Eastern bloc.

Reading this fascinating story I began to think more specifically about my own cultural context as a lesbian writer and critic working in the framework of the gay and lesbian press. Gay writers in America must also walk that tightrope between making ideological statements in the face of a dominant and hostile culture, and at the same time maintain a certain artistic standard and aesthetic integrity. I have sadly concluded that, at this stage of the game, that marriage is on the rocks. In what appears to me to be an attempt to manufacture, rather than reflect lesbian culture, like the Stalinists we have developed a sort of lesbian Socialist Realism which has come to dominate lesbian fiction.

There are many successful and popular lesbian and gay writers with full and satisfying careers. Most of them write primarily about straight people, or about gay people in the personas of straights. The few writers who produce openly gay material in a commercial setting are usually men, while the handful of lesbian writers publishing in the mainstream are primarily limited to subjects like coming-out stories. Very few have been able to write about primary lesbian characters where the story *assumes* lesbianism presented in the context of daily life and from a lesbian perspective.

For those of us who have decided to write about gay people in the same manner that heterosexual writers write about heterosexual people, for the most part even our best work will not be reviewed in the most prestigious publications nor sold in most American bookstores. Yet, we continue to write about the women in our lives and imaginations. Supposedly we do so because we are compelled towards these issues out of a political and artistic sense of urgency.

Enter the alternative presses, the underground culture, tiny theaters. Lesbian and gay writers have been driven to create, support, and produce work for these venues because of censorship, both economic and social. Hence, one would assume that these small publishing houses and literary magazines would be hotbeds of excitement and revelation where the secret life of gay America would be permitted to unfold. However, when I looked over the list of books I reviewed for the *Native* this past year, I found that I was almost uniformly disappointed in the work being published by movement presses. In fact, most of the lesbian books I read struck me as preachy and didactic, filled with stiff, one-dimensional characters. Additionally the writing styles and narrative structures were often uptight and repetitious.

It's hard to know whether these aspects are the products of the current crop of lesbian writers or whether they are the result of decisions made by editors. For whatever reason, I found the recent sampling to be quite narrow. From my reading and personal interactions I have since deduced some unwritten rules of lesbian publishing.

First, let us look at style. Stylistically, lesbian writing is usually naturalistic or realistic, narrative or confessional. For the most part confessional work focuses on the personal experiences of an author who came into contact with an issue considered "hot" on the political agenda of the lesbian-feminist movement. Early on these issues included coming out, sexual assault, and abortion. Later they became racism, anti-Semitism, and class oppression. More recently they have been about oppression of some kind *within* the women's community, particularly issues of sexual difference. Obviously these are all topics that need to be discussed in fiction. Until now, however, the required format has called for

specific analysis, pat conclusions, and one-dimensional explanations for experiences that are more multidimensional than any
single ideology has been able to accommodate. In addition, the
reader has been led to believe that any individual expressions of
these experiences should not be challenged or questioned because
to do so implies the reader's bigotry against people in that category.

Narrative work has suffered a different structural fate. There is
virtually no experimentation in language and form in contemporary lesbian novels. Early works used some fragmentation and
gender/pronoun ambiguities, but with the exception of books like
Dodici Apazdu's *Goat Song* or Audre Lorde's *Zami*, lesbian novels
today have an almost standard protagonist/conflict/resolution
format, with even-sized chapters, all told from uniform points
of view. Experimental formats invented by classical gay writers such
as Jean Genet, Jack Kerouac, Marcel Proust, etc.—which are so
standard as to be clichés—remain miles ahead of most small press
lesbian fiction.

In terms of content, it appears that the main purpose of our
fiction is not, as stated, to depict lesbian lives, but rather to argue
for a specific point of view. This perspective has to do with a
"chosen people" hang-up I see pervading lesbian culture in general.
Succinctly stated, content is required to show morally superior,
oppressed people confronting forms of social oppression. In order
to show morally conflicted protagonists or characters with cruel or
negative aspects, the author must qualify these descriptions by
implying that their ambiguities are the result of social oppression.
In other words, lesbian characters are not allowed to be real.

The implications of these unwritten rules go far beyond the
personal vanity of style of any one reader or writer. The rules reflect
a general stagnation in the lesbian-feminist political movement and
among lesbian artists in general. As a lesbian writer I understand the
necessity of raising these issues and do so myself, but I also think
they have to be discussed in a manner that reflects the variance of
human experience, because propaganda is not literature.

One of the many examples I can think of in which an author
successfully accomplished this balance of aesthetics and morals
would be James Baldwin's *Another Country*. It features black, gay, and
socially marginal characters in realistic settings that convey their
social realities as well as their individual personalities. Yet, I doubt
this book would have been published by a lesbian press today
because it starts out with the negative image of the suicide of a

black man. I understand and accept that anyone running a publishing house or magazine has the right to promote the kind of work he or she personally believes in. However, given that censorship of lesbian writing is so brutal and almost absolute, lesbian work rejected by our own presses will probably not appear anywhere else. We have to face this with a more textured response.

Like "proletarian music associations," lesbian presses and writers have, to a large degree, decided that their readers are not able to make choices for themselves. Instead of presenting a wide range of work, varied in style and perspective and letting readers choose what to relate to, decisions have been made that allow for only a narrow range of topics fit for our consumption. The result of such selection has been more and more of us looking to mainstream artwork for inspiration. For lesbians, that means reverting to our pre-movement process of learning to relate to crumbs, learning to superimpose our realities on heterosexual ones. Lesbian culture can be a growing place for artists, not an alienating and confining list of "shoulds."

I believe that if lesbian writers and publishers could let go of foregone conclusions and stop re-proving the same formulaic arguments, we could work honestly on the depiction of ourselves. Considering the paucity of gay characters in fiction and the wide variety of gay people in the world, there is a lot to depict. Then the complexities that make up each individual can inspire the vision of freedom we all long for. This would be a more productive and interesting reason to build lesbian culture.

COMMENTARY

Pre-movement lesbian writing was often formally inventive. I'm thinking of Djuna Barnes, Jane Bowles, Gertrude Stein, H.D., etc. And the early days of women's presses also featured experimental approaches by writers like Monique Wittig and June Arnold. But the association between conventional narrative and the women's presses was never transformed.

Fortunately a serious and quality lesbian literature has begun to emerge since this article was written, although, ironically, it takes place primarily (but not exclusively) in the mainstream presses, probably because, frankly, they don't care what you write as long as it sells, an attitude which ironically offers more freedom to the writer. But exciting, formally inventive, openly lesbian work has appeared in recent years from such novelists as Carolivia Herron,

Rebecca Brown, Jeanette Winterson, Carole Anshaw, and playwright Ana Maria Simo, among others.

As the years passed and I became more familiar with how publishing works, I began to understand the destructive impact of the closet and sexism on developing a mature lesbian literature. First, in mainstream book and magazine publishing, the vast majority of lesbian editors are closeted. This eliminates huge areas of potential intellectual and artistic (as well as marketing) development for lesbian literature. Second, the sexism of gay male editors is absolutely appalling. There are many who have never published a book by a lesbian (or a gay man of color, in many cases). And there appears to be only the most minimal interest in lesbian literature among straight men and women in editorial. So the combination of talented editors withholding their skills and overwhelmed small press editors unable or unwilling to publish more innovative literary texts has significantly slowed down the development of the literature. Add to this the hostile writing programs, the refusal of mainstream literary magazines to adequately represent lesbian work, and the unspoken quota system among book review assignment editors—in which lesbian writers have to compete against each other for review space instead of being compared to books by heterosexuals that their work may have more in common with stylistically. Add to this grant and funding programs that are either hostile to or maintain unspoken quotas for supporting lesbian work. Add to this the dearth of teaching jobs for openly lesbian writers. Add to this the creation of "The Gay List" which only advertises and promotes lesbian writing to gay readers. In short there are many factors contributing to the increasing number of lesbian writers who are producing books without any lesbian content in order to be taken seriously. Of course, writers must be free to choose their own characters and subject matter under any circumstances, but if you know that your work will be marginalized if there is lesbian content, can the decision to exclude it really be freely chosen? After all, no other group has to undergo this type of twisted positioning. There is not one book on the face of the earth by a heterosexual writer that has no heterosexual characters.

Wake-up, AIDS Hysteria Will Change Your Life

Womanews,
December 1986

The AIDS crisis is being used to take away existing social and civil rights from gay people. While the medical crisis doesn't affect lesbians, the social crisis will. If ever we intend to make a stand to defend ourselves, this is the time to do it.

I have been working as a reporter for the *New York Native,* the newspaper of NYC's gay male population. This experience has given me a proximity to issues and debates surrounding the AIDS tragedy. No one knows what causes AIDS. It appears to be transmitted by a combination of factors including repeat exposure via anal or oral sex, blood transfusions, or sharing needles for shooting drugs. But not everyone who does these things will get AIDS. Sometimes a man will die and his lover will never get sick. There is at least another factor involved which has not yet been identified. Some people feel that this may be related to the use of specific drugs, such as poppers, or overall immune deficiency due to too much partying, too many previous sexually transmitted diseases, malnutrition, or other possibilities.

However, state and city governments have decided that the primary response they wish to make is to close the baths. In my opinion there is no medical justification for closing the baths. The baths provide a central location where potentially men can obtain condoms and safe sex information should they desire it. When the organized meeting places are closed, gay sex will go completely underground—far from any health information.

Closing the baths contributes to the health crisis. It only serves one purpose—to confirm the fear of gay people as diseased and dangerous individuals whose sexuality is inherently filthy. If you read the articles in the daily papers about the recent closings of the leather clubs, you will find repeated references to whips and chains. None of these things have anything to do with AIDS. In fact, some sado-masochistic sex play is safe sex and should be encouraged as a healthy alternative. These articles condemn gay sexuality. They have nothing to do with the health crisis.

The closings are based on a set of guidelines issued by Governor Cuomo, shutting down "public establishments" where homosexual oral and anal sex takes place. He does not define the word "public." These guidelines lay the groundwork for the out-lawing of homosexuality on a medical, instead of moral, excuse. Testing is already going on in the military which has said it will discharge all homosexuals. The rights of employees in the public school system have been challenged. These witch hunts will be based on a test that has such a high rate of false results that the gay press nationally is recommending that no one take it. It is my belief that in the next few months we will see attacks on gay people's rights to work in education, food service, and the medical professions.

What is gay leadership doing about this? NOTHING. The heads of many of the gay organizations are in the pocket of the mayor's office. Some have or aspire to appointed positions. Instead of encouraging gay people to resist, they are taking a wait-and-see attitude. In addition to their complicity with the political machine, some "respectable" gay leaders want to be disassociated from the bath and leather people. They believe that their own assimilation will protect them and their illusions of political power.

A gap in leadership has also been created by the continuous sense of grief and shock throughout the entire community. People are trying to keep their lives together and care for the sick. At the same time, however, upper- and middle-class and upwardly mobile gays have bought the myth for so long that they would be pro-tected by the system that many still can't accept that the status quo has turned against them.

Anti-gay hate sheets like the *New York Post* are using lies to incite fear of gay people. They have created a panic among heterosexuals that they will all get this disease by sitting in the same classroom with a gay person. Beyond straight intravenous drug users, the number of heterosexuals who have contracted AIDS is very small. Although not enough research has been done on women, recent articles in the *Times* and the *Native* have implied that women may possibly not be transmitters of AIDS. If this is the case then the recent attack on prostitutes in the press is unfounded scape-goating. It is more likely for prostitutes to get AIDS from men than to transmit it. But no one seems to care about that.

171

What can we do? I believe that we are entering a very frightening time for gay people and we must be as vocal and visible as
possible. We must discuss AIDS at work, on the subways, and with
our families and neighbors. We must be prepared to challenge any
infringement on our rights and dignity. It is time to bring out those
gay badges and wear them on the streets to provoke discussion
about AIDS and to resist the temptation to fade into "safety." Finally,
we need to bring back the radicalism of the early gay movement,
ignore the homocrats and demonstrate, be angry and flaunt our
gayness. No one else is going to do this for us.

COMMENTARY

Of course the most glaring error here was the lack of recognition of lesbians
with AIDS. My error was a reflection of the general invisibility of lesbians with
AIDS in all areas of information, prevention, and care. When this article was
written, ACT UP had not even been formed yet, and information or analysis
about lesbians with AIDS was nonexistent. Although sexual transmission of HIV
through oral sex between women has never been anecdotally or medically
confirmed, there are many lesbians who have contracted AIDS through needles,
blood transfusions, sex with men and direct blood-to-blood contact with HIV.
There are still no adequate support services or medical access for these women.

Given the dearth of services, it is ironic that the focus of the lesbian
community on behalf of lesbians with AIDS has been to advocate dental
dams—pieces of latex—for use in oral sex. However, not only has HIV
transmission through oral sex between women never been proven as a mode
of transmission—but dental dams have never been confirmed for efficacy in
the inhibition of the transmission of HIV. Lesbian PWA AIDS activists like Kerry
Duran of Boston, Dee Deberry of Tampa, Florida and many, many more have
courageously battled for representation on all levels of policy making within the
government and within the AIDS activist movement. A national representative
gathering of lesbians with AIDS met with Health and Human Services Secretary
Donna Shalala during the weekend of the 1993 Lesbian and Gay March on
Washington but have, to date, received none of their demands.

The dental dam phenomenon is one of the most complicated chapters in
the history of the modern lesbian movement. A huge amount of material was
developed, in a number of countries, advocating the use of dental dams during
oral sex. However, the practice never really caught on—probably because
people had no anecdotal evidence in their personal lives that oral sex was
actually a mode of transmission. But the fact that very few women ever used

dental dams with regularity had virtually no impact on the official discourse endorsing them. Curiously, in this instance lesbians insisted on official scientific corroboration before abandoning the dental dam campaign. But this was the only time I can ever recall when lesbians looked to an official body to tell them what was going on in their own lives, instead of relying on their daily experiences for information as they have in every other instance.

Dental dams did fit the gay male condom model and so were perhaps easier to understand than a more complex, question-filled, and truthful approach to lesbians and AIDS prevention. But there was also an element of AIDS-hysteria about the dental dam campaigns that underlined how willing (for a time, at least) lesbians were to embrace obstacles to their sexual practices without concrete evidence that these obstacles were necessary. After all, gay men knew that there was an AIDS epidemic, even when the *New York Times* refused to cover it, because they saw their friends getting sick and dying. Lesbians have not had a comparable experience of seeing mass death in which the initial infection originated in lesbian sex practices because that is not where these infections have originated. Yet they were ready to vigorously endorse dental dams despite the lack of anecdotal or scientific evidence. Perhaps dental dams fit in with some kind of conflict or shame for lesbians about our sexual practices.

Additionally, these campaigns were so virulent that anyone who questioned them was accused of "causing the deaths of women." Of course, there were gay men, early in the epidemic, like playwright Robert Chesley, who opposed the first safe sex campaigns, and they, like Chesley, are now dead. But there was no comparable situation with lesbian oral sex. Some organizations went to great lengths with enormous expenditures to develop dental dam packets to hand out in bars, dental dam advocacy videos, and even entire departments of agencies designed to serve lesbians who had contracted HIV sexually from other women, sometimes without accruing a single client who even claimed such origin. All of this going on while actual lesbians with AIDS remained unserved.

QUEENS TRIUMPH AT WALDORF-ASTORIA BASH

Seattle Gay News,
July 1987

It was billed as "The Night of a Thousand Gowns," a $250-a-head fundraising event for selected gay organizations. But what made this party more fabulous than most was that the guests were invited to come in drag, and they paraded those gowns in the grand ballrooms of the Waldorf Astoria. In San Francisco, drag at the city's poshest hotel might be *de rigueur* but for guppified New York, this was a historic occasion. Drag was given its deserved place of honor.

Crowds gathered outside the Waldorf's Park Avenue entrance to cheer the arriving queens as they stepped out of stretch limos and luxury automobiles. Couples arrived from Calgary, Ontario, San Diego, Dallas, Atlanta, and Brooklyn. He, crisp in tux and tails, sprinkled perhaps with a few old army decorations. She, always divine, whether as Catherine the Great, Dolly Parton, or a wide variety of tramps, debutantes, royalty, and dance-hall girls. Their gowns ranged from bar mitzvah polyester to Robert Legere originals to one red plastic postmodern affair. The escorts ran the gamut from short, balding gents in glasses to studs to nice boys to graying, dangerous-looking, wealthy men who could easily work for NASA or the CIA. It was an all-American event.

Yet, amidst all the glitter, the reality of the AIDS crisis and the need for a radical, visible movement were never forgotten. Eagle Empress Nicole received the Lynn Carter Award (named for the well-known female impersonator who died of AIDS). Nicole said that this event was "an important chapter in our gay history as we recognize and pay tribute to the true pioneers of our movement—drag queens and female impersonators. Drag queens were Stonewall. They fought back and then others followed. They were the first to fight for our rights when others couldn't or wouldn't."

Then she called for a return to the radical tactics of the early movement. "It's time to march again, hold massive demonstrations. We drag queens of yesteryear long ago passed the torch to those of you more acceptable. Don't be afraid to return to the streets where our movement was born."

After the crowning of the new empress Sybil Bruncheon the festivities returned to fundraising for the evening's beneficiaries — the March on Washington Committee, National Gay Task Force, AIDS Action Council, Human Rights Campaign Fund, and the New York Lesbian and Gay Community Center. Quite a few celebrities were present including a dapper Vito Russo, Charles Busch in a white halter, Rollerina on the arm of Steve Ault, Miss Gay Great Lakes, Miss Connie Lingus (Trash Queen of the Poconos), Pandora Box, Clitoris Leachman, Rick Donovon, Cardinal Sin, Dora Jar, and Dolly Lama.

Miss Blaze Starr (Miss Gay America) summed up the feeling of the evening when she said, "AIDS is making us realize that every moment we have is extremely precious." After a perfectly rendered lip-synching of herself singing "The Impossible Dream," Miss Starr reminded us that "female impersonation is a gay art form, an art of which all gay people can be proud."

COMMENTARY

So, this call for action was coming from everywhere but the established leadership. It came from dykes, drag queens, people with AIDS on the front lines. That same month, August 1987, I attended my first ACT UP action, a silent vigil at Memorial Sloan-Kettering Hospital where administrators were not actively recruiting participants for existing experimental drug trials. ACT UP had been founded the previous March and was taking on an increasingly high profile, attracting friends and enemies in the government and in the rest of the gay community. Wealthy gays were outraged by our tactics, homocrats accused us of being counterproductive. Many people who felt that they owned or defined the gay movement were threatened by ACT UP.

Within the organization there was a uniting enthusiasm even though people came with a variety of agendas. For those of us from the feminist movement, advocating for equal access to resources for women and people of color topped our list of priorities, even though we were involved in every aspect of policy and strategy development. This question of access was to come up again and again throughout ACT UP's tumultuous history even though, ultimately, we were the primary advocates for representing the broad range of infected people, spawning prison projects, pediatrics advocacy, establishing needle exchange programs, pushing for access for women, leading insurance reform, and working for social protection for all people with AIDS.

175

WOMEN NEED NOT APPLY
INSTITUTIONAL DISCRIMINATION IN AIDS DRUG TRIALS

Village Voice,
February 1988

Last December Rebecca Cole, assistant director of the National AIDS Hotline, got a call at home from a woman with ARC (AIDS Related Complex) who wanted to get into a program testing the drug Ampligen. The woman had already been through two drug studies and proved to be a reliable participant. Like many others with ARC or AIDS she was interested in Ampligen because it appears to be a non-toxic, anti-viral drug and an immune booster without the side effects of AZT. There is only one barrier between her and treatment. She is a woman.

Currently all Ampligen testing is for men only. Of thirteen drug trials presently in NYC that are relevant to women, five are strictly for men. The trials that are open to both groups are primarily for AZT. But the most hopeful drugs for the future, Ampligen, Imuthiol, and Isoprinosine, remain off-limits to women. The hospitals and pharmaceutical companies justify the exclusion of women on the grounds that they are not reliable subjects for these drug trials.

According to Dr. Mathilde Krim, "Clinical trials for AIDS have been so few that investigators have chosen the most controlled conditions possible. Working exclusively with gay men accomplishes this because they are homogeneous in risk factors. Women are being excluded because of the assumption by doctors that they are IV drug users and therefore undesirable patients." Cole, a member of ACT UP (AIDS Coalition To Unleash Power) an AIDS activist group, takes a harsher view. "It's the good-old-boy approach to guidelines," she says. "The FDA and the drug companies are not concerned with making the drugs proportionally available to the populations that need them."

Ampligen was developed by HEM Research, a small company based in Nashville. HEM went into partnership with DuPont

Pharmaceutical in order to get the financing necessary to bring a drug through the complicated process required for FDA approval. HEM could not open the trials to women because they had not investigated the possibilities of birth defects, says DuPont spokesman Roger Morris. He said that DuPont was concerned about "reproductive damage" for which ensuing lawsuits can cost a company huge amounts of money.

Dr. Michael Grieco of Saint Luke's Ampligen Program cited some other reasons for women's exclusion. "The best patients," he said, "have been male homosexuals. Women have less compliance. There's less education, motivation, and understanding. It is different taking someone who is productive in the arts than someone living as a minority person. They're not going to have the same grasp." However, Grieco does admit that corporate sponsorship determines the accessibility of the trials to women. It is substantially cheaper to test drugs on a specific group, such as homosexual men, than to reflect in trials the diversity of people with AIDS. "As studies get funded by the government instead of by drug companies, they will include women. Now it's a question of economics."

DuPont claims to be moving in this direction as well. "There is a small supply of the drug," says Morris. "So we can't move as quickly as we would like." But his company is planning to open a future trial at the University of Pittsburgh that will be open to women. However, there are very few women with AIDS in the Pittsburgh area. No plans are being made for such a project in New York.

DuPont has other arguments for male-only protocols. Morris claims that most researchers want an easily handleable group and in many cases women with AIDS are IV drug users. That leaves approximately 2,000 women nationwide who have contracted the disease through other means. Yolanda Serrano, president of ADAPT, an advocacy group for IV drug users and their families, says, "Many women with AIDS are recovered users. Many people in drug treatment programs are workers, homemakers and mothers, who have a lot of responsibility. They should have the same chance as everyone else to live out their lives."

Refusing experimental drugs to women did not begin with the AIDS crisis. A 1981 report published by the American College of Physicians entitled *Under-representation of Women in New Drug Trials* found that women have been generally ignored since the Thalidomide scandal of the early sixties, where women taking the drug during pregnancy gave birth to children with missing limbs. According to the report the results are two-fold. Women who are sick cannot be treated with drugs. And, in the long run, drugs are put on the market without ever having been tested on women. This can be the fatal flaw because women may have lower tolerance than men due to size, nutritional background, and hormonal fluctuations. Seven years after the AIDS crisis began, only one drug, AZT, has been approved by the FDA. Krim says AZT was never tested on women, although it is now being prescribed for them.

The gay community has been able to mobilize so that there is now a strong network where men can get information on new drugs. But this is not available to women with AIDS who do not have the same financial and social access to health care. In 1988, women with AIDS live an average of 298 days after diagnosis; men live 400 days. While 63 percent of men with AIDS are white, 72 percent of women with AIDS are black or Hispanic.

The Women's Committee of ACT UP intends a major campaign to open up the trials and make the drugs available in large numbers. "I have not been working in AIDS every day and gone out on the streets in order to get drugs released for men only," Cole says.

COMMENTARY

Ironically, Ampligen turned out to be worthless, but I continued my emphasis on writing on behalf of the most under-served people in the AIDS community, following this with a piece on AIDS and the Homeless in the *Nation*. The *Nation* magazine, a straight liberal weekly, had almost uniformly ignored the gay and lesbian movement and AIDS. When they finally did notice us, it was in an anti-ACT UP piece.

Using the liberal press to condemn ACT UP was becoming a nasty habit among self-appointed gay "leaders" who hadn't had to be accountable to anyone for years. Especially in the media. They resented the arrival of a grass-roots movement because it stole their thunder. Richard Goldstein, the insulting and destructive *Village Voice* editor had recently assigned the first of many articles trashing ACT UP. Activists met with Goldstein for years, begging him to use the paper to build activism, to do investigative stories and publish treatment information. Instead he devoted a series of full-page articles to musings on his own sex life and other irrelevant topics. We fought for almost five years before getting a regular AIDS column in the *Voice* and even that was exclusive to articles that Goldstein agreed with. Given the huge numbers of gay readers and writers at the *Voice* and their supposedly progressive pose, the fact that Goldstein's ego kept the *Voice* from becoming influential in the fight against AIDS is shameful. It was in this climate that the *Nation* published the following piece which focused safely on the homeless and not on homosexual rights or sexual practices.

THOUSANDS MAY DIE IN THE STREETS
AIDS AND THE HOMELESS

The Nation,
April 1988

Two years ago Ralph Hernandez was kicked out of his New York City apartment after his AIDS-related symptoms cost him his job with a window replacement company. Since then he's lived in building stairwells or in the waiting room at Grand Central Station. At one point he went to the Ward's Island Men's Shelter, but he could stay only one night because of the threats from residents who saw his skin lesions in the group shower. Living on the streets has aggravated the sores on his legs, making it difficult for him to walk or stand in line—things he must do to get food, use a shower, or find a change of clothes. "I was told by the VA hospital to keep the sores on my legs and body clean and to get plenty of rest and good nutrition," Hernandez says. "I told them I was homeless, but they gave me no referral to a place to stay. Nor was I given any treatment or medication. Workers at the shelter never approached me about my condition or offered me assistance or advice, so I returned to the street."

According to the Partnership for the Homeless, of more than 90,000 homeless people in New York City, up to 8,000 have AIDS or ARC. To date, the city has provided 66 beds for their care. Last October Mayor Edward Koch announced that an additional 838 beds would be made available by 1991. But with an estimated 400,000 New Yorkers currently testing positive for HIV and a majority of them expected to develop AIDS or ARC, the Partnership estimates that by then there will be between 130,000 and 180,000 people with AIDS or ARC in need of housing.

New York City is the most extreme example of the emerging crisis, but the convergence of AIDS and homelessness is becoming increasingly evident around the country. Few cities have undertaken projects specifically designed to address the emergency in part due to the overwhelming burdens already shouldered by AIDS service organizations and homeless advocacy groups. At present,

Los Angeles has only three shelters with a total of 25 beds for homeless AIDS patients. The San Francisco Health Care for the Homeless Project has set up one city-funded residential program for homeless intravenous drug users with AIDS, which serves between five and seventeen clients. According to Cynthia DeLouise of Columbus House, a shelter in New Haven, Connecticut that also serves homeless people who have developed AIDS, "There is an increase in those who must use our shelters because there are no adequate services in the city. People are discharged from the hospital and come directly here."

Who are the AIDS homeless? No one knows how many were forced out on the street after the disease wiped out their jobs, homes and savings—or how many were infected after they lost their housing. In an attempt to address the gap between their increasing numbers and the lack of adequate housing in New York City, last July the Coalition for the Homeless filed a class-action suit charging that the city was not fulfilling its mandate to find emergency housing appropriate to the medical needs of all homeless people. The suit was filed in the names of Ralph Hernandez, Kenneth Mixon, Michael Snyder, and Wayne Phillips who, as Vietnam veterans, members of racial minorities and drug users are perhaps most representative of homeless people with AIDS. In January, State Supreme Court Justice Edward Lerner granted a preliminary injunction agreeing with the Coalition's complaints and urging the city and state to take immediate action.

According to Judith Berek, Assistant Deputy Commissioner of the Division of Adult Services of New York State's Department of Social Services, there is no problem. "In New York," says Berek, "when HRA (the Human Resources Administration) determines that a person has AIDS and requires special housing, it provides such housing. In addition, medical care is provided." But 66 beds hardly provides adequate care. Moreover, Berek is referring only to those diagnosed under the official definition of full-blown AIDS as established in the early 1980s by the U.S. Centers for Disease Control (CDC). Dr. Stanley Yancovitz, Director of Clinical AIDS Activities for Beth Israel Medical Center, disputes this definition. "In terms of vulnerability to infection or how ill a person may be, a distinction between CDC-defined AIDS and other symptomatic HIV infection is artificial and illusory. Many persons have become ill and died from HIV-related illness without ever meeting the criteria for CDC-defined AIDS." So, while New York City's Division of AIDS Services provides rent support and placement assistance to twenty percent of the AIDS homeless, it refuses to help the vast majority who have ARC or are HIV positive and have tuberculosis or chronic diarrhea, for example. "I don't know how many times," states Ginny Shubert, a lawyer involved with the Coalition's class-action suit, "I've heard someone say, 'Your client would be a lot better off if he had full-blown AIDS.'"

New York State's Department of Health does require that any shelter resident who gets close enough to a doctor to be diagnosed as having AIDS must be hospitalized until appropriate housing is found by the Human Resources Administration. As a result, many people with AIDS stay in hospitals for longer terms than are medically necessary. Dr. Ernest Drucker, Executive Director of Montefiore Medical Center's drug treatment program, estimates that on any given day, at least 250 AIDS patients are in the city's public hospitals because they have no other place to go. According to Dr. Jerome Ernst, Chief of Respiratory and Infectious Diseases at Bronx-Lebanon Hospital, more than one-third of these patients die before housing is found.

At present there are thousands of people with suppressed immune systems living covertly in shelters or on the streets and receiving no medical attention or special services. The New York City shelters house as many as a thousand people each night in a large single space. These warehouses are noisy, dirty, smelly, and are often either brutally hot or underheated. Flu, pneumonia, and tuberculosis are rampant, and adequate rest and nutrition are impossible. Because the shelters close during the day, people with symptoms such as chronic diarrhea are forced out onto the street.

Deniece Clarke is a thirty-five-year-old black American born in the Bronx. A longtime IV drug user, she and her nine-year-old daughter have AIDS. Another child of hers has already died of the disease. Deniece has Kaposi's Sarcoma, an AIDS-related cancer found more often in gay men than in drug users. She has had two lesions surgically removed, paid for by Medicaid and applies a salve to her skin. She does not know the name of her medicine. After becoming homeless, Deniece and her children were placed in the Martinique Hotel, a notorious single-room occupancy establishment on West 32nd Street, only recently shut down by the city. They lived in a one-room fortress where the ever-playing T.V. set drowned out the violence of the hotel's hallways and staircases. Deniece is beginning to develop neurological disorders and is no longer in control of how she frames her sentences.

New York City paid $1,600 a month for Deniece's room. For appliances she brought a refrigerator from the Bronx and a hot plate. Her diet commonly consisted of pickles, hot dogs, and applesauce, although meals were available in the hotel's cafeteria. Now that the Martinique is closed, she has been relocated to another one-room apartment in Manhattan. This one also costs the city $1,600 a month, at least twice the market rate. Yet, if her "buddy," a white lesbian volunteer from Gay Men's Health Crisis, or her social worker were to find a larger apartment at a lower rent in better condition, the city would not subsidize the cost, preferring to pay HRA-approved landlords.

Deniece's daughter is lucky to be staying with her mother. Many children with AIDS have parents who are dead or in jail or otherwise unable to care for them, most often because of drug addiction. There are also significant numbers of these children who have been abandoned to the hospitals. While children represent only a small percentage of AIDS cases in the United States, their numbers have doubled annually. In New York City, one out of eighty newborns in 1988 tested positive for HIV antibodies. About half of these babies will develop HIV-related illnesses. In neighborhoods where drug use is common the rate was one in twenty-five. Up to 900 infected babies will be born in the city this year. "Children beginning their lives on the margin of society," says James Hagerty, a medical student at Harlem Hospital, "are often isolated from the love and care they deserve. Our nation must develop a coherent, comprehensive program that includes improved housing, home care, and respite care for these disadvantaged and chronically ill children."

The largest group of AIDS homeless is single men. Traditionally AIDS has been discussed in terms of middle-class gay men on one hand and "underclass" IV drug users on the other. However, a survey done by Reverend Julio Torres, the Director of Community Support Services at the Franklin Avenue Shelter in the Bronx, found that while only five percent of the residents said they were exclusively homosexual, fifty percent reported having had homosexual sex. Thus, while a few in the homeless population may have gay identities, many have gay realities. Only one third said they used IV drugs. For this reason, groups like ACT UP are advocating the distribution of free needles and condoms in the shelters.

New York City, which is the largest landlord in the nation, holds thousands of empty apartments while real estate prices continue to guarantee mass homelessness. Comptroller Harrison J. Goldin admits that out of the more than 200,000 city-owned apartments, 3,540 are empty. He claims that 1,700 only need minor repairs and could be rehabilitated for fifteen million dollars. Repairing all the city-owned housing would cost only sixty-three million dollars, Goldin said, and could be completed in little over a year.

But so far, despite the real emergency in the streets and shelters, the city's response has been negligent in the extreme. On March 28 thousands of AIDS activists plan to besiege City Hall to protest the Koch administration's inaction in the face of the imminent collapse of the city's overburdened and underfunded health care system. Such protests are vital. Without them, the combination of racism, homophobia, health care for profit and a firmly entrenched social psychology of denial virtually guarantee that thousands of people will have nowhere to die but the streets.

THE LEFT AND PASSIONATE HOMOSEXUALITY
PRESENTED AT THE SOCIALIST SCHOLARS' CONFERENCE

*Gay Community
News,*
May 1988

The progressive community's response to the AIDS crisis has revealed how incapable it is of addressing any issue in which homosexuality is central. After twenty years of occasional lip-service and no honest investigation, the theoretical foundations of the contemporary left are apparently irrelevant to AIDS activism.

For example, the left has only been able to say the words "lesbian and gay" in the context of laundry lists like "blacks, women, and gays." We never saw laundry lists like "South African freedom fighters, Palestinians, and gays" because of the obscene distortion—propagated by the left for years—that bringing up gay people would alienate Irish revolutionaries, Central American refugees, and anyone in the working class. When the left did say "gay" it was always followed by "rights."

"Gay rights." I remember a few years ago when a contingent of lesbian and gay journalists asked the *Guardian* to change their heading from "lesbian and gay rights" to "lesbian and gay liberation" and they refused. I've always assumed that their rejection of the word "liberation" was based in a refusal to fully imagine a world in which heterosexuality would be freely chosen instead of imposed by force as it often is today. That step required too much personal investigation on the part of the *Guardian*—the same paper, by the way, that when interviewing for a reporter to cover "women and gays" began the interview with the question, "What is your line on Kampuchea?"

The left has never come to terms with the passion of homosexuality. And AIDS cannot be adequately discussed if you cannot say "ass-fucking." Furthermore, how can somebody who has never fully explored the scope of his or her own sexuality deal with it in the social discourse? For this reason, self-affirmed lesbians and gay men are the best equipped people to create a movement that can openly discuss and affirm sexual practices because each of them has gone through the singularly difficult process of coming out, an experience that has no parallel in heterosexuality.

An overly theoretical left has been unable to accept that the infamous "cutting-edge" on which they wish to stand is overflowing with faggots and dykes who are coming from a millennium of rule-breaking, underground culture, and the survival skills oppression engenders, with lives revolving around cultural defiance and self-awareness. Can leftists, used to the image of the male industrial worker, make their stand with angry fairies? And know that some of them are male industrial workers?

The fact that the gay community and a sense of gay identity were already in place has enabled the AIDS movement to be as strong and unified as it is today. There is a tradition of bonding between gay people and a traditional aesthetic of gay confrontation which includes direct action, flamboyancy, humor, anger, and style. These elements bring a humane and emotional content to political issues that other groups often treat with dry rhetoric.

Every week, here in Manhattan, 300–400 people show up at the ACT UP meeting. Along with the black community, ACT UP is the largest truly grass-roots activist movement in NYC. The room is filled primarily with gay men, then women both straight and lesbian, many of whom work in AIDS-related fields. There are virtually no straight men in ACT UP. I think the overwhelming explanation of their absence in this case is homophobia.

Lesbians have long been alienated from gay men because of gay male separatism, unequal access to material and social power, and sexism. And yet this crisis has changed gay men and has dramatically changed that relationship. Lesbians are playing strong, visible roles in the AIDS movements primarily because lesbians had political skills and organizing experience that many gay men lacked. Most gay men were politically inactive during the last two decades while the women's movement was at its height.

Straight women have a historically special relationship with gay men that is particularly strong around moments of personal need and sharing. But straight men of the left, who are willing to march for every nation in struggle in the world, will not walk into a room full of queers and make a stand with them. Speaking as a lesbian who worked in the abortion rights movement for years and was purged from CARASA (Committee for Abortion Rights and Against Sterilization Abuse) by homophobic leftist women (eight lesbians were forced out of the organization), I have to concede that the men of ACT UP have been more concerned with learning from lesbians than straight women ever were. This is because the men of ACT UP are fighting for their own survival and are fighting from the heart of their own experiences, not from the text of some book or endless theoretical debate. ACT UP is growing in size and emotional breadth everyday because ACT UP wants to end the AIDS crisis. To them, nothing is more important.

COMMENTARY

In the audience for this talk was Dan Cohen, one of the straight editors at the *Guardian*, a long-standing leftist weekly. He was very annoyed by my criticisms and objected to them vociferously. A few weeks later Dan came to ACT UP to see for himself and ended up staying for a couple of years, becoming one of the very few straight men to ever take an active role in the group. The *Guardian* consistently supported ACT UP and AIDS activism as well as expanded their coverage of gay and lesbian issues until they folded in 1993.

Ironically, ACT UP never really needed the support of the left because they did not operate within their confines. Many ACT UP members had real world power and so took their case directly to the general public and the government, using direct action to generate a high level of media exposure. Tiny coalitions and ghetto organizing were not the forum for the efficient, necessity-organizing style that ACT UP continues to use to this day, where it is a major player in the international development of AIDS research strategy.

CHILDREN AND AIDS
DEBATE STIRRED OVER PLACEBO TESTS

New York Native,
August 1988

There are at least two thousand children with AIDS or ARC in America today. Eighty-five percent inherited their condition from parents who are intravenous drug users. Eight years into the AIDS epidemic, the federal government has just begun its first funded experimental drug trials for pediatric AIDS and related conditions. Almost thirty hospitals nationwide are beginning studies on intravenous gamma globulin (IVIG), a combination of processed plasma for children. The testing methods have come under criticism from members of patients' rights groups and from within the medical community.

According to the IVIG protocol developed by the National Institute of Child Health and Human Development, half of the children included in the study will be receiving four-to-eight-hour monthly intravenous applications of IVIG while the other half will be receiving four-to-eight-hour monthly intravenous applications of placebo. Considering that the average patient is eighteen months old, critics maintain that applying extended intravenous treatment of no medical value to sick toddlers and infants may not be the most ethical medical practice.

Dr. Aryeh Rubenstein, a pioneer in pediatric AIDS, conducted a preliminary investigation at Albert Einstein Hospital in New York, comparing fourteen infected children given IVIG with fourteen untreated children. Two of the fourteen treated patients died by the end of the study while all of the untreated patients died.

"For symptomatic children," Rubenstein said, "our experience indicates no necessity for placebo comparison."

If Rubenstein's findings were conclusive, there would be no need to subject sick children to placebo today, but physicians prominent in AIDS research have questioned his findings.

"The preliminary data suggests efficacy but is generated by a small number of patients," said Dr. Keith Krasinki of Bellevue

Hospital, one of the authors of the protocol. "As long as efficacy hasn't been demonstrated, using placebo is the most expeditious way to answer the question."

Dr. Mathilde Krim, founding chair of the American Foundation for AIDS Research, recently testified before a federal subcommittee that "no trial in CDC-defined AIDS should use a placebo in control groups." Krim suggested that AZT be used in the comparison group when new medications are being tested.

The Community Research Initiative (CRI) is an independent organization carrying out their own protocols. According to Christopher Babick, a person with AIDS affiliated with CRI, "When a promising new drug comes along, it is imperative that it be made available to all people with AIDS. It may take a little longer for researchers to come to their conclusions, but giving someone a placebo when the drug has shown results is immoral."

"We really care about patients," responded Dr. William Borkowski, Associate Professor of Pediatrics at New York University Medical Center. "And those of us taking part in this study feel that placebo makes the trial of greater use in the long run. However, there are differences of opinion about what an appropriate placebo would be. I favor an oral placebo."

The protocol lists a number of justifications for the use of placebos on small children. It claims that during the long IV treatment, "Not only will the patient receive better clinical assessment, but the family will have access to the entire pediatric team. For the patient who receives oral or no placebo there is simply no realistic way to provide the same in-depth care."

Iris Long, a pharmaceutical chemist and an activist with ACT UP objects to the reasoning surrounding this protocol.

"The fact that HIV-infected children outside clinical trials receive insufficient health care is deplorable. But, to sell a placebo trial to a parent as the easiest way to secure better health care for a child is potentially coercive."

Although participation in the IVIG trial requires parental approval, questions have been raised about the nature of consent when there are no other options.

"Informed consent is a real trap," says Maxine Wolfe, author of *Institutional Settings in Children's Lives.* "It subtly coerces people into thinking that placebo will guarantee their child better medical care."

According to the interim report of the Presidential Commission on the HIV Epidemic, providers are encouraged to "decrease the need for placebo-controlled studies by immediately beginning data collection for AIDS." The report goes on to suggest that doctors "utilize placebo-controlled studies only for patients without immediate life-threatening disease." Yet, the National Institute of Child Health and Human Development protocol claims that being on a placebo will "result in significant benefits for those who receive it."

"We believe," continues the protocol, "that families who agree to enroll their children will do so with the hope that their child will receive the IVIG treatment. We believe that when there is hope, an individual's response to disease is improved."

"Despite the protocol's claims," said Long. "I do not see how sick infants experiencing lengthy infusions will have their spirits raised. Any indirect benefit that a child could enjoy from partic-ipating in a trial does not depend on placebo infusion."

"Being seen frequently is a benefit," said Borowski. "The question is whether you need to be seen frequently with an IV in your arm."

TAKING RESPONSIBILITY

Outweek,
August 1989

Co-Dependence and the Myth of Recovery
by Kay Hagen

Despite the recent flood of gay self-help books in the chain stores, the tradition of gay and lesbian underground publishing flourishes. While some forms of queer writing have recently been permitted commodification, some will never be seen in B. Dalton's window. Whether it is a poetry chapbook in an edition of fifty, *My Comrade* for the drag set or xeroxed political pamphlets, gay and lesbian writing remains primarily a grass-roots event.

It would be hard to be alive today and not know that twelve-step programs have widespread appeal within the gay community. Since virtually every homosexual has been told at some time in their life that they are bad, we have learned well how to destroy ourselves. In recent years more and more communal efforts have been made to identify and stop abusive behavior, particularly alcoholism and drug abuse.

These programs have become so popular among women that the recent Michigan Women's Music Festival, an annual gathering of 6,000 lesbians, offered extensive twelve-step meetings in the following categories: Alcoholics Anonymous (AA), Adult Children of Alcoholics (ACOA), Survivors of Incest Abuse (SIA), Smokers Anonymous (SA), Narcotics Anonymous (NA), Overeaters Anonymous (OA), AL-ANON, Debtors Anonymous (DA), Sex and Love Addicts Anonymous (SLAA), Co-Dependents Anonymous (CODA) and generic twelve-step meetings six times a day. So, in a culture in which coming out is considered an act of mental health, anonymity has re-entered the foundations of many gay people's lives. Twelve-step and the language of recovery are influencing gays and lesbians in a big way. But clearly it has spread beyond physical addictions. Now twelve-step is being used as a way to "recover" from emotionally destructive patterns as well as physical ones. Both are referred to, in-house, as "addictions."

While clearly AA is the only system that works for millions of people who want to stop drinking, only time will tell if applying that program to relationship issues like "co-dependency" will have the same effect.

Kay Hagen, a writer from Atlanta, Georgia, has published a pamphlet in Samizdat form under the series heading *Fugitive Information* (Escapadia Press). Her piece articulates a clear and informative critique of the twelve-step movement and its impact on the lesbian community. Hagen, a self-defined Adult Child of Alcoholics, spent five years in an ACOA program that she says "affected me almost as profoundly as my personal awakening to feminism" fifteen years before. However, she viewed her feminism and ACOA experiences as distinct from each other until the term "co-dependency" was introduced into the canon.

The phrase was coined initially to represent men and women who were involved with lovers or family members addicted to alcohol or narcotics. It has since taken on a broader definition as behavior that supports another person's more obviously de-structive patterns. Hagen zeros in on the definition proposed by Robert Subby, a family-systems therapist well known in the co-dependence field. He describes it as:

> An emotional, psychological, and behavioral condition that develops as a result of an individual's prolonged exposure to and practice of a set of oppressive rules which prevent an open expression of feeling.

Hagen goes on to dissect this definition, focusing on the word "oppressive" and attempts to redefine "co-dependency" according to the tenets of feminism. She concludes that "co-dependence" is a euphemism for internalized oppression in intimate relationships.

> Internalized oppression occurs when the subordinate takes in the beliefs of the dominator. The dominant group defines meaning, morality and value, permeating society with images, institutions, structures, laws and customs which re-enforce these definitions.

In this way we come up with such social distortions as gay people being "narrow" while heterosexuals are "universal" or lesbians live in a "ghetto" while straight women live in "the world." Hagen posits that "co-dependency" is a more acceptable and benign term than "internalized oppression" even though they share many of the same definitions. For example, a woman who defers her needs to the needs of men, defines herself in relation to others, sees herself as a victim, denies her own feelings, is "a woman perfectly socialized into a male-supremacist society." Such a woman knows that defying these behavioral limitations means being punished in a wide range of ways from physical abuse to being ignored or shut-out. Calling this condition "co-dependency" is a de-politicizing use of the language.

> Co-dependence is no accident. Nor is it a disease, nor an individual character disorder. . . . When we do not recognize the relationship co-dependency has to the dominant culture we risk falling prey to another aspect of our training in which we accept personal responsibility . . . in a culture of dominance [where] the oppressed is always at fault.

The book *Co-Dependent No More* by Marie Beattie is now finishing up two years on the best sellers list. Critical literature on the subject has only begun to appear. Hagen's slim leaflet is a strong foundation for a much larger discussion that will inevitably surface wherever gay people fight only their personal "disease" and not the culture's as well.

Aids and the Responsibility of the Writer

Presented at Outwrite: The First National Lesbian and Gay Writers' Conference. Other panelists were Essex Hemphill, Susan Griffen, Pat Califia, and John Preston. San Francisco, March 1990

First I want to talk about writing and then I want to talk about responsibility. I've just published a novel *People in Trouble,* about the AIDS crisis. I spent three years working on it and in the process confronted a lot of questions relevant to AIDS fiction. When I began working there were very few books about AIDS. They were mostly about facing one's own illness or the death of a lover. I knew that I was not writing from either of these perspectives and so identified for myself the category of "witness fiction," so that I could understand the position of my words in this event.

To be writing about something of this enormity when it surrounds you leaves those of us who write about AIDS no possibility of objectivity. Nor can there be any conclusiveness since the crisis and our responses to it change radically and daily. So, I knew that I was committing to ideas and impressions that would already be history by the time the book actually reached readers.

In *People in Trouble* I imagined a small demonstration by AIDS activists outside Saint Patrick's Cathedral in New York City. Two-and-a-half years ago I imagined forty nervous men cautiously standing up to disrupt a religious service. By the time the book was published, there had been a real life demonstration of seven thousand angry men and women confronting the Cathedral. In this case, the community I was writing for and about made the boundaries of my imagination obsolete.

There is no existing vocabulary for discussing AIDS. To expect one would be unreasonable since this is an event that we will be spending generations trying to understand and define. In order to discuss it in novel form, I needed to identify a series of words that were generally resonant. This is a challenging task in a culture that does not acknowledge truth and a community that is emotionally overwhelmed. I started out by making lists of hundreds of details pertaining to the crisis. Rock Hudson at the airport being whisked off to Paris. Watch alarms going off in public places reminding their bearers to take their AZT. Men with teddy bears. Friends spreading AL721 on their toast in the morning. People spending their life savings on Ampligen or Dextrane Sulfate. Finding out later that those drugs were worthless. Then I chose fifty that I felt would be meaningful symbols to large groups of people, symbols that might have lasting resonance. It was an attempt to identify a vocabulary while understanding that to establish this group of words is perhaps all that the first generation of AIDS writers can do in the hope that future writers can use this foundation to develop a comprehensive and challenging literature. I also had to reject words. Words that were being used to distort. Words that were lies. Words like *innocent victim*. Words like *general population*.

I also made a decision for myself personally that I was not writing a novel documenting the life and death of a single individual. Instead I wanted to use the examples of people's lives to express a precise political idea—namely, how personal homophobia becomes societal neglect. That there is a direct relationship between the two and that this nation needs to confront this configuration in order to adequately address this crisis.

In the past I've written novels about the interior lives of people in marginal communities, and this enabled me to have some approval from the straight press because my work could be read voyeuristically. This time I knew I wanted to accuse straight people— to bring them into the literature in a manner equal to the role they play in this crisis: one of apathy, neglect, and denial. For that reason I had to write a primary character who was a straight man. That's when I discovered that just as literature has distorted women into the virgin/whore dichotomy, straight men have been distorted into the hero/villain dichotomy—neither of which I find generally appropriate. So, when I committed to violating these conventions by describing someone unaware of how other people are living and unaware of how much power he wields, I found myself vulnerable to being dismissed with, "Oh, she's a lesbian, she hates men." There does not yet exist a way for lesbian and gay male writers to address the straight male character and his societal power without being subjected to this dismissal. The fact remains that marginal people know how they live and they know how the dominant culture lives. Dominant culture people only know how *they* live. And so the people with the most power have the least information. And to state this is still considered didactic or extreme.

I had more surprises when I began touring with the book. Since, except in New York and San Francisco, men do not generally come to my readings, or those of lesbian writers in general, my audiences are mostly women. In cities where AIDS is not as much in people's daily lives as it is for us in San Francisco and New York, I found that people no longer wanted to talk about writing or books. They wanted to talk about AIDS. They asked me various questions about transmission in addition to expressing levels of discomfort with the politics of AIDS activism. One question that came up over and over again is, "If the shoe were on the other foot and this were happening to lesbians, don't you think the guys wouldn't help *us*?" And of course I had to answer *yes*, but, at the same time, not give in to the homophobic stereotype that gay men hate women and assert, instead, that this lack of reciprocity exists between all men and all women. Straight men are noticeably absent from the battle to win full abortion rights for straight women—and they're *married* to them. It's more about being raised male in this culture which insists that the male experience is the objective, neutral experience from which all other experiences can be generalized. This is why we see so little awareness or advocacy by gay men on women's behalf. Not only with regard to AIDS but also with regard to sexual assault, economic oppression, cancer, and abortion. However, I know at the same time that gay men have been allowed to die because they are *gay* not because they are men. And I also know, from two years of involvement in ACT UP, New York, that there is a general understanding in that organization that sexism is not only wrong—it is politically inefficient.

On a human level, the fact of the gay community going co-ed is something that has certainly enriched my life personally and intellectually, although it has been a strange experience, in a country where women earn half of what men earn, to go from a movement of all women to a movement of men. I guess it is something akin to experiencing heterosexual privilege for the first time because we now have access to the money, power, visibility, and resources that men move with in this culture, and I hope we can use these resources to benefit all of us.

I'd like to say one more thing about responsibility. There are people in this room, many people, who would not be alive today if it weren't for ACT UP. There is no book that got any drug released, any drug trial opened, or any service provided. Reading a book may help someone decide to take action, but it is not the same thing as taking action. The responsibility of every writer is to take their place in the vibrant, activist movements along with everybody else. The image created by the male intellectual model of an enlightened elite who claim that its artwork *is* its political work is parasitic and useless for us. At the same time I don't think that any writer must write about any specific topic or in any specific way—writers have to be free of formal and political constraints in their work so that the community can grow in many directions. But, when they're finished with their work, they need to be at demonstrations, licking envelopes and putting their bodies on the line with everybody else. We live in the United States of Denial, a country where there is no justice. The way we get justice is by confronting the structures that oppress us in a manner that is most threatening to those structures. That means in person as well as in print.

OUTING
THE CLOSET IS NOT A RIGHT

Village Voice,
April 1990

As for the morality of dragging gay public figures out of the closet—well, I'm not sure. What I do know, though, is that to call this an invasion of privacy is distorting and dishonest. Most gay people stay in the closet—i.e., dishonor their relationships, because to do so is a prerequisite for employment, housing, safety, and family love. Having to hide the way you live because of fear of punishment isn't a "right" nor is it "privacy." Being in the closet is not an objective, neutral, value-free condition. It is, instead, maintained by force, not choice.

Obviously the more gay people come out the better life will be for all gay people. "Privacy" has nothing to do with it. I think the question is really if gay people are a *people* and have responsibilities to each other. And, when homophobia results in mass death, do those responsibilities become more compelling? The closet is not a right. It is something we want to make unnecessary, not claim and cling to.

IS THE NEA
GOOD FOR GAY ART?

Outweek,
August 1990

The government is using homophobia again as an instrument of social control. We need to focus on homophobia and not on "saving the NEA." Of course, museums and boards of directors find it easier to articulate "Save the NEA" than to engage in fighting the oppression of gay people. This euphemism might even make the fight more palatable, but when the crisis over the NEA is resolved one way or another, no political impact will have been made on our behalf.

At the same time, the organized arts community has a lot of soul searching to do about its own history of exclusion. Before Helms, many other biases existed in the funding and presentation of artwork. Historically, the rewards system in the arts has been reserved primarily for white people from the middle and upper classes whose work fits the aesthetic agenda of critics and arts administrators. Yet, the majority of artists previously admitted to the reward system never spoke up about this institutionalized discrimination until it affected us. Obviously, it is not acceptable for artists who are gay to be excluded from federal funding. Nor is it acceptable for rewards to be demanded by one group at the expense of another.

For any minority artist, part of being admitted to the reward system is that while the benefits are great for the individual, the price for the community is tokenism. I know this firsthand having personally benefitted from the "exception" distortion because I fit the criteria for tokenism. It is important to remember that people get rewards like grants, gigs, and reviews, not necessarily because they are "the most deserving" but also because of things like personal connections and how well they play the art game. Of course, recognition doesn't always equal betrayal, but I think it is important not to blindly accept someone as our representative simply because he or she has been selected by a government agency, publishing company or corporate funded art venue.

Up until about five years ago, lesbian artists were almost completely excluded from the reward system. In fact, some of the gay men currently involved in the NEA scandal participated in that exclusion. Lesbians were not reviewed in mainstream publications, were not presented in prominent art venues and almost never received funding for explicitly lesbian projects. As a result, the work remained invisible, and many women were unable to develop their talents, while others could and their work thrives. This is still the case with the small exception of the thirty or so out lesbian artists, across all disciplines, who have access to the new tokenism. However, before funding, work was supported by the audiences and determined by the lives, needs, and experiences of the community.

Now, through the new tokenism, a few political and apolitical sensibilities are permitted to be contained within the dominant culture. Individuals are even easier than political movements to contain. As a result, a single style is declared to be representative of a hugely diverse community that it cannot represent. At the same time racism, class bias, and the emphasis on trendy, marketable genres (like detective novels and stand-up monologues) keep other voices from the public arena. When the frustrated community pressures the token to be more accountable to its needs for expression, she often declares herself "independent," puts down the community as "p.c." or "narrow," and disengages herself for her own artistic and career development. In the end, the permitted aesthetic encourages new artists to work in precisely the same styles so that they too can be rewarded. In this manner, much of the development of lesbian arts is taken out of the hands of the audience and given instead to a small group of critics and administrators. This year, the NEA panel that recommended the artists whose grants were later rescinded was composed of six arts administrators and one artist.

Media reporting on the NEA scandal further distorts the picture. A *Village Voice* cover story by critic Cindy Carr entitled "The War on Art" focused only on the exclusion of artists whose work she had previously championed. Although I deeply respect and admire the work of Karen Finley, there are entire communities of artists who have been systematically silenced. They too deserve C. Carr's attention, even if they don't meet her aesthetic agenda. Attaching the "censored" label to artists whose NEA experiences are bringing them publicity and audiences far beyond what they might have otherwise achieved, takes the underdog position away from everyone who really is. It accepts the distortion that the art world is *the* world. When Karen Finley stands up at a national press conference and says, "A year ago I lived in a country of freedom of expression, now I'm not," there is a refusal or ignorance about the history of this country in which most people have been systematically denied expression. I find a disturbing subtext to some of these arguments—that white artists "deserve" to retain our race and class privileges even though we're gay. Artists could, instead, use this attention on funding as an opportunity to discuss a real democratization of the reward system as well as the passive complicity with the state that has dominated North American arts.

The *Village Voice* ran photos of the four artists whose grants were rescinded over the caption "Defunded" even though they receive more funding, exposure, and institutional support than 99 percent of the artists in this country. When Cindy Carr said in a second article that she "may now be forced to conceive of a new demimonde—a bohemia of the unfundable," I got really angry. Doesn't she know that 99 percent of the artists in this country already live in the world of the unfundable? And that this invisibility is due, in part, to the role played by critics like her? I certainly think that these artists should receive the grant money that they were rewarded, but I do object to a kind of fetishized egomania that depoliticizes the events. We are living in a city of 90,000 homeless people. No one is getting the services and funding that they need. I wish that these artists could see themselves in relation to their own society and place the NEA support in a broader political context.

While we must support lesbian and gay arts, we must also refuse the distortion of calling it "censorship" of the rewarded, while ignoring the thousands who are systematically excluded from support because they don't fit the profile for privilege. Every out gay artist loses grants, gigs, and opportunities and faces bias and limitations throughout his or her career for being gay. This needs to be addressed politically with a recognition of how homophobia works on all levels, not only in the case of the most visible.

Obviously artists want recognition. I apply for grants and I like getting approval. But the NEA scandal is giving us all an opportunity to rethink the values we've created as well as the ones we've been handed. At the same time that we won't lie down for a homophobic, anti-sex NEA, neither can we roll over for elitist exclusionism in our own community. The fact is that there is a huge backlash going on against gay visibility. This includes increased street violence, restrictive immigration, and continued negligence in the face of the AIDS crisis. In response, a variety of grass-roots, community-based movements like ACT UP and Queer Nation are arising. Despite the historically apolitical stasis in which many artists have festered, we can still rise to the occasion and participate as activists in these movements, working in community to end the oppression of gay and lesbian people instead of working to maintain an exclusive tokenizing NEA.

COMMENTARY

Absurdly, this article on the NEA put me under more personal pressure for expressing an opinion than I had ever experienced in my public life. This was more than an intellectual debate because at stake were huge amounts of money, the canonization of careers, and opportunities for publicity and prestige that some obscure artists would never be offered again. The arts community was expected to strictly follow the line that the people in question were being "censored" and to champion them as heroes. It was absolutely forbidden to talk about the corruption and exclusion of arts funding in the first place or to question the rhetoric behind the campaigns.

The first signs of trouble came a week before the above article was set to appear in *Outweek*. My editor Sarah Petit called to say that she had received pressuring phone calls from Cliff Scott, the publicist for some of the NEA Four. He was demanding that she kill my story. Sarah replied that he had no right to tell a gay woman what she could publish in a gay magazine and that, more importantly, he was part of an *anti-censorship* campaign and so was behaving abhorrently. I had a series of encounters with people stopping me on the street telling me not to publish the story—which most of them had never seen— and even an incident in which individuals were pressured not to attend my birthday party because of my position on the NEA. Even a year later, one of the Four called the director of Outwrite, Amy Scholder, and told her that I should not be allowed to speak at the conference on this subject. Of course she ignored him.

This is one case where I feel sure that history has justified my position. Not only did the NEA Four adjust their rhetoric but, more significantly, two years after these events, Sapphire, a black lesbian poet, published a poem about the Central Park Jogger rape case, "Wild Thing," in a small magazine, *Portable Lower East Side*. Some right-wingers took one line of her poem out of context and circulated it in the Senate. Since the magazine had received $5,000 in

NEA funds, the head of the agency, John Frohnmayer, was forced to resign. Because Sapphire was black, radical, and difficult to commodify, the *New York Times* reporting on this very significant event never even mentioned her name—while the white performance artists continue, to this day, to be regularly promoted on the basis of the NEA action.

Even with increasingly negative and restrictive policies towards sexually explicit work by government agencies, I wonder if gay and lesbian artists are actually receiving less funding now than before the scandal erupted. Because, after all, only a handful were ever funded in the first place. If anything, this event gave more publicity to gay work even though the mainstream media still requires that it be under attack by the right wing before they'll report on it.

EILEEN MYLES

Interview,
December 1990

Eileen Myles is forty, sober, in great shape and in every way beautiful. Her small apartment is a mess. Her large dog is chewing on my leg. I only see one coffee cup. A poet for twenty years, Myles has just published her first major collection *Not Me,* out this month from Semiotexte.

SARAH   *So why do I make more money interviewing you than you did publishing your life's work?*

EILEEN   Yeah, I got a hundred dollar advance. But every time I write a poem I'm filled with joy about how lucky I am to be a poet. One day last week I wrote this very fast poem and knew it was one of those beautiful ones written in a moment of heat.

SARAH   *What is your perspective on the NEA debate?*

EILEEN   If anything comes out of all this strife around censorship and art, it should be that the art community starts to talk to the world, starts to want to know about the world. Sure, we should tell them who we are, but we should find out who they are too, because they're not dying to meet us.

SARAH   *What are you thinking about sex lately?*

EILEEN   I've been thinking that what I really want to do is enjoy women. Appreciate them, admire them, listen to them, talk to them. I met someone recently and suddenly felt drawn to her. It turned out she was a poet. We went to a coffee shop and I decided just to listen to her and not think about whether I wanted her to be my girlfriend or how to get her into bed. I had this whole new sense of freedom.

SARAH   *Are you ever going to paint your apartment?*

EILEEN   It's a depressing color, huh? Should I move?

SARAH   *How much rent do you pay?*

EILEEN   Two hundred and forty dollars.

SARAH   *Forget it.*

WHAT IDEALS GUIDE OUR ACTIONS?

Outlook,
Winter 1991
Excerpted from
a speech at
Outwrite, 1991.
Other panelists
were Craig Harris,
Ana Maria Simo,
and Robert Gluck.

I believe that the National Endowment for the Arts (NEA) funding crisis has its roots in three different arenas. It is the result of ten years of Reaganism and the right-wing coalition that has kept Reagan and Bush in power. It is part of the broad homophobic backlash to the visibility that has accompanied AIDS. And it is a reaction to years of artists' isolation from other communities.

If artists really believe all our talk about racism, sexism, and class privileges, then we must articulate a clear and inclusive vision of how we want to live. This vision can include an arts reward system that does not perpetuate the special privileges for an elite and the institutional neglect that have become normal for an increasing number of Americans. This vision means that as we oppose the exclusion of gay artists from NEA grants we must, with equal vigor, oppose the systematic exclusion of entire communities of artists—an exclusion that many of us have previously accepted as normal. Acknowledging and dismantling these exclusions is equally important and must be done hand-in-hand with our opposition to Helms and homophobia.

Marketing, nepotism, and racial exclusion have always been taboo topics for discussion in the arts. And some are saying that this is not the strategic moment to "open up this can of worms." But I would argue that, strategically, this is the perfect time because this is when the attention is on funding and this is when we are all scrambling to find out what it is we stand for. We know we are opposed to Helms but what ideals guide our actions? Do we want to "Save the NEA," i.e., return to the status quo of exclusion that existed quietly a year and a half ago?

We are artists in a political battle and our role can be similar to the role of the old left—that is, to be radical, to be challenging, to propose a vision. Look at how that structure has functioned in the gay movement. Since ACT UP came along and stretched the parameters of gay politics, suddenly we see an issue like domestic partnership given enormous credibility. Before ACT UP and gay civil disobedience, the simple request for a legalized gay family was considered absurd. ACT UP has made it seem reasonable. Why then are artists and the centrist arts establishment taking the same position—that is, a return to the status quo? True, the most established artists have the same interests as the institutions, but what about the vast majority of us? Shouldn't we be constantly pushing for more minority representation in arts organizations, stronger community relations, and more equitable distribution of resources? Let's articulate a visionary agenda of concrete reforms that we want to see put in the place of the current corruptions. OK, we know these won't be instituted next year or the year after, but an agenda can give us some clarity about what we are working towards. For example, how many people of color were awarded grants by the NEA panels in question? Ten percent? Twenty percent? Alright, let's propose that next year the panel should proportionally represent underfunded communities—so the panel would be eighty to ninety percent black, Asian, Latino, and Native American. That would guarantee a more diverse spectrum of recipients. Besides, history has shown that disenfranchised people are much more likely to select ecumenically than dominant culture people. So panelists of color or women are more likely to include white men in their selections than the other way around.

Or, how about real peer panels? We're told that the NEA has peer panels now but that's not really the case. Panels should be 100 percent artists. Arts administrators and critics receive salaries, have their own agendas, and their own professional debts and alliances. Administrators and critics are also overwhelmingly white, far out of proportion to artists. Besides, once a critic or administrator is associated with an artist, his or her own prestige grows along with that artist's career, creating even more bias in funding choices. The person who reviews your work should not be the same person who decides whether or not you get grants. Keep critics and administrators out of funding. They have too much power as it is.

Third, people who sit on panels should not be allowed to receive grants from their own panels. That's where conflict of interest and cronyism sink deepest into the most obvious corruptions.

These simple reforms would change a lot of things but the fact remains that no white majority industry is going to provide real equity to others. Those of us who have access have to use our connections for democratization. White artists must refuse to co-operate with segregated panels, festivals, and programming.

Another challenge to building a movement is to take the NEA issue out of the province of arts-only advocacy groups and instead build with other communities along the shared experience of repressive legislation. How many times have I heard someone say, "Artists need health insurance"? Don't we all need health insurance? Besides, history has shown us that single issue organizing never works because social change requires a social context. Gay art came out in the first place because of gay liberation in everyday life, not because of a small group of gay lobbyists going to Washington. We artists need to use our skills to confront the widespread lack of funding and services affecting a diverse and growing spectrum of people in this country.

Some immediate tasks have to do with reclaiming the vocabulary imposed on this event by the press. This is probably the first time in history that the media has defined a gay and lesbian issue before we had time to figure it out for ourselves. In this country the government and the media exist in a dialectic of power. When the government takes away a grant and the media replies with millions of dollars in publicity, it would be false to call this simply "censorship." Without any compromise, people who had their grants taken away should receive the money that they were rewarded. But because we're facing a complicated system of career inflation under the title "censorship," we need even more to clearly articulate our opposition to all exclusion. Just as artists should not be cut out because they're gay, neither should they be excluded because they're the wrong color, they have no friends on the panel, or their work isn't trendy enough. We fight homophobia, not because we think gay people are superior, but because we follow a larger principle of equal access for all without bias. I know it is virtually impossible to get a complicated message out through the simple-minded media, but in our own territory we can use words like *de-funded, censorship,* and *blacklist* more truthfully to describe people's differing levels of access to visibility and support.

Finally, I want to say a few words about sex. Another complex issue in this debate is the role of sexual material in the funding of gay and lesbian art. While it is true that most gay artwork continues to be excluded from the upper echelons of power, there is a handful of artists who receive extensive institutional support.

Ironically, in a number of fields, programmers, critics and funders are more likely to support sexual content than openly gay work without sexual content. This bias reflects the stereotypes that the proper role for a lesbian artist is to talk about sex and the proper role for a gay male artist is to talk about AIDS. As a result, many people receive no institutional support, with or without the Helms amendment, because their gay and lesbian work confronts subjects such as male power and race.

We have to build a vibrant, resonant alternative that can feed our activist movements. Right now we're being offered two choices: Helms or the Same Old Thing. We have to say no to both.

COMMENTARY

At Outwrite I organized this panel on censorship to more broadly define the parameters of the debate. I invited three other respected writers to discuss the topic in their own terms.

Robert Gluck is a well-loved, San Francisco-based experimental writer who has been influential on two generations of formally inventive work. Part of the New Narrative school, Bob has always been on the margins of the literary establishment because of the experimental nature of his work. He spoke eloquently about the absolutism of conventional narrative in the criteria of reviewers, publishers, and funders and the role this had played in his life as a writer.

Ana Maria Simo, a Cuban-born experimental playwright, librettist, filmmaker, and fiction writer spoke about her experiences as a token Latina invited onto funding panels. Ana exposed, quite starkly, the kind of cronyism and nepotism involved in nominating artists for grants. She also detailed the way in which minority representatives on panels are expected to choose the one Latina or one lesbian who can get funding under the unspoken quota system. She told how she was not expected to have any influential input into the choice of which majority culture writers would be granted. Ana described how friendships between panelists, class and ethnic similarities, and even having attended the same college were all factors in determining who would be nominated for funding.

Craig Harris was a writer I knew from early days at the *Native*, and he had gone on to work at Gay Men's Health Crisis as a staunch advocate for people of color with HIV and AIDS. When I called and invited him to be on the panel, I had no idea that he was extremely ill with AIDS himself. And so it was shocking to see him appear in San Francisco, barely able to walk, covered in

KS and afflicted with severe diarrhea. Outwrite was to be his last public appearance. He could barely stand at the podium and was unable to raise his voice. But Craig talked about attending Vassar College and how he was unable to even get *into* the creative writing classes there. In a whisper he chronicled a lifetime of exclusion and a few months later, he was dead.

Delusions of gender

Village Voice,
January 1991

Phyllis S., a thirty-nine-year-old Bronx resident, tested positive for HIV two years ago. In August she developed a severe, recurring urinary tract infection that has made it impossible for her to work. But Phyllis, who has three children including an HIV-positive three-year-old, isn't eligible for social security. She, and thousands of women like her, are denied disability and other AIDS benefits because their illness does not meet government standards.

The U.S. Centers for Disease Control's official definition of AIDS requires individuals to have HIV plus at least one from a list of opportunistic infections or cancers. The list, which is derived from studies of gay men, does not include gynecological infections such as vaginal thrush or pelvic inflammatory disease (PID). Even life-threatening diseases like cervical cancer are omitted.

The CDC so far has rejected complaints from activists that the definition is too narrow. When ACT UP's Women's Committee descended on the agency in November, Ruth Berkelman, chief of AIDS surveillance, told them, "When we start talking about changing the case definitions, we get a lot of screams from scientists, from all kinds of places, saying, 'We can't track trends every time you do this.'" But it is not just convenience that makes the agency hesitate. "These conditions, like yeast infections, are common in all women. Science does not tell us that certain women's conditions are related directly to HIV," says CDC spokesperson Kent Taylor.

Not so, says Maxine Wolfe of ACT UP, arguing that gynecological infections thrive in women whose immune systems are suppressed by HIV. "We have been told over and over again that, 'Well, women get those things.' That's not a good enough answer. We know what *normal* is. When a woman is treated over and over again and it still does not go away . . . you don't have to be a genius to understand that."

Medical studies across the country do suggest that gynecological infections occur with unusual frequency and severity in HIV-positive women. The CDC insists its own data show that cervical cancer occurs *less* often in women with HIV. But studies outside the agency say otherwise. In one, researchers at the University of Miami reported that sixty-three percent of HIV-positive women have abnormal pap smears, compared to five percent of uninfected women.

And such problems can occur long before AIDS-defining symptoms. One little-noted Brown University study last year found that as many as two-thirds of women with HIV suffer from severe and chronic gynecological infections before any officially recognized AIDS symptom appears.

One study conducted at the CDC itself found that of 1,100 women age fifteen-to-forty-four with HIV listed on their death certificates as the underlying cause of death, only half met the definition. "And that's only the cases we know about," says Linda Meredith of ACT UP/DC. "A restructuring of the definition would at minimum double the government's AIDS expenditures."

At stake for women like Phyllis is much more than social security and other benefits. "Most doctors are not aware of the relationship between PID and HIV," says Dr. Vicki Alexander, medical director of the Community Family Planning Council. She says the narrow definition means frequent "under-diagnosis" of women with HIV, leading to delayed and inadequate treatment. It also limits access of women with HIV to experimental therapies since many drug trials continue to require an official diagnosis.

In the days of illegal abortion, some women claimed psychological disorders in order to qualify for the procedure. Francine Wilson of Harlem Legal Services says the narrow CDC definition has forced women with HIV into a similar strategy today. "They have been forced to go into court with documentation of severe depression or even schizophrenia to qualify for benefits," says Wilson.

Terry McGovern of Mobilization for Youth Legal Services and others have filed a class-action suit against the U.S. Department of Health and Human Services on behalf of men, children, and women denied assistance due to the CDC definition. The case is currently in federal court under Judge Miriam Cedarbaum, a Reagan appointee. The government has moved for dismissal. Others have taken more aggressive measures: 500 activists demonstrated at CDC headquarters in Atlanta in early December, demanding a recasting of the definition. Ninety-two were arrested on charges of criminal trespass.

In response to such pressures, the CDC has now set up a committee to review its definition. But, unless the courts take action, the signs are not hopeful: the agency's new "Spectrum of Disease" study, which will track infections in 4,000 HIV-positive people, includes only 280 women.

COMMENTARY

In March of 1989 ACT UP-New York sponsored a Women and AIDS teach-in. They produced a xeroxed packet, later published by South End Press under the title *Women, AIDS, and Activism,* which included a list of symptoms experienced by women with AIDS. When Linda Meredith and Chip Rowan of Atlanta ACT UP invited them to come do an action about the sodomy laws, the New York group insisted that it be about the CDC definition and the sodomy laws. This was the beginning of the three-and-a-half-year campaign to change the government's definition of AIDS.

John Kelly, Mike Frishe, and David Z. Kirschenbaum went to meet with the CDC to talk about the definition in November 1989. At this time ACT UP decided that T-cells were not accurate indicators and should not be the sole basis for an AIDS diagnosis, despite a contingent within the organization continuing to push for a diagnosis based on 200 T-cells.

The first definition-related action took place in January 1990 primarily involving an affinity group called the Costas, named after an ACT UPer who had recently died. The group included Maxine Wolfe, Michael Naisline, Walter Armstrong, Sean Slutsky, Randy Snyder, Avrum Finkelstein, Lee Schy, Jo Ferrarri, Illith Rosenbaum, Marian Banzhof, Polly Thistlewaite, and others. They took over an office at the CDC, demanding a changed definition and a higher standard of care.

In May of 1990 ACT UP organized "Storm the NIH." Activists including Risa Dennenberg, Jean Carlomusto, Zoe Leonard, the Costas, Invisible Women (another affinity group), and others sat in at Dan Hoth's office demanding a women's health committee, the recruiting of women into clinical drug trials, and a change in the definition.

The international AIDS Conference was held in San Francisco in June of 1990. There were street actions outside focusing on issues of women and AIDS and inside, when Tony Fauci was speaking, activists unfurled a large banner "Form a Women's Health Committee." By August of that year, after a series of pressuring Zaps, fax and telephone campaigns, and other actions, Fauci and Hoth finally agreed to meet with seven lesbians from ACT UP DC and NY—

Maxine Wolfe, Risa Dennenberg, Heidi Dorow, Garance Franke-Ruta, Linda Meredith, Melinda Daniels, and Laurie Sprecher. They demanded a national conference on women and HIV with the government paying for women with AIDS and HIV to attend and participate.

In the meantime, Terry McGovern, an attorney for Mobilization for Youth Legal Services HIV Project, realized that many of her clients were not qualifying for disability benefits even though they clearly had advanced HIV disease. She came to ACT UP with the realization that changing the definition would dramatically impact on benefits. McGovern filed a lawsuit and tried to get mainstream gay groups to join it but no one would take her seriously initially. Once she did develop the lawsuit, however, a number of them did come on board. The suit was filed in October 1990 on the day of an ACT UP demonstration about women's issues at Health and Human Services in Washington.

On December 3, 1990, in the pouring rain, the first demonstration by HIV-positive women was held outside the CDC. It included Kerry Duran, Linda Awoayadei, Mary Lucy, and others. Laurie Cotter of ACT UP did the press work, beginning the advance phase of media pressure on the issue.

Ten days later, the Women and HIV conference was finally held, including participation by HIV-positive women. The first speaker was James Curran, Director of HIV Surveillance for the CDC. When he appeared activists started chanting "Change the Definition." Dr. Judith Cohen of the AWARE Program in San Francisco, which did street outreach to drug users and sex workers with HIV, pointed out all the contradictions in Curran's speech and lost her CDC funding a short time later. The women who attended wrote up and distributed a statement of unity demanding a change in the definition, a change in the criteria for disability benefits, and the immediate recruitment of more women into clinical trials.

In the Spring of 1991, activists discovered that the CDC intended to release a new definition requiring 200 T-cells or less for benefits, disregarding all the information about women's symptoms. In response, ACT UP spent the year getting a wide range of groups, about three hundred of them, to oppose this standard. The groups included Actors' Equity, the American Red Cross of Shreveport, the American Medical Association, NOW, and the National Association of Black Lawyers. Assemblywoman Deborah Glick of Manhattan got the NY State Assembly to pass a supporting resolution, as did the Maine state legislature.

In June 1991, ACT UP ran a full page ad in the *New York Times*: "Women Don't Get AIDS, They Just Die From It."

Every time ACT UP did an action, something changed, someone moved. Behind the scenes, the CDC added vaginal candidiasis to the list of symptoms, but still insisted on the 200 T-cells, while the presence of Kaposi's Sarcoma, for example (which appears more frequently in people infected by sex than by needles) did not require the accompanying T-cell count. So, even with the changes there were still higher standards for women to meet to receive benefits. A phone Zap to James Curran effectively stopped him from releasing it. At this point activists vowed to stop all behind-the-scenes lobbying and relied exclusively on grass-roots organizing.

At the International AIDS Conference in Amsterdam in June 1992, James Curran was zapped and forced to meet with women. This capped the accumulation of the largest amount of public comment ever received in the history of the CDC.

Then, the following September 1992, the CDC hearings were held in Atlanta. Activists Marybeth Cachetta, Terry McGovern, Linda Meredith, and others raised $10,000 to bring HIV-positive women from all over America. Here the definition was finally changed to include cervical cancer, TB, bacterial infections or 200 T-cells as the criteria for benefits and services. This was the first time that woman-specific or intravenous drug user-specific symptoms were included and that they did not have to be tied to a T-cell count.

In New York City, the first year after the new definition went into effect in January 1993, the official number of women and intravenous drug users who now qualified increased by forty to fifty percent.

After three-and-a-half years, this thoroughly grass-roots campaign triumphed. And even though there was a legal component, it was strategized consistently as a political battle. But, unlike traditional coalitions, this was a campaign run by ACT UP that got the info out to grass-roots organizations. They in turn, were not asked to be part of the coalition; instead they were just asked to endorse the demands. The result was a manageable and effective alliance between infected and uninfected women.

In terms of real impact on people's lives, the changing of the CDC definition was perhaps the most significant political victory in the AIDS crisis.

WHATEVER HAPPENED
TO LESBIAN ACTIVISM?

Presented
at the
Lesbian and Gay
Center, NYC
January 8, 1991

Millions of people have experienced the loss of someone they know to AIDS. But only a handful have taken action. So it is not the experience of loss, alone, that motivates activism, but rather a whole other set of beliefs and faiths that determine one person's commitment. Beyond the deaths of personal friends to AIDS I also came to ACT UP, over three years ago, because lesbians were no longer doing activist work. ACT UP was the only movement I could agitate in that permitted me to affirm my homosexuality. And it was the only organization addressing AIDS that was truly activist. I also came to ACT UP because AIDS is an event, which like abortion, encompasses social and personal liberation issues that are consistent with my own vision of what we need to have freedom.

However, coming to ACT UP also meant working with men who had never supported women's struggles for autonomy. Men who had never fought rape, marched for abortion rights, contributed financial support, or simply informed themselves about women's lives. And for many, but not all, gay men this is still true today. In fact, it sometimes seems that the reason some gay men who once ignored us, now praise us, is only because of our contributions to AIDS activism and not a recognition of our personhood.

At the same time, women working in AIDS have moved the issues of women and AIDS to visibility while continuing to work on every other AIDS-related issue as well. But many men who work in the full spectrum of issues (pediatrics, insurance, housing, etc.) have not fully integrated women's lives into their rounds of commitments. So, women have been made responsible to raise and maintain women's and AIDS issues in addition to all the other responsibilities we have committed to.

One of the greatest gifts I have received from ACT UP, and there are many, has been from men's higher sense of entitlement. They have always been told that they are important and so they expect a higher level of response. In the women's movements, while we challenged every power institution in the culture, we were unable to directly address them. We rarely knocked directly on the doors of the government, but I also believe that we never thought they would listen to us and the effort seemed futile. Ultimately this reticence hurt us because only the conservative lobbyists of NOW ended up with influence on policy while the radicals disappeared. Since working in ACT UP, many lesbian activists have learned how to challenge the government directly and are working with more effect than we once did.

My question is—how do we transfer this empowerment to our own community and our own needs apart from the context of AIDS? I am committed to ACT UP, and I will stay in ACT UP, but I also want to know how we can maintain this level of strength without being dependent on men. Well, I think the first step is to redefine what lesbian issues are. The media (an institution in which lesbians, unlike gay men, have zero power) has created a false agenda for us. They have told us that our issues are ones in the private sphere, an argument that facilitates our return to family and motherhood roles only. We have been told that lesbian issues are only custody, artificial insemination, adoption, and gay marriage. Well, I disagree. I think that the most pressing issue for lesbians in America is economics. In this country women still earn fifty-nine cents for every dollar that a man earns. That means that the women's movement is a poverty movement. One of the reasons that we are dependent on ACT UP and other AIDS organizations to publicize issues of women and AIDS is because of the gay community's huge financial resources. Of course it is wonderful that the community has made their funds available to activists, but a movement of men will always be on the opposite side of the economic power scale from a movement of women. It is men's salaries versus women's salaries. ACT UP has media attention because we do great actions and because there are men in the media who identify with the men of ACT UP. ACT UP produces great t-shirts because we have gifted creative artists and a constituency that has the discretionary income to purchase them.

In other words, women working in AIDS who wish to raise women's issues in addition to their other AIDS work, can only get resources and visibility because we are connected intimately to people with more money, social power, and sense of entitlement. Straight people call this marriage. Right now we call this coalition.

217

But if gay men prioritized women's lives and with the same commitment that women have made to them, then women's issues would be organic and homogenous to our organizing and not the special responsibility of the women in the movement.

At the same time groups like ACT UP are only responsible for women's issues to the extent that they are related to AIDS. Beyond AIDS, ACT UP cannot become the new women's movement. We need to do that ourselves. Do we need an activist lesbian organization? Do we need small Zap groups? Do we want to extend the women's cancer movement that is coming out of San Francisco? Should more lesbians come into ACT UP? I think all these things should happen. I hope that each woman will take the responsibility to become active again in the kind of group that is most appropriate for her. And, if that group does not already exist, I hope women will take the responsibility to start their own groups instead of waiting for someone else to do it for them. There is no one else.

There are many reasons why lesbian activism fell apart. It had a lot to do with Reaganism, because *deprivation of services disempowers any group of poor people*. It also had to do with the domination of identity politics and therapy over activism—which I consider to be retreat from directly confronting the government. And it had to do with divisions in the movement over racism, class, and sexuality. But I also think, looking back, that we were never fully empowered around our own issues. Even when we properly identified our agenda: rape, reproductive freedom, racism, sexuality and employment—we became mired in victim identities and could not sustain a commitment to direct action. Since the middle eighties lesbians have by and large withdrawn from activism. We write, publish, have cultural events, tell each other how we have sex, and provide services—all of which are important. But we are not in the streets. A few organizations have survived the Reagan budget cuts but none of them maintained activist movements to keep them radical. What is the meaning of a rape hotline without a Stop Rape movement? The time has come for a new lesbian activism—in or out of ACT UP. We have to fully participate in activism to create a country that *we* want to live in.

COMMENTARY

I had written this talk for a mixed audience. Unfortunately, only lesbians (and two gay men) showed up. I found that humiliating, especially considering my years in ACT UP and the gay press. After the talk some of us got together and decided to call a community meeting to see if people wanted to start a lesbian group. At that time I was still mired in some of the rhetorical traps of the pre-AIDS women's movement and so approached that first meeting with a structure that was doomed to failure. Instead of coming in with a proposal for action, I came in to that room of 150 women with an "open" agenda. This mistake enabled all the classic disempowered, obstructive lesbian behavior to surface. About half the women there had come to do something. About half had come to stop something. The whole project quickly fell apart, but it was an enormous learning experience that was to directly influence how the Lesbian Avengers began their organizing one year later.

WHY I FEAR THE FUTURE

In
Critical Fictions:
The Politics of
Imaginative
Writings
edited by
Philomena
Mariani
(Seattle:
Bay Press,
1991)

W. H. Auden wrote, "Not one of my poems ever saved one Jew." When the AIDS-activist organization ACT UP first began, we believed that hard work, education, diligent activism, and creativity would produce solutions to the AIDS crisis. We did not anticipate the extent to which the government would obstruct our every initiative. With 106,000 AIDS deaths as of June 1991, this nation still does not have a needle exchange or condom distribution program, explicit safe sex material, protection for people with AIDS, adequate health services, or an efficient and humane research procedure. The obvious conclusion that I draw is that the government does not want to end the AIDS crisis. As poet Kenny Fries says, we know that Silence Equals Death, but we have just recently realized that Voice does not equal Life.

As I was sitting in New York University Medical Center visiting my friend Phil Zwickler, I ran down a checklist in my mind of all the reasons why we massage the feet of dying people. Because they have been in bed for a long, long time and have poor circulation. Because they need to be touched but chest catheters and IV's get in the way. Besides, they can't sit up. Because, by rubbing their feet you can sit on the edge of their beds and they can see you. Because you can talk to them and touch them at the same time and they don't have to move. Because you can take one last look.

At Phil Zwickler's memorial service, I really had to smile because the guy was such a control queen that he had planned how we would memorialize him. In fact, there was even a moment when we had to sit and listen to Phil's favorite songs. He made us listen to Steely Dan. The food afterwards was coffee and Danish. When his mother stood up to speak, I was really worried because that is everybody's nightmare—to die and your mother has the last word. But actually it turned out that she really knew who he was. So often at these services the parents do not really know their child.

Phil Zwickler was a filmmaker, and one of his films, *Rights and Reactions,* was about the passage of the Gay Rights Bill in New York City in 1986. The bill finally passed after years of humiliating defeat. As I was watching the footage he chose for his own memorial, I suddenly realized, for the first time, that I had lived as an adult homosexual in a city without a gay rights bill. In fact, I was thrown out of two restaurants on two separate occasions in the early eighties for kissing women. They could do that then because there was no gay rights bill. Sitting there, at Phil's service, I suddenly started to cry, half for Phil and half for me because they threw me out.

This brings us to Tompkins Square Park, from which three hundred homeless people have been thrown out. I live one block from the park and my neighborhood is currently under police occupation. The city is spending $100,000 a day, in the middle of its worst fiscal crisis, to keep homeless people out of the park. So now there are police everywhere. They're in every coffee shop. They're in every store. They're talking on every pay phone. When you stand on a corner waiting for a light, you're standing in front of the police. When you run into a friend and have a chat on the street, it takes place right in front of the police. In the meantime, they do let people into the park if they are going to play basketball, walk their dog, or take their kids to the playground. But if you are homeless, you can't go in.

As Carla Harryman has pointed out, the definition of who constitutes the public is rapidly changing. Now homeless people— that is, people with no private space, people who must live in public space—are being told that their homelessness is their private problem. That they are no longer part of the "general population." What is permissible in the public sphere is also shrinking. Women who want abortion information can't get it in federally funded clinics, says the Supreme Court, *even if they ask.* Women who are nude dancers now have to wear pasties (which are far more lascivious than nudity). The Court has decided that it is really the nipple that is obscene. The *New York Times* reports that AIDS has not spread into the heterosexual, non-drug-using world and therefore is not a concern for the "general population."

But so many of my friends are dying.

I'm thirty-two years old. I read the obituary page first.

Recently ACT UP held a demonstration at the United Nations. We're asking the World Health Organization for disaster relief services. We're asking for food, shelter, and medical supplies. There's a small park across the street from the UN where people are allowed to demonstrate. But the police would not let us walk on the sidewalk to get to that spot. They began to arrest ACT UP members simply for standing. Usually, we *try* to get arrested to attract media attention since the deaths themselves are not newsworthy enough. But this time, people got arrested for no reason. We had joined the ranks of the non-public: the people who are not allowed to be seen on the sidewalks, not allowed to go into the park, not allowed to discuss abortion, not allowed to show their nipples. We are on the losing side of the great divide.

My friend Bo Houston calls from San Francisco. He can't walk or swallow.

I don't know which issue is more significant for gay writing—how we are to represent AIDS in our literature or the fact that so many writers are dying. I cross my fingers hoping that George Bush will die of a heart attack soon. I can't imagine any other scenario that would actually get rid of him. I know it's humiliating to be reduced to crossing my fingers, but I have to try everything I can.

At the Lambda Literary Awards, Allen Barnett, author of *The Body and Its Dangers,* arrived in a wheelchair from Co-Op Care to receive his award. He announced that he had picked out his tie to match his Kaposi's Sarcoma. Then he took his Hickman catheter out of his chest and started talking into it as though it were a microphone.

At that point I realized that when I first began to comprehend the enormity of what was happening to my community, I anticipated only that we would lose many people. But I did not understand that those of us who remain, that is to say, those of us who will continue to lose and lose, would also lose our ability to fully mourn. I feel that I have been dehumanized by the sheer quantity of death, so that now I can no longer fully grieve each person—how much I love each one and how much I miss each one.

However, knowing that no large social gains can be won in this period, I still remain politically active. I do this because small victories are meaningful in individual lives. I do this because I don't want to be complicit with a future in which people in need will die and everyone else will be condemned to a vicious banality. But also because I believe that in long, hard struggles, there is a value to what Gary Indiana calls "the politics of repetition." Even if it takes all of our energy, I still intend to do everything I can to at least keep these issues alive.

LAYING THE BLAME
WHAT MAGIC JOHNSON REALLY MEANS

Guardian,
London
November 19, 1991

For eleven years Americans have been pressuring our government to take action against the AIDS virus. The response has been two inadequate drugs (AZT and DDI), increased stigmatization of people with AIDS, and no condom distribution, clean needle, or explicit safe sex campaigns. All of this, of course, has taken place in a two-tiered health care system in which only the wealthy can obtain treatment and care.

Then, in the midst of this static state of neglect, a much beloved basketball star, Earvin "Magic" Johnson, announced on November 7 that he has tested positive for HIV antibodies. Suddenly the media snapped to attention. Information on how AIDS is transmitted appeared in daily newspapers for the first time. Hotlines have been overwhelmed by concerned people clamoring for information. Even President Bush felt compelled to assure voters that Johnson is "a hero to me" and that, as far as AIDS goes, "I don't like the allegation that I don't care . . . because I do, very, very much."

Johnson is the perfect candidate for America's first acceptable spokesperson with AIDS. He is young, black, charming, wealthy, and a record-breaking athlete. He has led his team, the Los Angeles Lakers, to five national championships and has been awarded Most Valuable Player trophies three times. Even more indicative of his broad credibility is the fact that he has been chosen by a number of major corporations to do product endorsements for such emblematic American brands as Pepsi.

However, the most crucial element enabling Johnson to maintain his credibility, even with HIV, is that he has repeatedly assured the public that he became infected through sexual contact with a woman. It is this fact that underlies the media's implications that Johnson's life is more important than the lives of the 125,000 Americans who have already died of AIDS. Some of these dead were also celebrities and some were minor sports figures. But they were also homosexuals, bisexuals, IV narcotics or steroid users. If Johnson were to admit to any of these he would be immediately transported, in the public mind, into the category of "guilty victim."

This split between "guilty" (homosexuals, bisexuals, IV drug users and anyone who has sex with them) and "innocent" (babies and hemophiliacs or other people who have had blood transfusions) has been set in stone by the U.S. media. For over a decade, the national press has been the primary enforcer of this division. They have systematically presented white babies and white heterosexual women with AIDS on the covers of weekly magazines, on television talk shows, and incorporated into the plot-lines of popular television programs. At the same time, gay people and drug users have been depicted as dissipated deviates who are a threat to the health of the nation. This division is so strong in the American mind that even someone of Johnson's reputation would probably not be able to disrupt it.

The evening of his announcement Johnson went on the Arsenio Hall Show (a popular late-night talk show with a black host) to assure America that "I am very far from being a homosexual." Johnson said he had been infected by a sexual encounter with a woman (not his wife) two months earlier and had learned about his infection the day before the public announcement. He then assured viewers that he had offered his wife of eight weeks a divorce which she had refused. He said that his wife had tested negative as had her seven-week-old fetus.

It's a nice story, but it is filled with flaws. First of all, it is generally agreed that it takes between three and six months (in what is called "the window of infection") after transmission for HIV antibodies to register in an Elisa Test. So his claim of testing positive two months after infection is clearly untrue. Second, there is no way to test a seven-week-old fetus for HIV. If the mother is negative, the child will also be negative. If the mother is positive, the child has a thirty percent chance of being positive. But even that cannot be clearly determined until up to eighteen months after birth when some infants discard HIV antibodies inherited from the mother.

Even more troubling, however, is the fact that the Magic Johnson case once again raises the lack of scientific resolve with respect to the question of female-to-male transmission. It has never been completely confirmed in America whether women can sexually transmit HIV to men or other women. Fewer than two percent of U.S. AIDS cases are men who claim to have contracted

224

the virus sexually from women. Deduct from that the number of individuals who do not want to admit either to having gay sex or to shooting drugs and the resulting numbers are quite minimal.

Since HIV requires semen-to-blood or blood-to-blood transmission, it would theoretically be possible for a woman to infect a man through sexual activity. But, in that scenario the man would have to have open sores or skin breaks through which her blood could enter his. It is unlikely that someone as healthy as Magic Johnson would be having sex with open sores. It has never been proven that oral sex with a woman puts her male or female partners at risk for HIV transmission. Vaginal fluid, like saliva, can contain HIV but many feel that the amount contained is too low to trigger contagious infection. Which is why kissing cannot spread AIDS.

AIDS educators and activists have long debated the social issues involved in a fuller discussion of female-to-male transmission. On one hand, some feel that if heterosexual men did not perceive themselves to be at risk, they would never use condoms. So, maintaining the myth saves women's lives. On the other hand, others point out that the widespread but distorted belief in easy and frequent female-to-male transmission results in anti-prostitution hysteria and increased government harassment of sex workers. In some cases, HIV-positive prostitutes have been charged with attempted murder—a crime that might actually be impossible to commit.

Most importantly, however, Magic Johnson's claims have reignited a particularly loathsome rhetoric that views women solely as "modes of transmission," bringing AIDS to men and children. It denies them as human beings with AIDS who are, in fact, the most underserved AIDS population in America. A story on the front page of the Sunday *New York Times* sports section was headlined "Fast Lane Could Be AIDS Lane." The piece quoted a number of prominent sports figures expressing fears that prostitutes were endangering athletes when it is probably the other way around.

Magic Johnson's announcement will encourage many black and Latino teenagers to take AIDS seriously for the first time. It may inspire significant progress in fundraising for research and advocacy for extended services. But all of these improvements may be maintained within a severely enforced AIDS double standard in which women, IV drug users, and homosexuals—that is to say, the vast majority of people with AIDS—will continue to be left out in the cold.

THELMA, LOUISE, AND THE MOVIE MANAGEMENT OF RAPE

Cineaste Magazine,
December 1991

In 1976 my university feminist organization shocked our campus community by spray-painting "A Woman Was Raped Here" on the actual sites of thirty reported rapes. Such a tactic would have little effect today because the word "rape" is on the front page of every tabloid in the nation. Rape is now an open topic of conversation.

The presentation of rape in the movie *Thelma and Louise* differs from its presentation in other contemporary films such as *Wild at Heart* or *Last Exit to Brooklyn* in that *Thelma and Louise* acknowledges the presence in the viewing audience of women who have been raped. It presents rape, not as a voyeuristic entertainment, but instead as the real life experience that audiences can relate to both as victims and as rapists. The public outcry about the film breaks down precisely along these lines of identification.

In the movie, however, as in real life, there is still no justice for women who have been raped. And there is still no public consensus about punishing rapists. *Thelma and Louise* reflects this unease by couching the protagonists' response within a double message about women's lives and their relationships with men. This dichotomy is built into the representation of the two characters as two different "types" of women. Thelma (Geena Davis) is in the tradition of the cinematically constructed female stereotype. She fits recognizable behavior patterns from television and movies. She is the overwhelmed, sloppy, not too bright, sexy housewife about to have an adventure. Her passivity makes her watchable, easily enjoyable, and not threatening. Never once in the movie does Thelma really get angry.

Louise (Susan Sarandon) is much more authentic. She has boundaries. Traditionally this used to read on screen as "cold," but by breaking character-type Louise is allowed depth and self-knowledge. Louise does what she wants. Louise smokes. She knows what good sex is. She is able to talk to her boyfriend as an intellectual equal. "You get what you settle for," warns Louise. Thelma, on the other hand is an accommodator. "He [her husband] is an asshole," she says. "Most of the time I just let it slide."

Even though it is Thelma who is beaten and sexually assaulted, Louise delivers the anti-rape message of the film, not only by killing the rapist, but also by making a clear statement directed at male viewers. "In the future, when a woman is crying like that she's not having fun." It takes Thelma until the end of the film to actually come out against rape.

Directly after the assault, her knees are covered with bruises, but Thelma exhibits no other physical or emotional reaction. Instead, her character continues to evolve along the lines of fake movie logic. From rape to murder to saying "Fuck you" to her husband on the phone, to an affair with a hitchhiker, all in twenty-four hours. In real life, of course, very few battered and assaulted women would leap, the next day, into a light-hearted passionate and sexually awakening one-night stand with a man they do not know. This is designed to make the film more palatable.

Compare it, for example, to Alain Tanner's very similar 1978 black-and-white film *Messidor*, in which two Swiss women hitchhikers kill a rapist and become fugitives. But, unlike *Thelma and Louise*, they also become lovers. Or Marlene Gorris's *A Question of Silence* in which three humiliated women band together in murder and then laugh in the face of the courts. Of course, there is an intimate pleasure for the female viewer in watching two women live, travel, and make decisions together. This depiction is far more resonant than the artificial sensual/intellectual dichotomy that *Thelma and Louise* offers when positioning each of them in relation to men.

In *The Accused* Jodie Foster and Kelly McGillis (playing rape victim and prosecutor) hold hands and stare, smiling, into each other's eyes once their boyfriends are conveniently out of the picture. Likewise in *Thelma and Louise*, once the men are disposed of (having firmly established each woman's heterosexual credentials), these two are able to fully confront each other as equals. However, that equality is established only by the revelation that Louise, too, has been raped. The screen is then filled with an image that occurs regularly in daily life but is never depicted in art or entertainment— the coming together of two raped women.

"I'm not sorry that son of a bitch is dead," says Thelma finally. "I'm just sorry it was you who did it and not me."

Then they kiss. Then they die.

FAME, SHAME, AND KAPOSI'S SARCOMA
NEW THEMES IN LESBIAN AND GAY FILM

Presented at the Brattle Theater in Boston as a Benefit for *Gay Community News.* Other panelists were Michael Bronski, Jenny Livingston, and Daryl Chin. January 1992

In 1987 Jim Hubbard and I founded the New York Lesbian and Gay Experimental Film Festival. We made our commitment to experimental, personal, and independent film because we believe that every person sees the world differently. Today, you can walk into fifty Hollywood movies and see a variety of plots, but the look is almost always the same. It pretends a homogenous view. But, if you come to our festival and watch fifty experimental films, the variety of the human imagination will be confirmed. Each artist's individual relationship to timing, texture, sound, framing—to the broadly visual and sensual—is celebrated in experimental film.

But "experimental" also has significance for a lesbian and gay audience. These rough, handmade films are consistently a far more visceral and accurate presentation of how we really live than the commercial films prepared for a straight audience. Even though experimental film is an obscure art form, gay experimental film has been able to attract a broad-based popular audience. Indeed, in five years, we have shown over 300 filmmakers to almost 15,000 people. This is because, as gay people have had to interrogate and invent themselves, films that re-imagine the world resonate for us with deep and familiar emotions.

The area that most clearly highlights the difference between personal and commercial images is in the representation of AIDS. To date there have been very few commercial films addressing the epidemic. But one thing that they all have in common is that the look of AIDS is whitewashed from the public eye. Viewers are protected from seeing people who are really sick, really angry, and really abandoned by the general public—the same public that the distributors feel dependent on for the film to make a profit.

Compare this, for example, to the depiction of AIDS in experimental film. *Viva Eu* by Tania Cypriano, a Brazilian woman, is a portrait of Wilton Braga, an artist living for nine years with AIDS. His body is covered with Kaposi's Sarcoma, yet he is filmed casually nude. He is filmed in a sleeveless sequined shirt dancing at a party. In *DHPG Mon Amour*, Carl Michael George uses a Super-8 camera with sound on cassette, to show the reality of a gay male couple living with AIDS. Joe has to infuse his lover David with DHPG through a chest catheter. The film was shot, and then three months later Carl tape-recorded the two lovers as they reacted to the footage. Only, by this time David was blind and so the soundtrack consists of Joe explaining the images to David as the film is being projected before them. *Elegy in the Streets* by Jim Hubbard is a forty-minute silent film about ACT UP. Instead of that endless familiar footage of demonstrators chanting, we watch their faces, their expressions and gestures. The individual humanity is revealed.

In the five years that we have done this festival, fifteen of our artists have died of AIDS. As the crisis intensifies, there has been a dramatic shift in the work produced. At first the men's films were focused on sex and the perfect male body. In this year's film festival, there was not one new men's film that showed sexuality out of the AIDS context. The major subjects for male filmmakers were death and nostalgia.

For women the story is quite different. In the beginning women were very concerned with breaking stereotypes of normalcy—something that men are just beginning to address. The women have consistently placed their work in a larger political and social context. They acknowledged the world of other people. The men's films, on the contrary, have historically excluded women, children, and other men who did not fit into the young, robust, and white example. However, as men have abandoned the sexual subject, their view has become broader in terms of what kinds of people are depicted and also broader in terms of the emotions expressed. In the meantime, lesbian films of the nineties have become obsessed with their sexual experiment. This year we saw more films than ever before that dealt with trying to capture lesbian sexuality on screen. Interestingly enough, however, most of them fail in their quest to be sexually stimulating to the lesbian audience.

Since Jim and I have watched hundreds of hours of gay and lesbian sex films over the years, we have had an ongoing discussion about why the men's sex films succeed and the women's fail. It is a complicated question and our answers are just preliminary. But, it seems logical that when you see a man in gay porn get hard and come on screen, you can guess that he really did, thereby assuring the gay male viewer that homosexuality really does exist.

In many of the women's films, however, sex is simulated. The knowing lesbian viewer recognizes it as false and experiences yet another example of obscured sexuality, another chapter in the history of the faked orgasm. When filmmakers highly stylize lesbian sexual imagery, it does not resonate as authentic. This is because the filmmakers are trying to imitate gay male and straight porn—when actually, it appears that many lesbians respond erotically to visual cues that they can identify with as potentially real.

Unfortunately, the technology of film is not refined enough to record what women recognize as authentic signs of sexual arousal. A red flush over the skin, hardening nipples, and a swelling or wet clitoris and vagina are hard to replicate in a film or video that does not have highly sensitive and precise contrast. So, what lesbian audiences respond most favorably to is not genital shots or explicit sex acts but rather preparation and suspense, which often require a higher level of sound and editing skills than a low-skill porn style demands. But this identification question also contains a high level of shame on the part of the lesbian audience. No single event underlined this for me as clearly as our screening of the 1973 film *Near the Big Chakra* by Anne Severson.

Severson, a straight woman, was living in Berkeley in the early 1970s. One day she realized that she had never seen another woman's clitoris and so she made a twenty minute silent film of several different clitoral shots filmed starkly and straight on. The lesbian audience that we showed this to was so deeply embarrassed that they started making comments to the silent projection in an attempt to disassociate themselves from the images.

Later, very surprised, Jim and I tried to understand what was at the core of their embarrassment. First, the only female genitalia seen in the public sphere are in porn and usually these women are shaved, young, and do not have vaginal infections, tampax strings, or contraceptive cream visible in their vaginas as some women in the film did. But lesbians, who have seen many real cunts, know silently the private truth as opposed to the public lie. The film revealed the audience's deep secret: that real cunts are hairy and diverse, real cunts are what dominant media calls ugly. I think that the audience was responding to being exposed as people who see, touch, taste, and have vaginas that don't look the way they are supposed to. As long as the audiences are ashamed, the films will only be able to minimally achieve the goal of depicting lesbian sexuality in an organic manner, visually analogous to the way we experience it.

Entering from the private into the public is taking place off-screen as well. Many times in history it appeared as though gay and lesbian subject matter was just about to burst into general acceptance. But actually we never seem to get beyond tokenism. The number of gay and lesbian tokens permitted into the mainstream is very small, and is still restricted along race, class, and formal lines. But at the same time, the awards available to these tokens are greater than they have ever been. It is the trickle-down theory of gay liberation. So, I think we have to be much more vigilant about how and why our representatives are chosen. Once the mainstream selects a representative from a minority community, what we really know and feel about that person's authenticity cannot be expressed because they are representing us at a level where we do not have a voice. Are our representatives chosen because their work resonates with us and we trust and support them?

Take the example of Audre Lorde's novel *Zami*. Many gay people will cite *Zami* as one of the most influential books they have ever read. Yet *Zami* was never published by a mainstream press, never reviewed in the *New York Times*, and is rarely available in a mainstream bookstore. Surely the reason why all these avenues have been available to me, for example, and not her, had nothing to do with quality and everything to do with racial, class, and formal exclusion. Similarly, the films I mentioned earlier will never be seen in commercial distribution. They are being represented by *Longtime Companion*. In the same way, Marlon Riggs's film about black gay men, *Tongues Untied*, will win no prestigious Hollywood awards, will not earn huge financial returns, will not gain him access to the most exclusive arenas of cultural production as Jenny Livingston's *Paris Is Burning* has. Within the rigidification of officially sanctioned gay culture and officially recognized gay artists, the true diversity of our work which is knowable within the underground becomes obliterated.

Let us look for example at *Longtime Companion*, a movie that the mainstream press has called the most important film about AIDS ever made. All of the films I've described here are far more honest, truthful, and resonant descriptions of AIDS, but they are not palatable to straight audiences. They do not confirm those audiences' already existing beliefs about gay life. A nude man with

KS is not the image of AIDS that the media machines will permit into the world—and yet this image is a reality that we gay people live with on a daily basis.

As for the artist who is offered a place in the mainstream, there are many questions we must ask ourselves. What does my community really think of me? It's one thing to go on T.V. wearing a red ribbon, but how have I really treated people with AIDS in my own life? What is my relationship with community organizations? I raise this because the sad fact of tokenism is that at this point a gay artist could have absolutely no credibility with the people he or she speaks for and still be propelled into positions of access and power. Because class, race, and formal choices are prerequisites for mainstream recognition, we (both artists and community) must insist that personal opportunity is not the same thing as systemic change and never let the glamour of tokenism, or our own desire to be accepted, obscure the varied truths of how we really live.

CONSUMED BY NEGLECT
WHO IS TO BLAME FOR THE TB EPIDEMIC?

Village Voice,
January 1992

As tuberculosis rages out of control in New York City—with one third of the cases resistant to treatment—the press and government officials are placing the blame on patient "non-compliance." They say the failure of people with TB to complete therapy has led to the development of the new strains that don't respond to standard medications. But the causes of the current crisis are much more complex. Demolished social services, lack of low income housing, inaccurate doses of medications, and a tight-fisted drug policy have made compliance impossible for patients most at risk. And rather than take responsibility for these systemic problems, officials are proposing ineffective and even sinister solutions.

In the late 1960s the New York City Tuberculosis Program spent forty million dollars annually on twenty-eight clinics and provided over 1,000 hospital beds for TB patients. Doctors regularly prescribed two concurrent medications to insure that if resistance developed to one, the other would kick in. Tuberculosis was considered 100 percent curable.

But just as TB started to come under control, the city faced a budget crisis and cut health programs across the board. Funding for TB remained flat through the 1980s despite signs that, fanned by AIDS and homelessness, the disease was spreading rapidly. By 1990, 3,520 cases were reported in New York City, an unprecedented 38 percent annual increase.

Yet today, just nine TB treatment clinics remain open. There are zero hospital beds for long-term TB care in the entire public system. As a result, treatment has increasingly fallen to general practitioners. And, according to Dr. Karen Brudney, Director of the HIV clinic at Columbia Presbyterian Medical Center, drug-resistant patients treated in nonspecialized settings have often been prescribed just one additional medication at a time, when only a combination of drugs would be effective.

Besides beds, clinics, and adequate medications, the most critical need is housing. As long as there are 90,000 homeless people in New York, no health crisis can be solved. "The shelters are undoubtedly *the* focus for TB transmission," says Virginia Shubert, advocate for the homeless, pointing to outbreaks of rare strains of TB among residents of the same facility. Yet the city and state have fought lawsuits by Shubert demanding non-shelter housing for HIV-positive people. Gary Burke of the state AIDS Institute told the court that people with HIV contract TB in the shelters due to the dormant infection in their own bodies and that using housing as a medical-preventative measure is "erroneous."

Meanwhile, Lloyd Novick of the Department of Health told a congressional hearing last month that the state now favors the creation of three new shelters for homeless people with TB. Other proposals are no more encouraging. Newly named city health commissioner Margaret Hamburg recommends that patients with TB be given four concurrent medications. That means a regimen of a dozen pills a day for six months, something that few homeless people will be able to complete. Hamburg has proposed increased staffing, but approval is unlikely and even one-on-one staffing is not a substitute for housing.

Still other suggestions lean towards the Big Brother side of the bureaucratic imagination. Mark Goldberger of the FDA says the agency is reviewing plans for a skin implant that will release TB medication gradually over a period of months. But a patient having a bad reaction would be unable to stop the drug without a physician's intervention—an especially frightening prospect for a homeless person. And the move would establish mandatory implants as public policy. Consider the implications for birth control.

Overwhelmingly, the government's approach is to seek to control patients rather than to serve them. Though half of the drug-resistant cases could be served by Streptomycin, that drug hasn't been available in the city for six months. The FDA ended U.S. production after the discovery of fungal spores in the raw materials imported from France. Goldberger says the agency has found another manufacturer who can provide a "sterile" version, but not for several months at the earliest.

This delay is terrible news for drug-resistant patients who are forced to go to second-line treatments like Kanamycin, a highly toxic pharmaceutical that can cause hearing loss and renal failure and is administered through painful daily injections. Doctors

234

treating indigent patients have put in a request to the DOH to make available a novocaine-like substance to accompany the injections. But to date those requests haven't been approved.

City officials throw up their hands saying they can't do more without a federal bail-out. Although Congress authorized thirty-six million dollars for tuberculosis control nationwide, less than half of that has been appropriated. The city has received only about three-and-a-half million dollars, one-fifth of its request. The state has announced up to eight million dollars may be allocated to TB, but this includes already committed Medicaid funds. At least two million dollars of this funding was diverted from AIDS prevention.

THE DENIAL OF AIDS AND THE CONSTRUCTION OF A FAKE LIFE

Presented at an Outwrite: National Lesbian and Gay Writers' Conference panel *Is There An AIDS Fiction?* Other panelists were Bo Houston, Adam Mars-Jones, and Wayne Corbett. Boston, March 1992.

Two hundred thousand Americans have died of AIDS and not one of them committed a political assassination. If they all had, America would be a better place today for those of us who have been left behind.

Today, we who have been left behind meet in a state of emergency. It is not our fault that we have been victimized and persecuted. However, it is equally clear that the persecution will only end if we are brilliant and courageous and dedicated enough to stop it. It is this burden of change that I would like to address.

Why do we stand alone? Well, one of the most obvious reasons is that our biological families have abandoned us. Our parents are not protecting us. Our siblings are not supporting us. Our children are not defending us. The America that is against us is composed of and maintained by our families. By ignoring our lack of rights and continuing to exercise theirs, our families are participating in the construction of a fake life. They happily continue to kiss on the street, march in the Saint Patrick's Day parade, have weddings, and qualify for health insurance without any concern about obtaining these same privileges for their blood relations. When Magic Johnson is wildly applauded for saying, "I'm far from being a homosexual," who was in that audience clapping? When Benetton uses a photo of a man on his deathbed with MAI Wasting Syndrome to sell sweaters, who buys them? Our families propagate an official culture in which our lives are denied.

The spiritual price is, for us, immeasurable. No other group of people has been so abandoned. As a result, we come to each other without true foundations of support. We come without permanence. We come to each other as people who have experienced the most brutal betrayals. And, somehow, from this, we are supposed to be ingenious enough to save our own lives.

What is AIDS literature? I began writing about AIDS in the early

236

eighties. In 1985 I covered the closing of the bathhouses for the *New York Native*. In 1987 I began writing AIDS fiction and have been doing so ever since. What have I observed? AIDS is not a transformative experience. AIDS makes people become themselves but ever so much more so. If the person was selfish and abusive before, they also will be after diagnosis. If they were generous and visionary before, they will be after. Unfortunately we have constructed expectations for AIDS literature based on this myth of transformation. By holding it to a standard based on the model of religious conversion, we expect AIDS literature to reveal profound insights into life and death that people without terminal illnesses would not be able to conjure up on their own. But in reality, the opposite is true. People with AIDS who write long pieces of fiction often do not feel well, are depressed, and are writing against the clock. These are actually the worst conditions for fiction writing. As a result much of the work is hasty, panicked, and seems unfinished.

The same is unfortunately true of our political movements. I came to AIDS activism in July of 1987, and I came in good faith. I came from a feminist movement whose goal was a multiracial community in which the needs and experiences of all women would be broadly addressed. It was quite a leap for me to come from that framework into an organization like ACT UP in which the majority of men had never been politically active before, that is, had never been moved to action on behalf of anyone before. I come to this relationship with an open heart and an open mind. I do not insist that the entire feminist agenda be embraced. I see gay men organizing from the reality of their oppression, and I believe that by confronting the truth of your own life, a person is better able to realize other people's truths.

ACT UP has accomplished great things and will continue to accomplish great things, but I can say, simultaneously in praise and in criticism, that AIDS activists too remain essentially unchanged. Gay men who strove to be at one with other people before AIDS advocate for a broad agenda and a democratic process within their organizations. Men who were oriented exclusively towards power and money before AIDS treat the floor of ACT UP like the floor of the stock exchange.

The challenge for AIDS activism and for the whole gay and lesbian movement today is to find an overt and effective manner for interrupting the modes of domination within our own movements. No individual can single-handedly end the AIDS crisis.

Only a large number of people working in loose agreement and democratic process can make broad social change. When ACT UP first started, most HIV-positive people who came there felt that they would not survive. They wanted to, but it seemed impossible. So, they wanted the community to survive. Today, there are people who don't care if there is anything left after they're gone. This is not the majority of people working in AIDS, but the majority will not stand up to the few. After four years in ACT UP, I have observed that many gay men have a hard time confronting male authority, even when it is destructive.

Also, I think they fear alienating the elite who have access to highly technical information about treatments that others feel they need in order to stay alive. But in reality there are drug and treatment combinations that most PWAs may never even hear about let alone have access to. Occasionally, AIDS activists end up endorsing government sponsored trials for treatments that they themselves abandoned long ago.

Although lesbians have never entered AIDS activism in large numbers, we too have become increasingly tempted by the scent of mainstream approval. For white women especially, the integration of gay women and gay men has meant capitulation of the worst kind for racial segregation. The temptation is to have a degree of presentability by standing next to white gay men and creating a co-sexual illusion, one that makes us much more palatable to America and to our families. I was struck by the photograph of the staff of *NYQ* (New York's gay weekly) that appeared recently on the business page of the *New York Times*. There were attractive white men and attractive white women standing together like one happy white family. The editor of a highly financed new gay glossy *Out* was quoted in the same article saying that he wanted to create a magazine that he could show his mother.

As the AIDS movements have grown, lesbians have been uncharacteristically hesitant to develop our own activist organizations and have expressed realistic suspicion at the prospect of working with gay men. But at the same time, a new viciously homophobic mainstream feminism is emerging—most obviously represented by the phenomenon of Susan Faludi and her best-selling book *Backlash*, published by Crown Publishers. Faludi, who was recently on the cover of *Time* standing behind Gloria Steinem, is a writer for the *Wall Street Journal*. She managed to construct a 550 page book about women's oppression without mentioning the word "lesbian." Since she won't recognize that lesbians even exist, her analysis of such subjects as "never married career women over the age of thirty-five" becomes absurd. She mangles the complexities of such categories as "female headed households" and "the feminization of poverty." This lies in sharp contrast to the brilliant article by Anne-Christine D'Adesky recently published in the *Advocate* in which she shows that lesbians are over-represented among homeless women and identifies different ways in which their lesbianism contributed to their homelessness. This includes exclusion from family support systems and lack of access to men's incomes. So, the new straight feminism of the nineties doesn't seem to be offering lesbians a place of personhood either.

Why do our movements continually fall into pits of duplicity and corruption? It is as though our movements can only go as far as our visions and they fail when we come to the end of our consciousness. Why is it that white gay men and lesbians consistently ensure that every single social and political unit we construct excludes people of color? Why is it that gay men refuse over and over to use their male privilege and earning power to advocate for lesbians? Why is it that wealthy gay men repeatedly build institutions from which other, less powerful men are excluded? And why do the less powerful men refuse to challenge them? These are the places where we come to the end of our consciousness. These are the places where we are too patriotic.

We do what every good American does in 1992, we refuse to think for ourselves. Oh, new ideas come along. This week we are socially constructed, next week we are biologically determined. This week we have identity politics, next week we have deconstructed identities. But swallowing and regurgitating ideas is not the same thing as thinking for ourselves. Without vigorously demanding an organic process of imagination, we cannot grow beyond our current state of consciousness.

Recently I've been reading a lot about other politically radical movements in history. In the Vietnamese example, Ho Chi Minh knew that for Vietnamese people, anger was the forbidden emotion. He knew that if he could, in violation of centuries of conditioning, provoke his people to anger, he could make a revolution. For gay people today, imagination is our secret weapon. Every social institution in this country is against us and yet within our own community we recreate over and over the systems of domination that oppress us. We replicate these systems by practicing white exclusionism and male exclusionism and we permit others to practice it, when instead it is cultural violation, what Adrienne Rich called being "disloyal to civilization" that is the only way to avoid the fake life. The burden of change is ours alone. We are the ones who must imagine different relationships to each other in order to force the changes necessary to our own survival.

TOKYO ROSE

QW,
May 1992

In early March I had the opportunity to visit Japan for free. Who could refuse? The occasion was the First Tokyo Lesbian and Gay Film Festival. Jim Hubbard, with whom I had organized the New York Lesbian and Gay Experimental Film Festival, and I were invited as guests of the Stance Company, the private distribution firm that was producing the event. What I found was confusing, depressing, and I'm sure, subject to much misinterpretation on my part, but fascinating nonetheless.

The first sign of trouble emerged a month earlier when, while doing a reading in Toronto, I ran into Paul Lee, curator of that city's gay film festival. He told me that there were *two* "first" festivals being planned for the same month. One, by the International Gay Association, which had asked him to do the programming and one by the Stance Company, whose staff was all straight.

By the time I arrived in Tokyo, Jim had already met with the IGA. They were all men, very friendly, and pleased with their small, underground festival which had taken place two weeks before. Paul Lee told Jim that the IGA had cut most of the lesbian films from his program, rendering it an essentially separatist male event. The straight Stance Company, on the other hand, had a woman curator who had created a gender parity program. She highlighted the work of American lesbian filmmaker Su Friedrich in the festival catalogue.

In order to uncover as much as possible about Tokyo gay life in the five days of our short stay, Jim had made an appointment with the gay organization AKA for the following afternoon. AKA, which was founded eight years ago by five high school boys, is currently suing the Tokyo municipality for equal access to public facilities. We arrived to be greeted by a sullen young man wearing ACT UP buttons. For the next four hours we found ourselves in the middle of a high pressure pow-wow with AKA's central committee, four serious, arrogant young men.

Jim and I were accused of having committed "serious crimes" by assisting Stance—a straight company—in producing gay art. Our AKA detractors demanded that we denounce the Stance Company on the festival's opening night. While we agreed with them that gay arts festivals should be community-based, Jim and I also felt that any open public expression of gay life was beneficial. I tried to encourage AKA to use the festival to make its literature available and to recruit for the organization, but its position was that the kind of gay people who go to arts events do not make good political organizers.

For our views we were subjected to a vicious tongue-lashing which included being called "Columbus," "cultural imperialists," and "stupid." Yet our questions about why a straight company was so interested in gay film went unanswered. It certainly wasn't for the money, since Stance was taking a loss on its first year endeavor. AKA then suggested that *we* only ran *our* festival to make money off of gay people. When we informed them we *lost* money running our festival, they replied that we were "even stupider" than they had imagined.

For some reason Jim and I persevered with these fellows. The social worker in me was painfully aware that here were young gay men who had rarely been taken seriously. By simply respecting them, I thought we would somehow be able to move the conversation on to the more practical level of how to make the festival work for gay people. But, by the end of the exhausting day, nothing had been accomplished. We were surprised when they insisted on another meeting the following afternoon. Wearily we agreed.

That night we attended the Stance Company's pre-opening party which was totally straight except for one lone dyke festival volunteer—Hiroko Kakifuda, the first Japanese to come out on television. One of the guests at the fête was the straight editor at Magazine House, publishers of the Japanese translation of my novel *After Delores*. "There's someone I want you to meet," my publisher said, "the translator of Andrew Holleran." My translator Ochiichi Augustmoon was an out lesbian and the Japanese translator of Gertrude Stein. So I was quite surprised when the editor introduced me to another straight women in her thirties, chicly dressed in designer ensemble and handbag. "How do you do?" I asked, getting more confused by the minute.

Fortunately Hiroko invited me to go out after to a once-a-month lesbian dance held in the basement gymnasium of the commercial Shinju-ku district. So, I invited the editor, translator, and Stance Company curator—all straight—to come along.

There were about thirty lesbians in that room that night. About seven of them were American. I saw a couple of Western style Japanese dykes in recognizable coded poses. But whatever aesthetic united and identified Japanese lesbians to each other, I could not perceive it and no one could explain it to me. Some people danced. Some couples made out, but mostly the gathering was for talking with friends. The straight curator promptly drank a bottle of gin and passed out on the floor. A significant number of those present had read my novel (being one of the very few lesbian novels available) and soon my editor and I were surrounded by a barrage of questions. Not questions like, "Do you write every day?" but questions like, "How do I reconcile my lesbianism and my Catholicism?" Intense, serious, non-stop questions. Later my editor told me that she had never encountered people who "needed" their books so ferociously before. Afterwards Holleran's translator claimed women had made passes at her. Considering the demure atmosphere in that gym, I had my doubts.

The next day Jim and I unhappily headed out for round two with AKA. Once again they sullenly met us at an old coffee shop. Then, to our shock, they announced that after discussing all of our arguments until midnight, they had decided there *were* gay people coming to this festival who needed to know about AKA. Jim and I smiled at each other with relief. Taking them seriously had paid off. They handed over a stack of flyers for us to distribute before the films. Then, not knowing at all what was going to happen next, we followed them for a few blocks to a classroom where about forty gay men and two lesbians sat waiting. We were brought to the front of the room, offered tea, and again proceeded to answer rapid-fire questions for a few hours.

The rank and file was very different from their leaders. Their questions were much more basic and a lot more poignant. "Monogamy, non-monogamy," asked a bespectacled young man. "Which is better?" Another shy but friendly guy asked, "Should a gay person's lover be like them or different?" Like most homosexuals in the world, these people just wanted to find a boyfriend and be happy. But they live in such a state of invisibility and deprivation that they could not even imagine the basics of gay life. Furthermore, living in a prescribed society like Japan, these gay people just wanted to know the rules for being homosexual. "It's a personal decision," we answered over and over again. "Each of you has to decide for yourself."

Absurdly Jim and I were suddenly being held up as examples of the free and integrated homosexual. We were supposed to recite the rules for successful gay life. But despite our own personal chaos, simply regurgitating the basics seemed to be extremely helpful. "What do you do," asked one fellow, "if your lover insults you all the time?" "Listen," we answered in our worst psychobabble, "gay people have been told that we are bad and don't deserve to be happy so we punish ourselves instead of loving ourselves." This reverberated through the room to smiles and nodding heads, even though I felt like a walking Hallmark card.

Later they took us to a restaurant for beer and food and there the conversation got more intense. I spoke for some time with the two representatives of the larger lesbian section, which unfortunately had a meeting at the same time as our talk. Typically, they had fallen in love and lived together for eight years without making contact with other gay people. They were planning their first trip to San Francisco for the spring.

San Francisco is like Mecca for Japanese gay people.

"Does New York have rice bars?" a few men asked, hopefully.

"I don't know," I said.

"We want to go to San Francisco and go to rice bars," they said.

"Look," I answered, "the whole gay community of San Francisco is for you. All of it. You don't have to just go to rice bars."

"I'll go to rice bars," one insisted. "I have all the addresses."

"Do you have any friends who are HIV-positive?" one man asked me.

"Hundreds," I said.

A discussion quickly developed in which a number of men with HIV at the table started shyly and then insistingly asking me questions. I was shocked to discover that in the country where people have information about everything from the names of Madonna's back-up singers to restaurants in the East Village, these men had never heard of PCP prophylaxis. They had virtually no information about options for AIDS treatments, and had all been handed AZT at the 500 T-cell count with no further instructions.

"What can I do to live?" a number of men asked me. I tried to sound as confident as I could even though I was thinking, *These guys don't have a chance*. I told them that the people in America who live the longest are the ones who make their own decisions about their treatment instead of passively accepting whatever they're told. I wondered whether this would be possible in a Japanese context, but wrote down the names of a number of different medications and treatment options, encouraging them to show these to their doctors and demand information. When we left the restaurant I noticed that most of them left the lists on the table.

Finally it came time for the film festival's opening night. It was held in the middle of a popular shopping mall. The audience was eighty percent straight women.

"I know Japan doesn't want to confront AIDS," I said in my opening remarks. "But ignoring the virus will not make it go away."

Later Jim and I went out to dinner with my editor, Holleran's translator, and the translator of Edmund White, Michael Nava, and Paul Monette—also female, straight, and unmarried. These women specialize in male homosexuality. They subscribe to *Christopher Street* and *Lambda Book Report*.

"What's the deal?" I finally asked, hours later when we were all, in typical Japanese fashion, reeling drunk. "Why are straight women here so obsessed with male homosexuality? Why are straight people showing gay artwork to straight people when the real lesbians and gay men are underground, oppressed and dying of neglect? What is going on here?"

"Japanese women are changing very quickly," Edmund White's translator said. "But Japanese men are not catching up. For us, images of male homosexuality are the only picture we have of men loving someone else as an equal. It is the kind of love that we want to have from them."

"But what about feminism?" I asked. "Instead of retreating into voyeuristic fantasies about gay men, why don't Japanese women go to feminism to force change?"

"Those feminists," she said disdainfully. "They just want to be men."

"No," I answered. "You want to be men."

We ended up our evening at a "gay bar." There are different kinds of gay bars in Tokyo. There are places men go for sex, most of which are closed to foreigners primarily because of the illusion that you can't get AIDS from a Japanese. But actually, foreigners are more likely to insist on condoms than Japanese men are. Then there are bars like GB's or Zip which cater to Asian men who want to meet whites. There are also hustler bars and one lesbian club called Mars which I did not get to. But our hosts took us to a gay

245

bar building. A long stark corridor featured thirty or so doors, lined up next to each other like entrances to nuns' cells. Behind each door was a cubicle containing a bar, about five stools with the wall directly behind the stools and a bartender. In this case it was a "gay" bar because there were photos of gay men on the walls. The same five friends will go to their bar every night after work. It is like a second living room. As we sat there with our umpteenth round of drinks I realized that this was yet another phenomenon I would never understand. Why would hundreds of gay people choose to come to the same building night after night and then divide up into privatized units of friends thereby ignoring the possibility of community contained within those walls? The next morning, bewildered and exhausted, I boarded the plane for home.

COMMENTARY

Well, the straight festival curator came out and started running the Tokyo Lesbian and Gay Film Festival independently from the Stance Company. Andrew Holleran's translator came to New York to visit Fire Island for research purposes. Edmund White's translator came to the New York Lesbian and Gay Film Festival and then made a special trip to Washington, D.C. to pay a visit to Lambda Rising Bookstore. And Hiroko Kakifuda, the first out lesbian in Japan, began a newsletter that, one year later, had 800 subscribers.

COMING TO TERMS
AN INTERVIEW WITH CAROLE DESANTI

Lambda Book
Report,
August 1992

Carole DeSanti, Senior Editor at New American Library/E.P. Dutton, is currently the only openly lesbian editor in mainstream publishing who is actively acquiring lesbian fiction. She is responsible for bringing writers like Dorothy Allison and Sarah Schulman into the mainstream and has also worked with John Preston, Jennifer Levin, and the late James Kirkwood. DeSanti, 33, grew up in a Croation-Canadian family in a westside suburb of Cleveland. She attended Smith College and the Radcliffe publishing program. Carole began her career selling ads for *Sojourner* (a feminist newspaper), and after an abortive volunteer stint at Persephone Press (an early lesbian publisher), she began at Henry Holt. Then, at E.P. Dutton, she worked with legendary editor Bill Whitehead, the late pioneer of gay male publishing.

Here she is interviewed by Sarah Schulman with whom she has worked on three novels over a six year period.

SARAH   *How many novels can you acquire in a year?*

CAROLE   There really isn't a quota. Ideally three to six a year.

SARAH   *And how many submissions do you receive annually?*

CAROLE   Of exclusively lesbian/gay material, 150–200.

SARAH   *What kinds of manuscripts are you getting?*

CAROLE   Manuscripts I can't publish. A lot of people never
          look at themselves clearly and critically to determine
          what really is at the heart of their book. Are you
          writing simply for approval from others, or because
          you think this is a quick route to fame or money—
          neither of which is likely to happen. Publishing is a
          process fraught with setbacks and disapproval and
          irrelevant criticism at every point. There's a lack of
          the right kind of soul-searching in that there are a

247

lot of long elegies about break-ups or recovery, the kinds of subjects most appropriate to therapy. A novel is not the conversation you can have with your lover, it's not what you tell your recovery group. It is something that will only fit on these pages and nowhere else.

SARAH   *So let's say you only find a handful that you like.*

CAROLE   I don't find a handful at a time. I find . . . one.

SARAH   *Do you ask for rewrites before offering a contract?*

CAROLE   No, it's just not fair to the writer.

SARAH   *How do you convince the editorial board to go with a book you love?*

CAROLE   My enthusiasm is important. So are readings from other editors. Ideally the writer would have a track record. Sales figures between five and ten thousand books are preferable although there are always exceptions.

SARAH   *But the women's presses are angry about developing writers only to have them move to the mainstream.*

CAROLE   I made a policy of my own when I realized this was a problem. I do not "scoop up" anyone who does not want to make the break.

SARAH   *Do you see reasons why a writer should go to a small press?*

CAROLE   Absolutely. Some books would probably sell the same amount with a small press. The person editing and publicizing might have a better understanding of the issues involved. And, if you want a lot of hands-on care and attention, small presses are more interested in and able to do that.

SARAH   *Within the mainstream, it seems that lesbians receive smaller advances than gay men irrespective of sales.*

CAROLE   I think you have to take that apart. White gay men who are operating within the system and have done so all of their lives get themselves agents who will sell their books in a very aggressive way. This often means making the same kinds of claims that they would for a straight white male author.

SARAH *What about the fact that so few people even bid for lesbian books?*

CAROLE If there were more competitive bidding for lesbian books in the mainstream the advances would definitely go up.

SARAH *We're seeing a lot of nonfiction coming from the corporate presses with the words "Gay and Lesbian" in the title. Are they really representative of both men and women or is that simply a marketing technique?*

CAROLE Well, it varies, but more gay men are doing these kinds of books and in their desire to be inclusive they are sticking in that word even while omitting the experiences of lesbians. I see it more as gay men trying to market their work to publishers than publishers using it as a device to reach a wider audience. Most publishers aren't aware of the difference between the two groups.

SARAH *Speaking of inclusivity, there has been one out black editor, Connie Lofton at Dutton. She worked with Melvyn Dixon and Essex Hemphill.*

CAROLE Publishing has historically been an elitist white business. There is very little representation of minority communities at all.

SARAH *This gap is very destructive because the lesbians in the mainstream are not representative of the community. Most lesbians of color in print are in the women's presses with a few exceptions like Michelle Cliff and Paula Gunn Allen. The situation is reversed in the gay men's presses where men of color have been consistently ignored. Writers like Essex, Randall Kenan, Melvyn, Steven Corbin, Jaime Manrique, etc. are all in the mainstream. Assotto Saint self-published his anthology. Jewelle Gomez's The Gilda Stories was rejected by the mainstream and then won two Lammies for Firebrand.*

CAROLE Well, Linda Villarosa and Evelyn C. White just got a very substantial advance for their black women's health book, and I am publishing a book on black women and self-esteem next year. We just entered into a distribution agreement with a black press, Charles Harris Amistad. I know that the situation has to change. More editors of color would help enormously. Meanwhile, I want to see more fiction and nonfiction (not poetry) from gay men and lesbians of color.

SARAH   *Right now lesbian books are principally sold to lesbian read-ers. Who do you think is the most likely audience to cross over and read our work?*

CAROLE   I'm afraid it is probably straight men, especially as we editors keep encouraging writers to put more sex in their books. But for a spectacularly written lesbian novel with an individual voice, there certainly could be crossover potential.

SARAH   *I disagree with the assumption that we just haven't been good enough yet. I think* The Color Purple *is a lesbian novel. Its excellence was recognized but its lesbianism was repressed in the public discourse.*

CAROLE   There is no doubt about the fact that our society has not yet come to terms with lesbianism. Straight people still need to have their sexuality reinforced in books. I don't believe that white people feel their racial identities threatened by books about black experience, although the meaning of their identity can be challenged.

SARAH   *Only when black writers write about the interior of the black community can white readers colonize their books. But when Toni Morrison published a book on whiteness, she was insulted and attacked by the* Times's *white critic. Sexuality today is not as safely defined for straight people as race is for whites. That's why gay male poolside writing is the gay voice most palatable to straight people. It avoids the conflict with male power that takes place when we confront and make demands on heterosexuals about their behavior towards us.*

CAROLE   The best-selling genre of any cultural group is pornography and erotic material. There is still a tremendous need to identify sexually with what you are reading, to be validated by it. But racially, there are white readers of Toni Morrison, for example, who love to immerse themselves in her language. Even when she is writing about slavery, her books can actually serve as an escape for white readers.

SARAH   *It is so hard to imagine creating a book that can overcome the structure in which that book is contained. This is my greatest wish for lesbian writing and for AIDS writing—to break out of the closed world of community, relationships, the privacy of coming out. The demand has not been made on the straight world, the male world. We have not yet taken our place in the intellectual life of the nation. Instead we have observed or ignored it. I don't want to only show straight people how we live. I also want to show them how they live.*

CAROLE   But how do we get lesbians to start writing better books?

SARAH   *Women write first drafts and then have no place to develop them.*

CAROLE   So, we need support networks and uncloseted mentorship. One advantage for gay men is that their networks are built into the structure.

SARAH   *Well, in this country women still earn fifty-nine cents for every dollar a man earns. So our networks are weaker but they do exist. If I see a terrific writer, I tell you about her, try to bring her to Outwrite, recommend her for grants and readings, tell editors of anthologies about her work, write references for writers' colonies, etc. This happens every day.*

CAROLE   A lot of lesbians are closeted within the corporate hierarchy but even if gay men are closeted professionally . . .

SARAH   *They're not closeted on Fire Island. There is a free zone created by larger incomes. By the way, is the Publishing Triangle doing anything for women or people of color?*

CAROLE   Racially, the Triangle reflects the whiteness of mainstream publishing. A few lesbians attend meetings now. Most of the women are younger, still in the lower or middle reaches of the corporate hierarchy

251

SARAH   *But what about lesbian editor X at ___ or Y at ____ or Z at___?*

CAROLE   We've invited them but they won't come. I think they say they are overcommitted. Look, the closet is very real for these women.

SARAH   *In the meantime I keep hoping that gay men will share more of their resources.*

CAROLE   You're asking them to bond over gayness instead of maleness. But of course we must keep building networks and keep making our demands in every context, no matter how much they get brushed aside. But where do we go to re-charge?

SARAH   *That's what your lover is for.*

CAROLE   Yes, our relationships are asked to bear a lot of the burdens of this.

SARAH   *So, what is coming up in gay publishing?*

CAROLE   Here's my wish-list. More cross-pollination between the gay and the straight worlds. Gay and lesbian examples in self-help books, gay and lesbian sexuality in mainstream fiction. More nonfiction, history, biography. Books that are radically beyond shame and coming out. Gay and lesbian writers being held and holding themselves to the highest standards imaginable.

WHAT IS THE ROLE
OF GAY FILM FESTIVALS?

Delivered at
the New York
Lesbian and Gay
Experimental Film
Festival,
September 1992.
Other panelists
were Shari Frilot,
Jack Waters,
Sandy Dubowsky,
and Patrick Wright

Historically, gay film began with Dickson Sound Experiment
Number Three, a silent short of two men dancing that was made
in the 1890s. From the dawn of cinema, gay film was synonymous
with experimentation but soon branched out into its second genre
—pornography. Formal invention and explicit sexuality have been
the main expressions of and also the motives for gay film. This
seems logical since dominant culture provides a conventional
narrative for heterosexual life. Heterosexual film (whether it was
made by gay people or not) has overwhelmingly followed these
same structures. For women, the official story is heterosexual
romance, marriage, and motherhood. For men it is heterosexual
romance, war, marriage, war, and fatherhood. But dominant culture
has never provided a story of homosexual life and so no formal
structure was available for filmmakers to assume.

The first gay film festivals were porn shows and the next were
avant-garde screenings. But the first overtly stated gay film festival
came at the beginning of the post-Stonewall period. These events
have served a variety of functions, but for many years now the
desire for cultural assimilation has predominated in the aesthetic
choices of most gay film festivals. Specifically, for decades programmers have been promising the gay audience that the gay or
lesbian Hollywood feature was just around the corner. And in
preparation they ignored the century-long history of gay
experimentation and pornography and substituted, instead, the
history of the gay subtext in Hollywood film.

This was later expanded to include a variety of bad gay and
lesbian narrative features which have tried artificially to establish
a traditional narrative for gay life. But Imitation of Straight Life
has proven to be a very unsuccessful formula indeed. By looking to
the conventional structures as the only desirable model while
simultaneously avoiding formally inventive, emotionally complex

253

personal films, the festivals have been training gay audiences to be highly intolerant of our community's own indigenous art forms. So now, when highly imaginative and subversive films are shown in mainstream gay festivals, the audiences often boo, walk out, or exhibit indignant hostility towards the work.

Ironically, this reaction has occurred with work that is often the most original and emotionally accurate. Just some quick examples include Cecilia Dougherty's *Coal Miner's Granddaughter* at Frameline in San Francisco, Su Friedrich's *First Comes Love* in Toronto, and the Austrian lesbian feature *Flaming Ears* at New York's New Festival. Some of the most brilliant and resonant films that I have seen in recent years have been rejected repeatedly by the mainstream gay festivals. I'm thinking specifically of Jim Hubbard's *Elegy in the Streets,* a forty-minute silent hand-processed film about ACT UP, or his eight-minute short, *Two Marches,* which articulates the terrible loss of expectation and hope that came with the advent of the AIDS crisis. Increasingly programmers favor expensive, high-production value, slick film-school work with an eye towards Hollywood or features and traditional documentaries.

Of course we want and need expressions of gay and lesbian imagination in all forms, genres, and disciplines. And I do not believe that any one form is superior to any other. I too, look forward to quality feature films from lesbian and gay perspectives. But, the training of gay film audiences to reject formal invention, Super-8, hand-processing, silent film, and other experimental choices streamlines the collective imagination in an assimilationist direction.

This problem becomes even more dramatic because of the emergence, over the last few years, of gay features that have achieved mainstream approval and distribution. Ironically, none of these acclaimed films are sexually explicit—which reveals the most dramatic accommodation gay work has made for marketing purposes. The media has called these films "The New Queer Cinema." Ironically, the new queer cinema is also being made by women, people of color, poor people, video artists, and is emotional, sexually explicit, and formally inventive. The features that have been singled out as representative are often closer to the Old Straight Cinema than the vast majority of new lesbian and gay work being made today.

The film festivals, as community-based institutions, should be articulating an oppositional voice to the mainstream vision of what is acceptable gay cinema. But instead, they are playing catch-up by

featuring these expensive works over the more grass-roots productions. As gay images and issues come increasingly under the
control of the mainstream media we have to vigilantly think
through and articulate a presentation of work that best suits our
own visions. For this reason programmers and curators now have
a special opportunity to really provide creative alternatives to help
stimulate independent thought in our communities.

I WAS A LESBIAN CHILD

Unpublished,
September 1992

During the week of the Republican National Convention, Americans were subjected to the most overt display of homophobia ever to be broadcast over this nation's mass media. Simultaneously, vicious anti-gay legislation loomed in Oregon and the AIDS crisis continued unabated. So, I was surprised that this public hate-mongering provoked no phone calls of compassion from my straight relatives, friends, or colleagues about how personally awful it must be for gay people to endure this daily assault. Repeatedly it seems that homosexuals are the only community whose families will not take action in our defense.

This summer and fall the newspapers have been filled with the battle over multicultural education in the public schools. Conservative districts like Board 24 in Queens object to any mention of homosexuality in the public school curriculum. They have rejected the entire multicultural approach in order to keep homosexuality out of the classroom. These stakes are very, very high. Events at the Board of Education raise even more profound questions than the media has been unwilling to address. Namely, does society have a responsibility to lesbian and gay children?

History has shown over and over again that the families of lesbians and gay men are overwhelmingly unable and unwilling to protect and respect their gay children. The most notorious example is the fact that 91,000 gay and bisexual men have died of AIDS in this country, and that America that is composed of their families has still refused to take action on their behalf. According to *Newsweek*, only nine percent of people polled acknowledged having gay family members. Considering that more than nine percent of the respondents were gay themselves, that paltry number stands as firm evidence that America is denying the existence of gay and lesbian people, even in their own families.

For this reason the gay and lesbian community has had to act in loco parentis—reaching out and supporting other gay individuals in the kind of mutual aid society that families are supposed to be. We stand up for each other's civil rights, we provide counseling and support services for each other's emotional needs. We create literary and theatrical expressions of our experiences and imaginations as the dominant culture excludes us from theirs. All of this has become necessary because heterosexual America—i.e., our families—will not stand in our defense.

Children of gay parents have the right to see their realities acknowledged in their classrooms and school services. Lesbian and gay custodians, principals, and teachers are currently forced into the closet by lies depicting gay people as child molesters. Actually, over ninety percent of child molestation is committed by adult males against girls. But this is never used to justify depriving heterosexual males of employment. By being forced into the closet, gay teachers come to their students as truncated human beings and cannot offer the possibility of gay life to straight and gay students alike.

The consequences of the existing repression are dramatic. One third of all teenage suicides are by lesbian and gay youth. At the same time, most acts of anti-gay violence in New York City are committed by teenagers. Both of these tragedies are the direct result of the lack of humane and open discussion of homosexuality in the city schools.

Clearly lesbian and gay adults must take a strong, insistent stand for the inclusion of homosexual life in the public school curriculum. We must do it on our own behalf and on the behalf of lesbian and gay children, teenagers, and school employees who currently have no one else willing to be on the line for them. We must do this because parents have proven that they can't and won't commit the cultural violation of defending their homosexual children.

WHY I'M NOT A REVOLUTIONARY

Delivered at
the Publishing
Triangle's
Writers' Weekend,
October 1992.

In the vocabulary of the old left, the reason for living was revolution. In our time, however, we comprise the first generation who does not think that the future will be better. We fear the future. We live in a profound state of nostalgia. Concepts like *revolution* just become reminders of the impossibility of change. *Revolution* has come to represent everything we can't have and can't achieve. We know we won't make a revolution and so now we have to ask ourselves if there is anything else we *can* do. In my case, I favor resistance over the concept of revolution. One act of resistance every day is something I think we can all incorporate into our lives. Because, obviously, as far as lesbians and gay men go, the status quo is pretty awful for us at this time—so each of us continuing to live tomorrow exactly the way we lived this morning really just means more of the same.

One man whose act of resistance profoundly affected me is Derrick Bell. He is a black law professor who had an appointment at Harvard Law School. But Derrick Bell, having reached the most prestigious position in his profession committed a very unusual act. He refused to be contained by Harvard Law School. He announced that he would carry out a one-man strike; he would refuse to teach another day until Harvard tenured one black woman on their law faculty. Not only was Bell willing to risk all his prestige and salary and corporate power—for Harvard is a corporation—but, he was willing to do this to advocate for a group of people, black women, who had less power than he did in the academic hierarchy. Most interestingly for me, he refused to be a token. He refused to be the only one with access.

Well, in case you don't know the punch-line, Derrick Bell's teaching strike went on for four semesters and two summer sessions and finally he had to either resign from Harvard or go back to work in defeat because they had no intention of tenuring a black woman. So, he resigned. He did put those two years to good use,

258

however, by writing a book, *Faces at the Bottom of the Well,* in which he brilliantly describes what he calls "the permanence of racism."

Bell believes, as a result of his own life's experiences, that racism is a permanent institution of American life. It is an inherent characteristic of American culture and forms a crucial part of the economic, social, and political life of the nation. And, of course, this understanding can be applied as well to homophobia and to sexism, the final frontier. The permanence of these hierarchies of domination is a bitter pill to swallow—but, like substituting resistance for revolution—it can free us of many of the psychological strategies that keep us from taking concrete action on our own behalf.

In the past we believed that visibility and civil rights were the keys to transforming the lives of gay people, of people of color, and of women in this country. And that philosophy made sense because when we identify who does not have basic rights under the law, we are talking about the vast majority of Americans. We believed that if the legal system would recognize our full humanity and if people who despise us or, more importantly, resent us, could only get to know us better, our oppression would be reduced. We believed this process would improve our own lives and the many generations ahead with whom we identify.

Yet, this past summer, 24 years after Stonewall, 73 years after women got the vote, 19 years after the Civil Rights Act, this nation was subjected to the most vicious and vile public display of homophobia ever to be portrayed in the national media. Resolutions are currently pending in Oregon, Colorado, Tampa, Florida, and Portland, Maine that would significantly limit the rights of gay men and lesbians. Simultaneously, this nation continues to abandon people with AIDS and has no compassion for their survivors. Some cities have gay rights bills, but that doesn't stop gay bashings. Some cities have job protection clauses, but that doesn't stop people from being fired arbitrarily. We have huge numbers of people who are entirely open about their homosexuality, but they are ignored by the national discourse and excluded from the intellectual life of the nation. I think it should be obvious to all of us that actions directed towards convincing other people to like us have not worked as a strategy. Instead, we must focus, as Derrick Bell has done, on protecting our own community and strengthening that community's political power.

On September 26th a twenty-nine-year-old black lesbian named Hattie Mae Cohens and a forty-five-year-old white gay man named Brian Mock were at home in the apartment they shared in Salem, Oregon when a group of skinheads threw a molotov cocktail into their basement and these two members of our community were burned to death. Can you smell their burning bodies? These two martyrs were murdered five weeks before the state they died in was about to vote on the worst anti-gay legislation that has ever been seen in this nation. Even though this is the Emmet Till case of the nineties it was completely ignored by the national media. Even out gay people in major news organizations did not get this story into print. The only straight paper that reported on it was the *Oregonian*. And do you know what was on the cover that week of *QW*, New York's weekly lesbian and gay magazine? An interview with Susan Sarandon. Please *QW*, one act of resistance every day.

Lesbians, also, are under great pressure to be contained, to minimize or eliminate the lesbian content of our work, of our biographies in order to be invited into American culture. In the eighties a number of us tried to imagine a fiction in which the lesbian voice was the neutral, objective, and authoritative voice of the novel. But that is an effort that can only come from some illusion of empowerment. Today, in the midst of the devastation and pressure that is gay life in America, lesbian fiction across the board has become obsessed with our marginality. And those of us who are out look at the closeted and semi-closeted with more investment than ever.

One night I was hanging out with a bunch of friends flipping through the pages of *Vanity Fair* magazine. Annie Leibovitz had just published a series of full color portraits entitled "Heroes of the Gulf War," featuring a variety of killers in romantic poses. Thoroughly disgusted, we sat down and wrote her a collective letter. "We use our talents for peace," we said. "You are using yours for war." Of course she never responded.

Why do I take the actions of famous lesbians so personally? Sometimes it seems as though those of us who are out in our professions have gone as far as we will ever be allowed to go and are now standing, noses pressed against the glass wall that separates "us" from "them." Perhaps that's why I reacted so strongly to the recent *New York Times Magazine* cover story profile on Susan Sontag. The article carefully protected her closet. They didn't create fake husbands or faux boyfriends—but they collaborated with her in reinforcing the lie that brilliant and creative women must sacrifice sex and love in order to achieve.

In the *Times* profile, Sontag describes talking to her psychiatrist about her guilt over writing a romance novel instead of social criticism because she believes that fiction is not as useful a contribution to the public good. The doctor reassures her that giving people reading pleasure is also important. I wanted to scream. Why hasn't she asked these questions about her own homosexuality and the gay and lesbian community? Why isn't she concerned about the contribution she is withholding from us when she refuses—as one of the most respected women in the world—to come out as the dyke that she is? Lesbians suffer a real brain drain because so many of our great artists, leaders, and social thinkers are closeted. What does Sontag have to say about the struggle to build an integrated homosexual life? About how to build activist movements? About how to strategize to end AIDS? She did write a book, *AIDS and Its Metaphors*, but her closet kept her from addressing homophobia and its impact on the epidemic in precisely the way that her openness about having cancer *enhanced* her analysis of the stigmatization of disease in *Illness As Metaphor*. What does Sontag feel, sitting in *her* apartment when she hears about Hattie Mae Cohens? Can anything other than the desire to be accepted by straight people be at the root of Sontag's closet?

Many people argue that an artist's homosexuality is irrelevant to their work. But the way in which submerged lesbian content distorts artistic expression was made clear to me when I saw Anna Deveare Smith's play *Fires in the Mirror*, a smash hit one-woman show that ran at the Public Theater this year. Smith's piece addresses the conflict between Hasidic Jews and blacks in Crown Heights, Brooklyn. She recites, verbatim, testimony from a wide range of black and Jewish figures on the event and adapts a variety of personae to enact each character. But what really shocked me the most was the unspoken (and unacknowledged by critics) lesbian subtext that ran throughout the play.

To be specific, encoded in Smith's piece was a very subtle but persistent series of references to black lesbians. First of all, Smith plays the whole show in male drag. But the closet made its first overt appearance on stage in a short scene, early in the piece, where she portrays Angela Davis, the revolutionary black leader and teacher who is also a lesbian. Smith plays Davis wearing a black leather jacket as she is teaching in the History of Consciousness Department at the University of California in Santa Cruz. Davis is making a statement about how race is not sufficient enough of a category for her to use as the sole basis of community. "I am interested in community that is not static," Davis says. "I'm interested in coming together in a different way." Now, if the audience knew that Davis is a lesbian, her rejection of race as the only category for identity could take on a meaning that would be very challenging for homophobes of all racial groups. But, without this knowledge, the reverse impact occurs, where the audience can come away thinking that Angela Davis has mellowed, has become a liberal, is now a humanist. The closet here distorts a very important piece of information about the political and emotional life of one of America's most heroic figures.

Throughout the play Smith graciously avoids any mention of romantic love, sexuality, masculinity, or "the family." She never portrays a woman in a traditionally seductive or "feminine" manner. Instead, she emphasizes the intellectual life of most of her female characters—both black and Jewish. She actually remains quite gender neutral throughout. Additionally, when playing Jewish males—who are usually seen as less masculine than dominant culture males—she essentially plays them almost as herself—with little affectation of vocal tone or body movement that would traditionally signify masculinity.

In fact, the only overt discussion of black sexuality comes from Big Mo, a rapper based in Crown Heights. Mo complains that too many other female rappers are capitulating to dehumanizing images of black women's sexuality. She acknowledges that she has been put down for taking this stance but confidently asserts that, despite the criticism, she knows that "I'm not man-bashing. I'm female-asserting." Of the two women Mo points to as heroic exceptions to this collusion with dominant images of black women, one—Queen Latifah—is also widely believed to be a lesbian.

Obviously these questions of black lesbian identity are very important in Smith's life. But, by consciously burying them so deeply in her work, she is contributing to a huge pretense about events like Crown Heights. If we continue to insist that categories like black and Jewish are closed and not mitigated by other factors such as gender, sexuality, class loyalty, etc., then we will have a harder time imagining an alternative for human relations. The closeting of the controversy of homosexuality resulted in a more manageable and streamlined discussion of relations between blacks and Jews, but that containment is ultimately false. I'm Jewish and I have relationships with black people who are both homosexual and heterosexual. My homosexuality is a very significant mitigating factor in those relationships. I could not participate in a constructive discussion of black/Jewish relationships without including it.

I understand the desire to keep one's lesbianism out of the artistic product. I sit there like the rest of you and watch closeted women or semi-closeted artworks achieve a level of reward that is systematically denied the rest of us. I'm sure I'm not the only one in this room who sits home at night thinking "Should I write a straight novel under a pseudonym?" and other weird thoughts like, "Should I write for television?" because the approval is so seductive. But instead, I have to choose, every day, the path of one act of resistance. Once a day say something complicated, take on something difficult, challenge yourself, surprise the people around you, resist acting for the approval of straight people, of white people, of men. Talk about Hattie Mae Cohens at work tomorrow. Say her name.

COMMENTARY

In the fall of 1992, the gay and lesbian nation slowly became aware that fringe right wing organizations had placed anti-gay ballot measures for popular vote in a few selected locations around the country. Local gay communities did the best they could to fight the measures but some were unable to get the word out, even to the gay community nationally. The best organized defense campaign was in Oregon where experienced activists like Donna Redwing and Suzanne Pharr, among many others, strategized systematic responses to Proposition 9. The emotionally tense public debate in that state provided a lot of publicity for anti-gay propaganda and created a climate of overt hate.

On September 26 Hattie Mae Cohens, a black lesbian, and Brian Mock, a white disabled gay man, were firebombed to death by skinheads in the home they shared. Not only did Oregon police refuse to characterize this murder as a hate crime, but it received no national press attention. This is in the context of the aftermath of the Rodney King beating, which had rightfully resonated across America. But while Rodney King was beaten, these two people were murdered and there was not one word of media coverage—proving once again how cheap gay people's lives are in this country.

Because the Lesbian Avengers were committed to fighting the right, we decided to take on the job of gaining publicity for the murders. We developed a multifold strategy using a variety of direct actions and behind-the-scenes advocacy. Our first act was to build a large shrine to these martyrs and install it in the West Village. There we had their photos, paintings saying "Burned to Death for Who They Are," and incense, candles, and anything else that people brought. Avengers sat vigil from Halloween until Election Day when the vote on Proposition 9 would be taking place. Our opening ceremonies included a sermon by Avenger Lysander Puccio in which she said, "Fear aside. Sorrow aside. Even our fury aside. In total soberness, we take the fire into our hands and we take it into *our* bodies." At this point, before a crowd of about five hundred gay people participating in a Take Back the Night March organized by the Anti-Violence Project, about twenty Avengers swallowed fire.

Throughout the vigil people came and left mementos to Hattie Mae and Brian. They also left names of others who had been murdered for being queer like Marsha Johnson, a black drag queen and original Stonewaller whose body had been found in the Hudson River with her skull bashed in a few weeks before.

Behind the scenes we were desperately calling every lesbian we could find with any kind of inside position in the media. We were busily faxing information begging our handful of contacts to provoke some kind of news coverage. *Out* magazine sponsored a news conference at City Hall where openly gay council-members Deborah Glick and Tom Duane, as well as Comptroller Liz Holtzman, spoke out against the murders and against Proposition 9. Mayor Dinkins's liaison Marjorie Hill also spoke, but the Mayor reneged on a promised appearance.

Finally, the week of the election, Anna Quindlen, the esteemed *New York Times* columnist, published an op-ed piece about the Oregon murders, using language from our press release in her opening paragraph. This was accompanied by an equally impassioned column in the *New York Post* by Amy Pagnozzi, also on the Oregon murders. We had at least made record.

On election day, Proposition 9 was defeated by a frighteningly narrow margin. But two other anti-gay ballot measures did pass. The state of Colorado passed Proposition 2 prohibiting housing, job, or public accommodation protection for lesbians and gay men. And the city of Tampa, Florida passed a similar proposition. The Tampa community had been so under siege that we did not even know that the proposition was pending.

The Avengers did a second action aimed towards the lack of press coverage of the Oregon murders. We held a march, without a permit, at rush hour, down Fifth Avenue with posters saying "Do Not Let Them Rest in Peace" and flaming torches. The march was met by surprised police resistance, but no trouble except for a few citations for "illegal use of fire." We marched to Rockefeller Center where we had reconstructed the shrine and burned copies of the Tampa and Colorado propositions. Avenger Marlene Colburn addressed the crowd that night. "We, lesbians and gay men, have no more cheeks left to turn, so we will avenge these murders by any means we see fit."

Of course the most significant event of that November was the defeat of George Bush and the election of Bill Clinton. But the concrete results of this change were so obscure at the time that it hardly impacted on how the Avengers developed our strategies. We had faith in no man.

LETTER TO JENNIFER DUNNING

Turn-Out:
The Catalogue
of the Lesbian
Performing Arts
Festival,
November 1992

Turn-Out asked me to interview Jennifer Dunning, dance critic for the *New York Times*. Jennifer decided that she would rather respond to written questions instead of an in-person back and forth. Since this structure makes further probing or follow-up impossible, I decided to submit a statement and a few big questions for her comments.

SARAH   In the past, lesbian and gay choreographers who were not out in their work chose very different relationships to sexuality in their dances. Men have often used heterosexual partnering but draped it in a sensibility that other gay men could identify. But lesbian choreographers often refused sexuality altogether, focusing instead on purely aesthetic concerns.

In the seventies there was a transitional period in which the evolving feminist movement created a context for some artists to address womanhood and girlhood in an avant-garde framework, while still avoiding revealing their lesbian desires. At the same time, social realist dance companies like Wallflower Order addressed feminism and sometimes lesbianism in a more direct way. Edwina Lee Tyler and Roberta Stokes' 1980s company A Piece of the World was openly lesbian but was rarely seen in a traditional dance context, despite its founders' classical training, and performed primarily for the underground lesbian community.

Sporadically, playful sexuality and emotional/sexual bonds between women have emerged in postmodern dance in the eighties and nineties. I'm thinking specifically of Wendy Perron and MC Becker's duet at DTW around 1981, Susan Seizer and Jennifer Miller's duets as part of Johanna Boyce's Calf Women Company in the middle eighties, Barbara Hofrenning and Kimberly Flynn at Dancespace, Stephanie Skura and

265

Jennifer Green's duet in the Bad Play at PS 122, and Clarinda Mac Low's recent improvisations at Dancespace. But I think that these moments have been exceptions, both in the work of these specific choreographers and in postmodern dance in general.

Now that more homosexual choreographers are open about their emotional and sexual concerns, we still see a dramatic divergence between gay male and lesbian choreography. Many of the men seem to be overtly engaging concrete manifestations of gay life, whether using drag, re-claiming effeminate movement, or directly addressing the impact of AIDS. But lesbian choreographers are off in another direction. Often lesbian artists choose male and female dancers who are gender ambiguous or physically similar to each other. This tends towards an emphasis on gender neutrality instead of the arch faggotry or masculine exhibitions in gay men's dance. But, most importantly, lesbian dance seems, at this moment, to be focused on physical strength, muscularity, and endurance. We see this in the work of Elisabeth Streb, Jennifer Monson, and Cydny Wilkes among others. Of course, lesbian choreographers face many obstacles that gay men do not face such as cultural ideas about femininity, restrictions on the female role in certain dance forms, a dearth of openly lesbian critics, the cultural meaning of female display, and the intimidating factor of societal voyeurism on the lesbian body.

What, in your opinion, is the interplay between the emerging voice of lesbian choreography and the social context in which it is made? What would you like to say to these artists about their work? How can the broader dance world, critics, programmers, and funders be made to understand the meaning of lesbian dance to the larger society?

JENNIFER
DUNNING
RESPONDS

I initially regretted putting you through extra work Sarah, because of my neuroticism about public speaking. But I was glad I did when I read your musings on lesbian dance and its history. I should start off by saying that I am not quite sure what "lesbian dance" is. Is a dance "lesbian" by virtue of its choreographer's sexuality, or its subject matter?

Turn-Out was great news. It seems more than time for a festival celebrating art by lesbians, especially given the amount of work, or dance and performance art at least, that is being done by and about gay men today. I was amused to see that the people who put together the festival seemed to be men, though clearly committed and imaginative men. But looking through the roster of *Turn-Out* artists, most of whose work I know at least a little about, I was as puzzled as ever about how to define lesbian art. Should it be limited to work that deals specifically and in a fairly linear way with the experience of living as a lesbian?

Like you, I remember Johanna Boyce's wonderful girl-dances, and remember feeling sad, not that there was but that there seemed to have to be, a mention of a boyfriend lurking in most public conversations with the choreographer. I was bored by the wan polemics of Wallflower Order, whom I saw in a later and apparently less vital version. But most of all I remember being amused by the fact that while the earliest gay male dance I saw, by John Bernd, was very dreamy-touchy-feely, the "girls" were out there tussling on the floor, looking sometimes a little like soft-focus lingerie ads but never less than boisterously themselves.

And then that stopped for the most part. And there began to be more and stronger pieces about being a gay man. And I've wondered where the women are, in a time when "family values" and the plague of AIDS have made manifestos out of gay-identified art. Why has there been so much more of a lesbian presence in writing and popular or "women's" music? Is there a lesbian sensibility (for artists, audiences, or reviewers)? Have the energy and politicization needed to endure living in the age of AIDS made bold lesbian-identified creativity feel frivolous or irrelevant?

It is hard to believe that that invisibility has much to do with cultural ideas about femininity and female display or with pornography crusades. Why, for instance, might it be harder for lesbians to display their bodies than apparently straight women, who are stripping, increasingly, in modern dance today? Perhaps lesbianism is, deep down, far more frightening to most people than male gayness. The deeper, more inherent physical bonding of children with mothers may make it traumatic to identify comfort with "difference"? But a naked body is a body.

I'm not sure that a slew of confessional pieces about living as a lesbian would mean so very much after the first high. There is coming to be a sameness, I feel, in a good deal of that work by men. And if the aim is to challenge a suffocating, lethal status quo, it seems to me that the work is mostly preaching to or nose-thumbing at the converted, given the spaces it tends to be presented in.

If I give myself a kind of word-association test with the phrase "lesbian dance today" I think of something that is more performance art—a sliver of Jennifer Miller's Circus Amok in some PS 122 bouillabaisse program. Miller swallowed fire, eyes hooded and beardlet glinting, and generally occupied the stage space with all the dark, sardonic, threatening mystery that has attached itself to the idea of lesbianism, I think, in the popular mind. It was simultaneously a witty send-up and a celebration. But it was also very much of its kind.

So I don't know how to answer your question about how "the broader dance world, critics, programmers, and funders can be made to understand the meaning of lesbian dance to the larger society." I doubt if anyone can be made to understand anything, especially if the meaning isn't all that clear to start. Work by lesbian artists has to keep being made, whether it deals with living as a lesbian or more abstract themes, whether it is a confession, play, or celebration or just continuing on down an inviting or challenging road. And I guess what I would like to say to lesbian artists is, to paraphrase that recently infamous political bumper sticker, "annoy everyone and try to keep on working on the work you want to do without apology or explanation."

United Colors of Homophobia

February 1993

Months after the Campaign for Military Service's efforts to reverse the ban on gays and lesbians in the military fell to crushing defeat, the racial representation of the issue reverberates throughout gay politics. At the center are questions about the legacy of the civil rights movement and the crisis of leadership in the lesbian and gay community. These questions will transform identity politics in an increasingly polarized America and force both white gays and heterosexual blacks into choices that most have historically ignored.

According to the United States General Accounting Office Congressional Report on homosexuality in the military, white men are the group least affected by the anti-gay ban. For example, in the Marine Corps, black females were discharged for homosexuality at twice the rate of white males. Yet, of all the individual cases focused on in the high profile military debate, only one was black—Perry Watkins. National organizations coordinating the move to lift the ban like the Campaign for Military Service consistently featured white spokespeople. No women of color were put forward as media representatives and the increasingly conservative national gay press focused exclusively on white officers. So the actual impact of the military ban on people of color remained obscured by the white gay leadership and the white media.

Although the national media's depiction of gay life has grown more extensive recently, it has not grown more complete. Consistently, a white press corps has focused on the kind of gay people who most resemble them. White moderates who have salaried positions with gay and lesbian organizations get singled out as "leaders," while black gay and lesbian leaders are systematically ignored. This is true in the white gay press and in the mainstream. For example, a recent front page *New York Times* article on June 28th headed, "Blacks Reject Gay Rights as Equal to Theirs," quoted not one single credible black lesbian or gay leader.

269

It seems clear that a gay movement defined as all white is not the inheritor of the civil rights legacy. However, the gay movement as it really stands is that struggle's most natural offspring. But who is doing the defining? In New York City alone there are long term community activists such as Lidell Jackson, co-editor of *Colorlife: The Newspaper By and For Lesbian and Gay People of Color*; Haitian-born Assotto Saint, poet, editor and AIDS activist; Jewelle Gomez, novelist; Shari Frilot of the Lesbian and Gay Experimental Film Festival; Donald Suggs of the Gay and Lesbian Alliance Against Defamation. There are social leaders like Jocelyn Taylor, co-founder of the Clit Club, the only interracial lesbian club in New York, and many, many more. The list goes on and on forever. To both the mainstream and gay press such leaders often remain marginalized or invisible. And by extension, their work and issues are not presented as the organic parts of the whole that they actually are. "We do not get the attention of infants born to infected mothers," writes B. Michael Hunter in *Sojourner: Black Gay Voices in the Age of AIDS*. "We are not seen on Broadway stages, nor are we invited to address major political conventions." The right wing did not have to look very far to see where the gay movement is most vulnerable for further division and attack.

A well-dressed young black woman is speaking into the television camera. She tells the viewing audience that gays are trying to "elevate themselves to the level of minority." As the camera cuts to images of white drag queens, she explains how gays are using the victories of the civil rights movement to win "special privileges." The tape cuts to a chart as the black male narrator reveals the "average gay income" to be $55,000 a year. By the time the forty-minute tape is over, viewers have been told by implication or outright declaration that all blacks are straight; that gay people choose their sexuality and face no oppression or discrimination; that gays are manipulating the legacy of the civil rights movement to advance over other minorities, undoing whatever gains blacks have won.

The video is called *Gay Rights, Special Rights*, produced by the Traditional Values Coalition. This is the latest in the Christian Right's treasure trove of propaganda aimed at passing anti-gay measures. With 15,000 copies sold to date, *Gay Rights, Special Rights* carries a new, especially insidious message that black and white heterosexuals can unite and fight together against gay men and lesbians. All of whom are white.

Is it necessarily insulting to African-Americans to invoke the black civil rights struggle on behalf of the lesbian and gay movement? Historically, of course lesbians and gays—both blacks and whites—participated in the civil rights movement, but they were not allowed to be out. So there is that direct lineage. Of course people who oppose civil rights for lesbians and gays will not see our movement as a legitimate inheritor of the tradition of American freedom struggles. They would consider any association with homosexuality to be "insulting."

There is a long history of black lesbians and gays claiming both Stonewall and Selma. But this stand is facing a backlash from both black heterosexuals and white lesbians and gays. One particularly stark example has to do with a recent media attack on Donald Suggs, Public Affairs Director for GLAAD. Last year Buju Banton, a Jamaican dancehall singer, released a song called "Boom Bye Bye," which called for the murder of Jamaican gay men. "Two men hug up and a kiss up and a lay down in bed," he sang. "Shoot them now come mek we shoot them POW." Suggs, working in concert with Gay Men of African Descent (GMAD) led a protest against the violent demands of Banton's hit record. In the past gay black activists have often been hesitant to take a public stand against black homophobia because of racist attitudes among white gays ignorantly claiming that blacks are more homophobic than whites. His reward was a vicious attack in the October issue of *Vibe* Magazine, the hip-hop version of *Rolling Stone*.

In an article entitled "No Apologies, No Regrets," *Vibe* accused GMAD and Suggs in particular of being patsies for, and fronts for, gay white men. The article claimed that white gay men run the national media. *Vibe* even declared that Suggs's skin color was not dark enough for him to have credibility as a black spokesperson. The author of "No Apologies, No Regrets" was Joan Morgan, a black straight woman. *Vibe*'s editor is Jonathan Van Meter, a white gay man. Will disdain for black lesbians and gay men be the cement of the new coalitions of the nineties? Will anti-black homophobia prove to be the most inclusive ideology of them all?

A MODEST PROPOSAL

Presented at an
Outwrite '93
panel "Gay Books
Straight World."
The other
Panelists were
Jackie Woodson,
Reetha Powers,
Kenny Fries,
and John Scagliotti.
Boston,
October 1993

I have spent a great deal of time thinking through the structure of how lesbian literature is placed in the broader American context, and I have come to the conclusion that all of us involved in its production—writers, publishers, editors, publicists, marketing people, bookstore buyers, book review assignment editors, book critics, and readers—are complicit in maintaining the marginality of the work. Even though white Americans read black women writers and Christians read Jews, basically only homosexuals read homosexually themed books. This marginality is, ironically, absolutely contrary to the goals and visions of the political movement that made it possible for us to come this far.

For some time now it has been clear that we are functioning in a parallel world—in fixed and stagnant substructures of companies, bookstores, reading circuits, review pages, and readers' minds. I think the first necessary step to changing this is to eliminate the Gay List. Currently, lesbian and gay books are marketed in such a way that the homosexuality of the novel's characters is their primary defining attribute. Books with openly gay content are group advertised—even if the works have absolutely nothing else in common. For lesbian writers and straight writers to be advertised together is almost unheard of. The ads are placed almost exclusively in gay publications. Gay authors with openly gay content are almost never booked to read or tour with straight authors and are in no way sold to straight readers. In other words, the current, increasingly institutionalized, method for marketing gay and lesbian books inherently excludes this literature from the mosaic of American writing.

Obviously this exclusion has existed for all time and far precedes the invention of the Gay List. Throughout history straight people have, for the most part, disregarded our best and most talented writers, ignored them or treated them with condescension and contempt unless these writers removed homosexuality from their work. But now it is the habit of the publishing industry—both corporate and to some extent independent—to maintain this separation systematically. Integrating lists, integrating ads, integrating readings is an essential step that corporate publishers must take to counteract the ghettoization of the literature. Remember, "crossover" is a benign, deceptive word, standing in for the historical exclusion of gay and lesbian existence. To pretend that it is simply a marketing matter is to be short-sighted and ineffective.

This is not at all the fault or responsibility of open gays and lesbians in the publishing industry. They have been placed in untenable positions by the larger corporate structure as a gay management class, a substructure to contain gay authors. Often authors are unable to challenge or get to the larger corporation because to do so jeopardizes the very gay and lesbian people who courageously pioneered gay publishing in the mainstream. And of course they are people with their own shame and conflicts about their own homosexuality like the rest of us. Just because someone is out on the job at a publishing house or magazine doesn't mean they can or should stand alone in defiance of these exclusionary practices. It doesn't even mean that they can necessarily see them.

Reviewing presents its own obstacles. Currently in most liberal publications there are unspoken quota systems for lesbian, and, to a lesser extent, gay male books. That is to say lesbian books compete against each other for review space instead of competing against books of similar subject matter or formal concern. Let us say that five lesbian books are published within a two-month period. Only one of them will be chosen by the book review assignments editor for review based on the assumption that they are "special interest." Once the lucky book is selected it will be given secondary placement in the periodical's pages and will be assigned, in most cases, to another lesbian—probably the best friend of several of the authors of the other four books. The assigned writer is so thrilled to get a gig with a mainstream publication, even if it is a lesbian book, and is so intent upon showing that she can be "objective" in hopes that they will next assign her something she's actually interested in, that she will end up being five times harsher on the novel than any other critic would.

Publishers, both corporate and independent, and advocacy organizations like the Publishing Triangle, PEN, and the National Writers' Union must conduct an enthusiastic campaign to meet with book review assignment editors and let them know that this quota system has got to go. That openly lesbian and gay books deserve the same placement and assignment patterns as their heterosexual or closeted counterparts. The publishers need to stand up for their books and authors and treat this unethical behavior for what it is. Of course if the publishers are doing the same thing in their marketing patterns then they won't have any credibility in their dialogue with book reviewers.

There is an increasing quandary for experienced writers of gay and lesbian books with regard to the bookstores. From my experience of touring for ten years it seems clear that if I read in a women's bookstore, I will get mostly lesbians. If I read in a gay bookstore I will get mostly lesbians and some gay men. Straight people do not go to gay bookstores. If I read in a general interest store I will get a mixed audience plus gay people who won't go to gay bookstores. Therefore it is in my best interest to read in superstores whenever they will let me in. Ironically, my current needs are in direct conflict with the gay and lesbian bookstores who made it possible for me to be in print in the first place. At the same time, it is usually very hard for me to get a reading in a mainstream store. I have five books in print and have not been allowed into a mainstream bookstore in New York City for ten years except during Gay Pride Month. This winter is the first time that ban has been broken. And many of these stores feature straight, gay male and closeted writers with half the sales that I have. This is a situation about which I am absolutely furious.

The solution that occurs to me is a conscious and deliberate campaign by bookstores to tell the public that gay and lesbian books are for everyone. That these books are a legitimate part of the mosaic of American literature. But again, unless the publishers are also telling the public that gay books are for everyone, the bookstore will not be able to be re-positioned in the public's mind.

As a result of these frustrating conditions, increasingly our best, most talented lesbian writers, many of whom are out of the closet and have published books with gay content, are marginalizing or eliminating lesbianism from their books—and with good reason. I empathize with this phenomenon and struggle with it personally every day. The current situation is clear. If you want to be accepted as an American writer you must remove or obscure the lesbianism of your work. Otherwise you are condemned to the Gay List. This is the most dramatic symptom of the disturbing trap in which openly lesbian writing is currently mired. This is, in many ways, the most compelling reason to dismantle the current system. It is driving talented writers away from recognizable lesbian subject matter.

Lesbians are really the only remaining writers of American literature who do not appear in their own work. After all, there is not one novel on the face of the earth by a heterosexual writer that has no heterosexual characters. Writers must be free at all times to write whatever they wish. It is, however, necessary to analyze the reception of this work. The refusal to separate these two issues—writer's intention vs. reception of the work—has made it impossible to have free discussion on this topic to date.

The bottom line that I have clarified for myself over my ten years in print is that any differentiation in the way that my books, ideas, and person are treated in comparison to gay men, straight women or straight men is unacceptable to me. As an advanced writer I expect to be treated the same way that gay men, straight men, straight women, and closeted writers on my level are treated. I expect lesbian beginners to be treated like straight beginners, like gay male beginners. And I recognize that these exclusions multiply themselves when it comes to writers of color and to people working in non-commodifiable forms. Many of us were deeply shaken by the casual, passing notice, that took place in the mainstream press, of Audre Lorde's life and death, and it underlined yet again the understanding that our leaders, our geniuses, and our teachers can live and die without the respect and acknowledgement that they merit because our lives are simply not as important as the lives of heterosexuals. I expect lesbian geniuses and lesbian mediocrities to have the same opportunities as gay male and straight male and straight female geniuses and mediocrities, and I intend to be outraged and pursue concrete solutions when this equity does not occur—which seems to be every day.

275

THE LESBIAN AVENGERS

HISTORY MY AMERICAN HISTORY MY AMERICAN

2

THE LESBIAN AVENGERS
PART ONE

In the Spring of 1992 I sat down with five friends—Ana Maria Simo, Anne-Christine D'Adesky, Maxine Wolfe, Marie Honan, and Ann MaGuire—in Ana's living room to talk about starting a lesbian direct action group. We were each extremely politically experienced, with varied backgrounds in activist and community based organizing. We decided to approach this new group with great precision. We chose the name, the Lesbian Avengers. Ana's son, Thomas, came up with a logo—an old fashioned bomb with a lit fuse. We debated what the first action should be. Our original idea was to parachute into Whitney Houston's wedding. But we ended up deciding on an action on the first day of school in District 24, the Queens school district leading the viciously anti-gay battle against the recently proposed multicultural curriculum. Then, in June, on Gay Pride Sunday, the six of us, with Kathryn Thomas and Debby Karpel, handed out 8,000 lime green club cards. They said:

> WE WANT REVENGE AND WE WANT IT NOW!
> LESBIANS! DYKES! GAY WOMEN!
> There are many more lesbians in this world than men like
> George Bush. But cold-blooded liars like him have all the power.
> Let's Face It:
> Government, Media, Entertainment, the Money System, School,
> Religion, Politeness . . . are irrelevant to our lives as dykes.
> We're wasting our lives being careful. Imagine what your life
> could be. Aren't you ready to make it happen? WE ARE. If you don't
> want to take it anymore and are ready to strike, call us now at
> (718) 499-3802. We'll call you back.
> Think About It
> WHAT HAVE YOU GOT TO LOSE?
> The Lesbian Avengers

Because we wanted activists, we decided that the great filter would be to give the card recipients something to do, which was to call our tape-recorded announcement. Every caller was invited to a meeting at the Lesbian and Gay Community Center on July 7. The first meeting got about fifty people. Quickly, we were joined by a number of people who were to become the backbone organizers of the new movement's first year, like Marlene Colburn and Phyllis Lutsky—organizers par excellence; Carrie Moyer who designed the posters, t-shirts, and broadsheets establishing our distinct visual style; Lydia Medina—banner maker, whose work appeared in the mass media from *Newsweek* to *Newsday* as emblematic of the new lesbian movement; Kelly Cogswell, Sarah Pursley, and Anastasia Kedroe, who organized the historic Dyke March on Washington (more about that later); Sheila Quinn—fearless activist; Jenny Romaine and Eve Sicular of our marching band; Allison Frohling—imaginative, hard-working costume designer; Jennifer Monson—a choreographer who taught us our signature fire-eating techniques; Su Friedrich who ran the money, the phone tree, and other essential, administrative responsibilities; Janet Baus and Julie Clark of the video team; Rachel Shearer—tireless activist; Amy Parker—who used her various corporate jobs as xerox central for the Avengers; Lysander Puccio—Episcopal priest in training, go-go dancer, and devoted organizer; Mildred Gerestant; Kat Campbell; Carrie Higbie; Allison and Jillian Chi; Sue Schaffner—photographer for Dyke Action Machine, who designed our extensive wheat-pasting system; Leslie Majors who ran our extensive merchandise fundraising; Andrea Terrell; Cyn Riley; Lisa Reddy; Terry Maroney; Beth Trimarco; Lisa Springer; Melonie Fallon—who came from Barnard College to write a paper and ended up throwing stink bombs at fascists; Mindy Baransky; Ann Northrop; Karen Moulding—our lawyer; Francine Marchese; Justine Keefe; Gail Dotin; Susan Bueti; Kristina Deutsch; Carolina Kroon; P.N. Ryan; Helen Lang—the intrepid media coordinator; and many many many many more.

Fall was time for the Avengers' first action. We had been spending all summer getting to know each other, making fabulous posters, wheat-pasting them and otherwise announcing our existence and our premiere action. Remembering the experiences of earlier organizations who had become dependent on foundation or government money, we vowed from the beginning to do all our fundraising through parties at five dollars a head. That way, if we did good by the community, they would show their support. We held a party featuring the Maul Girls to raise money, and we even survived our first controversy. A number of people objected to our action being planned at a public school because they felt we were endangering the children. A furious discussion ensued about whether or not school and family were neutral, safe places for children and whether or not introducing children to the Lesbian Avengers was to the kids' advantage or disadvantage. We lost some people and gained many more. But the debate clarified that this was going to be a movement that was not for everyone.

At six o'clock on the morning of the first day of school, Lisa Springer, Marie Honan, Ann MaGuire, Catch Keeley, and I pulled into a parking lot in Middle Village Queens, unloaded two huge helium tanks, and started blowing up three hundred lavender balloons that said "Ask About Lesbian Lives." Then we waited. At about eight, fifty Lesbian Avengers appeared, waving the sea of balloons, wearing t-shirts that said "I Was a Lesbian Child" and accompanied by a kilt-clad marching band playing "We Are Family" as we walked half a mile to the school yard.

Middle Village was an Irish, working-class, right-to-life district, and they had never had a lesbian parade before. But, because of the balloons, the band, and our exuberant attitudes we met with very little hostility and no violence. I think people were so flabbergasted to see live lesbians there was no room for any other response. When we got to the school yard, the police were waiting and told us to go stand in a pen about a block and a half away from the entrance to the school. We refused. Well, the police had never considered that we might refuse and they had no contingency plan. Anne-Christine D'Adesky and Alexis Danzig argued with them for about ten minutes that we had the right to stand on public space, and quickly they allowed us to move to the front of the school yard. There, for an hour, we greeted each child coming to class on the first day with a balloon, a marching band, and banners imploring them to "Ask About Lesbian Lives." Some parents let their kids keep the balloons. Some refused. But every child who attended school that day heard the word "lesbian," and for some, it just might have been the most important day of their lives. It certainly forced the teachers to discuss the existence of lesbians, regardless of what restrictions had been placed on them by Mary Cummins, the bigoted chair of the local school board.

In many ways this action was emblematic of the stance the Avengers were to take in the coming year as we branched out nationally. We were willing to confront the greatest taboo in the culture—homosexuals in the school yard. And we did it in a creative, imaginative, and constructive way. It was a strong, radical, confrontational action. But it was friendly. It also set a pattern for our future of going directly to the sources that are attacking us and confronting them on their territory. This was a big step for the lesbian movement, away from symbolic actions or safe, comfortable critiques of other liberal organizations. It focused our work directly on the right wing, and established a new tone for lesbian politics—a post-ACT UP lesbian movement.

THE LESBIAN AVENGERS
PART TWO

With the advent of Clinton's election, there was a new aura of hope. Even though he seemed to bungle or ignore almost everything he had promised to women and to gay people (with the important exception of reinstating a range of abortion rights), it still was an enormous relief to not have the foot of George Bush on our necks. The Avengers had come along at exactly the right moment and lesbians were responding to our political style.

Shortly after Proposition 2 passed in Colorado, the mayor of Denver, Wellington Webb, came to New York City to promote Colorado tourism and trade—just as a national boycott of the "Hate State" had been announced. An anonymous lesbian faxed us his entire itinerary and the Avengers attended every one of his New York functions. When he met with CBS, we were outside, in the cold. When he had a power breakfast with the *Wall Street Journal*, the Avengers marched through the dining room chanting, "We're here, we're queer, we're not going skiing."

But the pièce de résistance was when Ana Simo, Ann Northrop, Julie Clark, Maxine Wolfe, Phyllis Lutsky, and Sheila Quinn went to the Plaza Hotel where Webb was having a press conference with the *Village Voice*. By this point Webb had asked Mayor Dinkins for special protection from us, so there was a police car assigned to him full-time. But when the Avenger Zap team arrived, the cops were in the coffee shop having a cup of coffee. The Avengers got all the way upstairs and into his suite, making his life really difficult for the second consecutive day. The action was a total success because, due to our presence, Webb was unable to discuss anything with the press beyond Proposition 2. He also was forced to acknowledge that 2 was part of a nationwide strategy by the right (one that he had opposed but not vociferously enough to have it be defeated). But it also taught the Avengers that, in the tradition of the Women's Liberation Zap Action Brigade and the ACT UP Zap group that got AIDS included in the Democratic Convention—a handful of people can do a strong, creative action that has broad impact.

That week, *Self* magazine, a slick Condé Nast publication, announced that they were holding a ski weekend in Colorado. Again, the Avengers went into action, invading *Self*'s Fifth Avenue offices. Within two days the weekend was canceled, although *Self* claimed that the Avengers had nothing to do with their change of plans.

We continued to do actions and continued to attract new members. And, we kept focused on the right wing, not forgetting about Mary Cummins and District 24, who were gaining power daily. Some Avengers attended a forum chaired by Cummins in a conservative Queens neighborhood. When Francine Marchese, an Avenger and a preschool teacher, stood up to speak, Cummins cut off her allotted time period, ordered her removed and screamed out "All you want to do is recruit!" which made it into the daily papers the next day. We were then provided with our slogan, "Lesbian Avengers, We Recruit," which promptly appeared on t-shirts. The phrase had even more meaning in the midst of the gays-in-the-military crisis, provoked by Clinton's announcement that he was going to lift the ban.

The press was starting to realize that we existed but had a hard time coming to terms with representing us. The *New York Times* covered the *Self* action but called us the Lesbian Agenda. The gay press, being totally misogynist, completely ignored us—with no coverage in the *Advocate* or *Out* magazine. But the mainstream finally caught on throughout the year with a piece in *Mademoiselle* by Louise Bernikow, followed by mentions in *Newsweek, New York Magazine,* and *Vogue.* The only journalist who accurately covered our movement was Donna Minkowitz at the *Village Voice.*

In January and February of 1993, I went on a book tour through the American South to promote my fifth novel *Empathy* which had been published by Dutton. I went to nineteen cities and showed the Avenger video and handed out Avenger materials in as many places as possible. By the end of the tour there were new Avenger chapters in Durham, North Carolina, Atlanta, Georgia, and Austin, Texas. By the end of my second book tour in the spring, people from Asheville, North Carolina to Birmingham, Alabama to Albuquerque, New Mexico to Tucson, Arizona to LA, Montreal, Toronto, London, Cork, Dublin and Belfast had seen the video. Maxine started an Avengers chapter in San Francisco and Carolina Kroon started one in Minneapolis. Next we were getting mailings from Avengers all over the world including Melbourne, Australia, an article in the French lesbian press, and a phone call from Japan.

Back in New York, the Irish Lesbian and Gay Organization was being trashed by the Catholic right in New York City and by a small gang of people inside their own community. Ann MaGuire, Marie Honan, Sheila Quinn, P. N. Ryan, and Catch Keeley had been hard-working Avengers and now they needed our help. Realizing that this event was a direct confrontation with the religious right, we threw all our organizational resources behind them. Carrie Moyer designed their posters; Marlene Colburn got arrested "queering" Fifth Avenue the night before the parade; Avengers organized stink bomb attacks; wheat-pasted; planned strategy; served as marshalls for the demonstration; and contributed lawyers and legal support. We had so much good experience working together that we were able to bring an entire functioning structure to this very large and complex political event, a structure that was to be put to use again a few months later in Washington.

Meanwhile other chapters evolved their own styles and carried out their own actions, but our first nationally coordinated event was in April 1993 as part of the National Lesbian and Gay March on Washington. Working together with some smaller organizations we decided to create the first ever Dyke March on the White House and set it for the night before the big Sunday demonstration.

This was the first time the Avengers had worked in a lesbian coalition and it was really tough. We had evolved a new kind of organizing style that was action-oriented, not ideologically based and had a way of working and speaking that was unfamiliar to the other groups. Furthermore, we now represented hundreds of people nationally and could bring out a hundred Avengers at the drop of a hat to do the real work of building an event. It was hard to deal with groups who didn't really represent anybody beyond their fifteen members, or didn't have the organization to do the necessary prep work. That old left style of organizing was foreign to Avengers, most of whom had never been politically active before.

About fifty Avengers got to Washington a few days early and started distributing thousands of club cards to the enthusiastically arriving crowd. The cards said, "Dyke March to the White House, Dupont Circle, Saturday at 7, Co-Sponsored by the Lesbian Avengers." No long-winded explanations were necessary. Over a million gays and lesbians had traveled to Washington for this event and the streets were totally homosexual. Many people had saved their vaca-

285

tion days and planned for months to attend and the enthusiasm was very, very high. Our little cards were received with overwhelming excitement and it began to occur to us that we were going to get more than the three or four thousand dykes we had anticipated.

That night we all gathered at DuPont Circle and the women kept coming and coming. We started marching (in true Avenger style— without a permit), and soon we realized that the numbers were absolutely huge. Around 20,000 lesbians marched through Washington, D.C. that night—the largest lesbian event in the history of the world. By the time we turned down Pennsylvania Avenue, we completely ruled the street. The Avengers stopped in front of the White House to eat fire and then we moved on to the Washington monument. You could see the ecstasy in the eyes of the marchers, many of whom had come from small towns and oppressed communities all over the country. One year before there had been six of us, now there were 20,000. It was one of the proudest moments of my life.

We did make the front page of the *Washington Post* the next day but they didn't print the name of our organization and they slashed the estimate to 6,000. Despite the work of our excellent media coordinator, Helen Lang, virtually no other mainstream press even mentioned this event but those 20,000 lesbians all went home and told their friends. At Washington we distributed 25,000 copies of a broadsheet developed by Ana Simo, Kat Campbell, and Lisa Springer, and designed by Carrie Moyer, with concrete information on how to start a lesbian direct action group. By the time we returned wearily to New York, Avenger chapters were springing up nationally.

The national network was to be used again in June when we learned that an HIV-positive lesbian from Tampa had received threatening phone calls and then had her trailer torched while she was in Washington at the march. In fact, she was one of a group of lesbians with AIDS who met with Health and Human Services Secretary Donna Shalala during the weekend of the march. Tampa, which had an anti-gay ballot measure in effect, refused to recognize the burning as a bias crime. Avengers from New York, Sarasota, Tampa, and Atlanta converged on that city, organizing a series of actions that created so much publicity for the case that the city's mayor was forced to appear with the Avengers to make a statement against hate crimes.

The Avengers represent a turning point in lesbian politics, a belief in the grass-roots, a commitment to direct action and creative organizing. But organizations alone do not make change.

Social change comes from creating a countercultural context in which large groups of people have the opportunity for mind expansion and political participation. For example, ACT UP transformed the self-image and group identity of thousands of gay people all over the world, whether they were ever politically active with ACT UP or not. In order to try to explain the philosophy and tactical choices of the Avengers, we published the following organizing handbook, hoping it would provoke new ways of thinking about activism, more than simply create new chapters.

Excerpts from

THE
LESBIAN AVENGER
HANDBOOK

A handy guide to homemade revolution

Compiled by Sarah Schulman with contributions from
Marlene Colburn, Phyllis Lutsky, Maxine Wolfe, Amy Parker,
Sue Schaffner, Carrie Moyer, and Ana Maria Simo.

Second Edition. Spring, 1993

INTRODUCTION

The Lesbian Avengers is a direct action group using grass-roots activism to fight for lesbian survival and visibility. Our purpose is to identify and promote lesbian issues and perspectives while empowering lesbians to become experienced organizers who can participate in political rebellion. Learning skills and strategizing together are at the core of our existence.

There is a wide spectrum of opinion in the lesbian community about what kinds of strategies to employ. Some people want to provide social services. Some people want to do theoretical development. Some people want to be in therapy groups. Some people want to work on electoral and legal reform. As a direct action, activist group, the Lesbian Avengers is not for everybody, nor should it be. It is for women who want to be involved in activism, work in community, be creative, do shit-work, take responsibility on a regular basis, have their minds blown, change their opinions, and share organizing skills. Other strategies are also valid but the Avengers' reason for existing is direct action.

The Lesbian Avengers was founded in June 1993 by six experienced political activists. They had a vision for a grass-roots lesbian activism that would go beyond visibility to a larger goal of movement building. On Gay Pride Day that year, these six handed out 8,000 fluorescent green club cards that said "Lesbians! Dykes! Gay Women! We want revenge and we want it now." Fifty lesbians came to the first meeting. Since that time, an increasing number of lesbians have come to the Avengers in the spirit of cooperation, negotiation and flexibility in order to build a community of skilled political organizers committed to action.

Since June we have found that certain organizing ideas help us keep our work pro-active, gratifying, and successful. One outstanding revelation has been to stay away from abstract theoretical discussion. It is so easy to create false polarities when there is nothing concrete on the table. But when our political discussions revolve around the creation and purpose of an action, it is much easier to come to agreement and share insights.

Another idea that has surfaced in our work is to encourage each Avenger to take responsibility for her own suggestions—in other words, be willing to make them happen. This way "Someone should . . ." becomes "I will" or "Who will do this with me . . . ?"

Because lesbians have been so excluded from power many of us have developed a negative stance where the only influence we have is to say NO. The Avengers is a place where lesbians can have their ideas realized, where we can each have an impact. A crucial part of that maturation process is to learn how to propose alternative solutions instead of just offering critiques. So, in our meetings if you disagree with the proposal on the floor, instead of just tearing it apart, propose another way of realizing the goal.

What follows is concrete information on how to organize a direct action group. The more efficient your frameworks are, the more encouragement and room there will be for creative, imaginative work.

Go girl!

DY

MANI

CALLING

LESB

WAKE

**IT'S TIME TO GET OUT OF THE BEDS,
OUT OF THE BARS, AND INTO THE STREETS
IT'S TIME TO SEIZE THE POWER O
DYKE LOVE, *DYKE* VISION, *DYKE* ANGER,
DYKE INTELLIGENCE, *DYKE* STRATEGY.
IT'S TIME TO ORGANIZE AND INCITE.
IT'S TIME TO GET TOGETHER AND FIGHT.
WE'RE INVISIBLE, SISTERS
AND IT'S NOT SAFE—NOT IN OUR HOMES,
NOT IN THE STREETS, NOT ON THE JOB,
NOT IN THE COURTS.**

by Anne-Christine D'Adesky, Kathy Darger, Brenda Miller, Carrie Moyer, and Ana Maria Simo

WHERE ARE THE *OUT* LESBIAN LEADERS?

IT'S TIME FOR A FIERCE LESBIAN MOVEMENT

AND THAT'S *YOU*: THE ROLE MODEL,

THE VISION, THE DESIRE.

WE NEED YOU.

BECAUSE WE'RE NOT WAITING

FOR THE RAPTURE.

WE ARE THE APOCALYPSE.

We'll be your dream and their nightmare.

LESBIAN

LESBIAN AVENGERS BELIEVE IN CREATIVE ACTIVISM:
LOUD, BOLD, SEXY, SILLY, FIERCE, TASTY,
AND DRAMATIC. ARREST OPTIONAL.
THINK DEMONSTRATIONS ARE A GOOD TIME
AND A GREAT PLACE TO CRUISE WOMEN.
LESBIAN AVENGERS DON'T HAVE PATIENCE
FOR POLITE POLITICS. ARE BORED WITH THE BOYS.
THINK OF STINK BOMBS AS ALL-SEASON ACCESSORIES.
Don't have a position on fur.
LESBIAN AVENGERS THINK CONFRONTATION
FOSTERS GROWTH AND STRONG BONES.
BELIEVE IN RECRUITMENT.

LESBIAN

LESBIAN AVENGERS BELIEVE IN TRANSCENDENCE
IN ALL STATES, INCLUDING COLORADO AND OREGON.
THINK SEX IS A DAILY LIBATION.
GOOD ENERGY FOR ACTIONS.
LESBIAN AVENGERS CRAVE, ENJOY, EXPLORE, SUFFER
FROM NEW IDEAS ABOUT RELATIONSHIPS:
SLUMBER PARTIES, POLYGAMY (WHY GET MARRIED
ONLY ONCE?), PERSONAL ADS, AFFINITY GROUPS.

LESBIAN

LESBIAN AVENGERS *scheme and scream.*
THINK ACTIONS MUST BE LOCAL,
REGIONAL, NATIONAL, GLOBAL, COSMIC.
LESBIAN AVENGERS THINK
CLOSETED LESBIANS, QUEER BOYS, AND

POWER

NOT BY THE ARMY. NOT OF STRAIGHT WOMEN. DON'T MIND HANDCUFFS AT ALL. LESBIAN AVENGERS DO BELIEVE HOMOPHOBIA IS A FORM OF MISOGYNY. LESBIAN AVENGERS ARE NOT CONTENT WITH GHETTOS: WE WANT YOUR HOUSE, YOUR JOB, YOUR FREQUENT FLYER MILES. WE'LL SELL YOUR JEWELRY TO SUBSIDIZE OUR MOVEMENT. LESBIAN AVENGERS DON'T BELIEVE IN THE FEMINIZATION OF POVERTY. WE DEMAND UNIVERSAL HEALTH INSURANCE AND HOUSING. WE DEMAND FOOD AND SHELTER FOR ALL HOMELESS LESBIANS. LESBIAN AVENGERS ARE THE 13TH STEP. LESBIAN AVENGERS THINK *girl gangs are the wave of the future.*

SEX

LESBIAN AVENGERS ARE OLD-FASHIONED: PINE, LONG, WHINE, STAY IN BAD RELATIONSHIPS. GET MARRIED BUT DON'T WANT TO DOMESTICATE OUR PARTNERS. LESBIAN AVENGERS USE LIVE ACTION WORDS : *lick, waltz, eat, fuck, kiss, play, bite, give it up.* LESBIAN AVENGERS LIKE JINGLES: SUBVERSION IS OUR PERVERSION.

ACTIVISM

SYMPATHETIC STRAIGHTS SHOULD SEND US MONEY. BELIEVE DIRECT ACTION IS A KICK IN THE FACE. LESBIAN AVENGERS PLAN TO TARGET HOMOPHOBES OF EVERY STRIPE AND INFILTRATE THE CHRISTIAN RIGHT.

TOP 10 AVENGER QUALITIES

(IN DESCENDING ORDER)

10. COMPASSION

9. LEADERSHIP

8. NO BIG EGO

7. INFORMED

6. FEARLESSNESS

5. RIGHTEOUS ANGER

4. FIGHTING SPIRIT

3. PRO SEX

2. GOOD DANCER

1. ACCESS TO RESOURCES
(XEROX MACHINE)

THE LESBIAN AVENGERS. WE RECRUIT.

LESBIAN AVENGER ACTION OUTLINE

The purpose of an action is to make our demands known, win change and *involve as many lesbians as possible in all aspects of organizing*.

Actions should be as well-planned as possible so everyone knows why we are there and feels involved. But, there is no way we can know everything in advance so we also have to be ready to make decisions on the spot in a quick and supportive way.

PLANNING

When Avengers have an idea for an action they can bring it to the group in two ways.

1) Bring a precise, specific proposal to the floor.

    or

2) Come to the floor with a vague idea. Pass around a sign-up sheet for those interested in developing the project. Then meet as a committee separately and return to the group with a specific proposal.

This way the large group discussion will revolve around a concrete proposal creating a framework for a more constructive and satisfying, task-oriented discussion. Once the large picture of an action is approved by the Avengers, the committee gets to work on specifics. Every action needs two coordinators who are responsible for following up everyone who took on tasks, and for presenting the action to the floor at each step. It is in committee that all the brilliant, wacky ideas can come to fruition.

Coordinators need to address the following questions.

CONCEPTS

What is the goal of this action?
Who are we trying to reach?
What is our message?

LOGISTICS

Time, date, place and length of action. Why?

The location needs to be scouted as early as possible. How much space do we have? Inside or outside? Obstructions? Entrances and exits? Security? Public or private property? How wide is the street for banners and props?

DEMO-GRAPHICS

What is the visual design of the action going to be? It should let people know clearly and quickly who we are and why we are there. NY Avengers have used a wide range of visuals such as fire eating, a twelve-foot shrine, a huge bomb, a ten-foot plaster statue, flaming torches, etc. The more fabulous, witty, and original, the better.

TACTICS

Type of action. Avoid old stale tactics at all costs. Chanting and picketing no longer make an impression. Standing passively still and listening to speakers is boring and disempowering. Look for daring, new participatory tactics depending on the nature of your action. NY Avengers have used overnight encampments, daring Zaps in the halls of the Plaza Hotel, an invasion of the offices of *Self* magazine, a torchlight march down Fifth Avenue at rush hour without a permit, handing out balloons to school children in an anti-gay district that said "Ask About Lesbian Lives," etc.

Type of Action: Symbolic? Disruption? Interference? Education? Group size and composition: Avengers only? Lesbian? Anyone?

CONTINGENCIES (WHAT IF?)

1. We can't get the spot we planned for?
2. Group is smaller/larger than we planned?
3. Bad weather?
4. Police interference?
5. Decisions about arrest need to be made on the spot?

How do we end the action?

Every task should be supervised by a member of the organizing committee. The two coordinators are responsible to follow up with each member of the committee and their responsibilities.

Remember—the point is to involve as many Avengers as possible in the organizing. One easy way to do this is if each committee member responsible for a task comes to the large group with a sign-up sheet (i.e., "Sign up to distribute flyers at the lesbian bars," "Sign up to learn baton twirling for the action," etc.) and then calls each person on the sheet to remind them of the time and place where the work will get done. The more organized the coordinators are, the easier it will be for people to participate.

A PRELIMINARY LIST OF TASKS FOR YOUR ACTION

Someone needs to take responsibility for each task. The coordinators will follow up.

- DEMO-GRAPHICS
- FLYER PRODUCTION
  (advertising the action)
- FLYER REPRODUCTION (xerox)
- FLYER DISTRIBUTION:
  (mailing, wheat-pasting)
- FACT SHEET
  (translation if necessary)
  to give out at action
- MARSHALLS

- SUPPORT
- MEDIA
- LEGAL OBSERVERS
- VIDEO TEAM
- MARCHING BAND
- CONTACTING OTHER GROUPS
  BEFORE YOUR ACTION
- TRANSPORTATION OF MATERIALS
- FUNDRAISING

AVENGER ACTION CHECKLIST

1. Why are we doing this action and what are we trying to achieve?
2. Who do we want to include?
3. Why this time, date, and location?
4. What is the action scenario from beginning to end?
5. Who are the coordinators?
6. What are the logistics of the location?
7. Who are our legal observers and what are our legal rights?
8. What decisions and preparations have we made about arrests?
9. Where and how are our flyers being distributed, wheat-pasted, and mailed?
   (At least ten days before the action.)
10. What other groups have we contacted?
11. When is the marshall training/pre-action meeting? Who will coordinate and chair it?
12. When are the poster/prop parties?
13. If needed, who is coordinating the civil disobedience training?
14. Who will interact with the police on site?
15. How are we letting people know about the action and encouraging them to attend?

HOW TO RUN MEETINGS

The point of the meetings is to keep them as short as possible, get work done in an effective manner, but still give people time for productive discussion about the politics and creation of the action. Since most of the hammering out of details and brainstorming for creative silliness happens outside the general meeting in committees, the role of the facilitator is crucially important for keeping things focused.

Facilitators volunteer from the floor and usually serve four weeks. We offer a facilitation training every few months, and women without experience cannot facilitate without first going through a training. We also ask people facilitating for the first time to invite someone more experienced to sit next to them and help them through their first few weeks.

The facilitator is responsible for setting the agenda at each meeting. But more importantly, she is responsible for creating an atmosphere of efficient respect. If people in the meeting that night are vague and inexperienced, the facilitator must listen closely and try to focus discussion around specific proposals for action. If people come to the meeting with rigidity or negativity, the facilitator needs to diffuse the tension and insure that the Avenger meeting is a place for free exchange of ideas. People have to be able to offer their perspectives without being jumped on and have space to explore ideas. Our meetings need to be flexible, negotiable, and conducive to creative thought. It is the facilitator's job to keep people pro-active, encourage them to make concrete suggestions, propose alternatives, and take responsibility for their ideas. She must insure that proposals are presented in a way that allows the largest number of Avengers to get involved.

The facilitator should set an agenda focused around the most important business—keeping things like teach-ins and announcements until the end. She needs to keep the meeting running smoothly and with focus on the task at hand. Usually discussion should not run longer than ten or fifteen minutes at which point she can offer the room the option to vote or continue discussion. If she sees that people are repeating each other, she can ask if anyone has something new to add.

Often the meeting will begin with people going around and introducing themselves. Sometimes we end with going around again but *not to say how we felt about the meeting*. Instead each person says what tasks and responsibilities they have taken on for the following week. Hopefully everyone in the room will have taken on some kind of responsibility.

FUNDRAISING

We decided from the beginning that we did not want to apply to foundations for grants and instead would raise our money in a grass-roots way from the community. We throw wild, creative, insane parties on a regular basis with really creative posters—usually following a great action. The better our action, the more people from the community attend to support us. Most of us are poor so our events never cost more than we can pay. On New Year's Eve we charged five dollars admission, twenty-five cents for coat check and two dollars for beer—and took in $5,000.

At our parties we usually come up with a fun theme, do really good preparation, have great music, and also provide a media room with videos and flyers from The Avengers. Parties become an organizing tool because we see how well the community likes us, have a chance to let them know what we are doing while they're having fun, and *we get them to sign up on our mailing lists.*

A good party takes about a month to organize. It requires two coordinators. The first thing they should do is come up with specific tasks and bring sign-up sheets to the large meeting so that as many Avengers as possible are involved in its creation.

THINGS TO TAKE CARE OF:

VENUE: Locate an unusual space, not familiar to your audience but large enough for dancing, lounging, and hanging out.

PUBLICITY: Generate an eye-catching flyer early enough to claim that date. Mail it to the mailing list. Distribute huge numbers of them early. Let newsletters, newspapers, and radio shows know in advance. Wheat-paste vigorously.

MUSIC: Music is the key to a great party. If no live DJ will volunteer her time then get someone with diverse and extensive musical knowledge. *A good sound system.*

DOOR AND SECURITY: Two women at the door to collect money and to be sure that every person who enters signs up on the mailing list. Someone else should pick up the cash regularly and store it in a safe place. A few Avengers on alert for security problems at all times.

FOOD AND DRINK: Locate nearest all-nite deli for extra ice and beer. Provide some non-alcoholic beverages as well. Large plastic garbage cans and bags are best for ice control.

SET-UP: Create clean-up, set-up, and decorating shifts. Have people working at different times to clear up bottles, etc. Have plenty of toilet paper and towels on hand.

MEDIA ROOM: Two Avengers in charge of fabulous video and propaganda devices.

SPECIAL EVENTS: Go-go girls, kissing booths, Tarot cards, etc., etc.

301

OTHER FUNDRAISING IDEAS:

> —At every meeting we pass around an envelope labeled *Actions* and ask each person to throw in a dollar or two.
>
> —We sell t-shirts and videos *but* they are also organizing tools. We don't want to get too weighted down in the merchandise business.
>
> —People can throw private parties for birthdays or whatever and ask friends to make a donation to the Avengers instead of presents.

IDENTIFYING RESOURCES

Lots of lesbians have resources they are willing to share with the Avengers, even if they don't want to come to meetings and organize actions. Find out who has access to free xeroxing at their offices, or a fax machine. Someone may be willing to do legal support or design flyers or just wheat-paste. In order to involve as many women as possible AVENGERS have to be cooperative, organized and—most importantly—*know how to use mailing lists as an organizing tool.*

YOUR MAILING LIST IS YOUR FRIEND

At every Avenger meeting we pass around a mailing list with names and phone numbers. New members are invited to add their names to the list. An updated activist list is presented every week. This is our activist pool. Whenever we have an action we call everyone on the list. Whenever we need people to leaflet, wheat-paste, work on a dance, or build props, we call the list.

At every dance or public event we are sure to have a supporters mailing list at the door. This is our constituent base. They receive mailings for all actions and events. Since these people have never come to meetings we wouldn't call them for activist tasks—but when it comes to filling the streets or our bank account—they are the ones we count on the most.

PHONE TREES

One Avenger is responsible for coordinating a phone tree, in which other Avengers are responsible for contacting groups of ten off of our activist list. Every action or call for help goes out over the phone tree. The main coordinator is responsible for keeping the phone tree updated each week and for being sure that the callers are following through. The phone tree can only be activated by a decision from the big group—that way arbitrary, half-assed, rumor-based attempts can be avoided. Ideally everyone who has ever come to a meeting will receive both a mailing and a phone call for every one of our actions. Anyone who has only come to our events will receive a mailing.

MARSHALL TRAINING

Actions need marshalls—that is, a group of women who take responsibility for big decisions like when to go into the street, when to sit down in traffic. Marshalls need to do a training before an action, learning legal issues involved, developing a method of communication and cooperation with each other. And preferably undergoing civil disobedience training (invite a trainer from your local ACT UP, Quakers, or peace group). Usually they are identifiable by brightly colored ribbons tied around their forearms. They serve as the wall between demonstrators and the police and also are the people who block traffic as the procession peacefully moves by.

SUPPORT

A coordinated support effort is necessary when there is the possibility/probability of arrest.

The goal of those doing support is to track the arrestees through the system and wait for them to be released. Support people have a *responsibility* and an *obligation* to remain until the last person is released. It is important for those on the inside to know that they have the support of those on the outside.

BEFORE ACTION

Get support sheets filled out in duplicate. One copy is for the support person on-site and one copy should be kept off-site in case the support person gets arrested by mistake.

DURING ACTION

Try to avoid getting arrested. Keep a list of people as they are being arrested. Ask them to shout out their names if you don't recognize them. If you see any violence by police try to get badge numbers. Politely ask police (white shirt if possible) what precinct they are being taken to. Once the arrestees are taken away, go meet them at the precinct. When the paddy wagons arrive, try to let the people inside know that you are there for them.

AFTER ACTION

Hang out and wait until the very last person is released. Check off their names as they come out and get information (i.e., are people being treated well, etc.). Contact attorney. Collect summonses for attorney while making sure that the arrestees know when to appear in court.

AVENGERS SUPPORT SHEET   *Fill out both halves*

NAME _____

ADDRESS _____

HOME PHONE _____ AGE _____ DATE OF BIRTH _____

SOCIAL SECURITY NUMBER _____ JOB TITLE _____

PLACE OF EMPLOYMENT _____

PERSONS TO NOTIFY IN CASE OF EMERGENCY:

NAME _____ PHONE _____

NAME _____ PHONE _____

PERSONS TO NOTIFY IF YOU MUST SPEND THE NIGHT IN JAIL:

NAME _____ PHONE _____

NAME _____ PHONE _____

OTHER: (Specify medical consideration, notify work, etc.)

_____

....

NAME _____

ADDRESS _____

HOME PHONE _____ AGE _____ DATE OF BIRTH _____

SOCIAL SECURITY NUMBER _____ JOB TITLE _____

PLACE OF EMPLOYMENT _____

PERSONS TO NOTIFY IN CASE OF EMERGENCY:

NAME _____ PHONE _____

NAME _____ PHONE _____

PERSONS TO NOTIFY IF YOU MUST SPEND THE NIGHT IN JAIL:

NAME _____ PHONE _____

NAME _____ PHONE _____

OTHER: (Specify medical consideration, notify work, etc.)

_____

MARCHING BAND

A marching band, drum corps, rhythm, section etc. can really aid all actions. Call them at least two weeks in advance.

SPANISH TRANSLATION

Fact sheets and press releases to the Spanish language press should be translated into Spanish. Translators need enough advance time to do a good job and get their draft to the designer without cramping her schedule either.

POLICE AND PERMITS

In general Lesbian Avengers do not apply for permits, do not ask for permission to do actions, and do not negotiate with the police in advance. Of course special circumstance may require changing this approach. All is subject to discussion in the group.

LEGAL OBSERVERS

Lawyers need to be contacted at least a week in advance. We usually need one lawyer and two students or observers for an action. Avengers need a clear understanding of our legal rights going into an event. Legal support Avengers should have ongoing communication with attorneys throughout the action.

XEROX

There are Avengers who work in corporations with massive xerox possibilities. But they need ample advance warning and assistance transporting the guerrilla copies.

FAX

There are Avengers who work in corporations that have access to unlimited FAX. They need advance notice and cooperative assistance.

FLYER PRODUCTION

The Avengers have a bevy of gifted graphic artists who can design beautiful posters, but they need to be alerted at least a week in advance and cannot be expected to pick up and drop off copy in addition to executing their designs.

DEMO-GRAPHICS

The visual design of our actions is a crucial part of Avenger work. In general we try to make each action look different from our previous events and have a style and presentation that has never been used by anyone before. Props play a huge part in this. Props, floats, shrines, burning torches, papier maché bombs, plaster statues . . . whatever! Demo-graphics need to be eye-catching, meaningful and visually exciting.

The more creative, imaginative and individual our actions look, the more eye-catching, inspiring, and fun they will be.

The design of an action usually begins with the preliminary flyer announcing the event to the community. Innovative design, contemporary, clever graphics, and even the color of the paper are all important ways to convey to the viewer how fearless, open, and new our approach is. To date our invitational leaflets have been one of the Avengers' strongest drawing cards.

Usually the flyer features a slogan or phrase that will be a consistent theme throughout the action. We try never to use a cliché or tired old rhetoric. Instead we've been able to come up with a wide range of eye-catching titles. When we built a shrine to the two gay people burned to death in Oregon, our demo posters said *"Do Not Let Them Rest in Peace."* When we dogged the mayor of Denver for 48 hours the signs said *"Boycott the Hate State."* When we held our New Year's Eve party, the poster featured a picture of seventies Blaxploitation film star Pam Grier, in hot pants, holding a rifle. The poster advertised *"Activist A Go-Go."* Our Valentine's Day Action honoring Gertrude Stein and Alice Toklas celebrated *"Politically Incorrect Domestic Bliss."* Our demo banners favoring the Multicultural Curriculum said *"Lighten Up! Teach About Lesbian Lives."* The banners for the torchlight parade down Fifth Avenue said *"Wake Up It's Happening Here"* and for the March on Washington said *"Lesbian Avengers: Out for Power."* So whether the theme is whimsical or angry, our slogans have been clear, clever, and strong.

Party Invitation, 1993

MEDIA

I. STANDARD MEDIA

Good, efficient media work is essential to any activist organization. The first thing you need to do is amass a list of media contacts. Go through all the daily papers and weekly publications in your area and identify anyone who writes stories with gay/lesbian themes or people behind the scenes or in other departments who might be openly or discreetly lesbian or gay.

Call every local radio and T.V. station and ask them directly for the names of people on staff (not only news staff) who are particularly interested in lesbian or gay stories. Make personal contact with anyone in any media outlet who is openly lesbian.

Four days before your action, FAX out your press release to your entire media list and then spend the next few days making follow-up phone calls encouraging the press to attend your event.

Use the set LESBIAN AVENGER press release format and letterhead (see sample).

At the action itself, speak to every member of the press and get their name and number. That way you know who has responded, who to add to your list, and who you can call afterwards for more follow-up. *Personal contact* is the best way to get coverage.

II. VIDEO

Every single action should be covered by an Avenger video team. In this way, even if we don't get television coverage we can always provide T.V. stations with our own footage after the fact.

Even more importantly, Avenger video teams can put together our own video compilations to be shown across the country and around the world. These videos have proven to be our best organizing tools for starting new chapters. Since the Avenger phenomenon has never been seen before, it is often hard for people to imagine the type of actions and spirit that define us. Videos are invaluable in communicating our work and attitude.

III. GAY AND LESBIAN PRESS

The gay and lesbian press ranges from glossy national magazines to typewritten bar rags. There are hundreds of newsletters and newspapers around the country and often they are the only way for gay people to communicate. FAXing and mailing press releases, communiqués, and newspaper clippings to the gay media is another good way of encouraging new Avenger chapters and, more importantly, the spirit of activism among lesbians. It also provides crucial coverage of our issues, something that can't be expected of the mainstream.

Rose is a Bomb is a Rose is a Bomb is a Rose is a Bomb is a

The Lesbian Avengers

along with representatives from

The New York Cultural Society and Friends of Bryant Park,

request the honor of your presence

at the unveiling of the Statue of Alice B. Toklas

by artist Dolores Departo,

in Bryant Park,

40th Street between Fifth and Sixth Avenues,

on Sunday, February 14, 1993

at 2 o'clock in the afternoon.

Invitation to Valentine's Day Action, 1993.

AVENGER LOGOS FOR REPRODUCTIO

the LESBIAN AVENGERS

The LESBIAN AVENGERS is a direct-action group focused on issues vital to lesbian survival and visibility

The LESBIAN AVENGERS is a direct-action group focused on issues vital to lesbian survival and visibility

the LESBIAN AVENGERS

The LESBIAN AVENGERS is a direct-action group focused on issues vital to lesbian survival and visibility

The LESBIAN AVENGERS is a direct-action group focused on issues vital to lesbian survival and visibility

The LESBIAN AVENGERS is a direct-action group focused on issues vital to lesbian survival and visibility

The LESBIAN AVENGERS is a direct-action group focused on issues vital to lesbian survival and visibility

COMMENTARY

By the summer of 1993, the Dyke March had caught on around the country. We held one of 3,000 marchers in New York (without a permit—of course) the day before Gay Pride. So did San Francisco, only they got 10,000. Denver, Colorado started a branch of the Avengers. The Austin chapter disrupted a session of the state legislature debating a gay rights bill and eleven of them were arrested. ACT UP got back in the news with an open-coffin funeral in Washington, D.C. for activist Tim Bailey who had died the previous week of AIDS. The Irish Lesbian and Gay Organization was in pre-trial hearings in anticipation of a jury trial. Clinton bombed Iraq and the Campaign for Military Service held a fund-raiser on the aircraft carrier the Intrepid sponsored by David Geffen, Barry Diller and Tom Stoddard.

The Avengers were producing t-shirts, broadsheets, a fifty-five minute video of highlights from our first year, and another edition of the handbook, still doing all our fundraising in five and ten dollar donations. A year ago I would have predicted that we'd be out of business by this time, but instead the opposite was true. A national, activist, lesbian movement. Now the question remained, what next? Would we be able to maintain our momentum? Would the grass-roots be able to have any kind of visibility or voice?

Photo of Lesbian Avenger Fire-Eater: Donna Binder, Impact Visuals

THE LESBIAN AVENGERS
PART FOUR—THE FREEDOM RIDE

By our second summer we had over twenty chapters, and so were ready to take on larger projects. The new round of anti-gay Christian ballot measures was underway with a number of defeats for us in Oregon, yet national organizations were still so focused on the military issue and Washington that there was no broadly coordinated response. Each small gay community was basically left to its own devices. Only the National Gay Task Force was offering even one-day "Fight the Right" workshops. But no one provided ongoing organizing support. This was a dramatic mistake since most of the small towns and rural counties facing these measures did not have the resources or the skills to defeat them. In many cases there were not enough gay people even out of the closet to publicly campaign against the measures. So, we decided to create a sixties model "Freedom Summer" organizing project focused on helping one of these small communities defeat the measure. I hoped that if we could help one community defeat the right, we could set a model for the rest of the country, of lesbians and gays crossing state lines to support each other in this vicious, desperate fight.

I got a list from the Task Force of upcoming ballot measures and systematically started calling the contact numbers all around the country. Most were in people's homes or stores and all had euphemistic names like Idaho for Human Dignity, Washington Citizens for Fairness, or Floridians Respect Everyone's Equality. None of the groups said the words "lesbian" or "gay" in their titles even though it was all gay people running them. Very few even returned my call. Not surprisingly no man who ever answered the phone had heard of me or of the Lesbian Avengers. But, if a woman answered, in every instance she was aware of one or both.

Finally, I got a return call from Jan Welch in Lewiston, Maine—a depressed mill town of 39,000 people—mostly Roman Catholic and mostly conservative. Their city council had passed a nondiscrimination measure which the right wing was actively campaigning to repeal, with the vote coming up on November 2. She knew the Avengers from the March on Washington but sounded highly suspicious and referred me to a male member of her coalition—Equal Protection Lewiston—who sounded even more suspicious and for three weeks never returned any of my calls. Finally, when I did find him at home, he expressed concern about outsiders coming in to Maine and specifically said he "did not want people with New York accents." Interpreting this to be veiled anti-Semitism, I answered that the Avengers have a wide range of accents and started calling every gay person I had ever met or heard of in the State of Maine until we got a response.

It came from Paula Aboud, at that time out-going Director of the Maine Lesbian and Gay Political Alliance based in Portland. She told me that Robert Bray and Scott Nakagawa of the Task Force were coming up to give an all-day statewide workshop on fighting the right and she invited the Avengers to come along. So Phyllis Lutsky, Ann Stott, Sara Pursley, and I drove up, eight hours, to convince Lewiston and the state of Maine that the Avengers could make a difference. This fear of outsiders seems to be a constant theme among gay people in these small communities—principally because they feel that the right wing will use that relationship to discredit the local gay community. However, at the same time, the Christian right's ballot measures are nationally coordinated, with nationally produced literature and nationally conforming language. In the Lewiston case, the measure listed all existing classes of protection such as disability, sex, race and religion—and then stated that no more groups could be added. They drew the line for civil rights.

At breakfast, in a local, surprisingly upscale diner, we read over the local papers, coming upon a paid advertisement by the Citizens of Lewiston for the Repeal of Special Homosexual Rights. They were announcing a brunch, to take place that week, featuring keynote speeches by right wing leaders based in Washington. We hoped that this blatant importation of national figures would help EPL warm up to our assistance.

Phyllis and I are two loud Jews. Ann and Sara are two blond WASPs from Minneapolis and Boise, Idaho respectively. We knew that we would be making different kinds of impressions and so, from the moment we entered the conference, we fanned out into different workshops, sitting next to different folks and trying to meet as many people as possible. From the beginning, the fear of outsiders was overtly expressed—even including activists from other cities in Maine.

Fortunately both Scott and Robert of the Task Force were immensely supportive and helpful to us throughout the day. Scott spoke very eloquently about the nature of the Right Wing, trying to give the audience a national perspective. He called the Christian right "the most influential radical movement in America," and pointed out that it is "as old as America itself." And then he made a point that has stayed with me ever since—something that I use in my personal life as well as my organizing. He analyzed the right's politics of resentment as being rooted in groups of people who have never had to acknowledge that they have rights because these rights have never been threatened. They object to having to acknowledge their rights as not inherently merited by their natural superiority and instead as an accident of birth. This was the most articulate explanation of not only the right's appeal, but also the roots of the increasingly tiresome "politically correct" and "reverse discrimination" accusations that I hear, not only in the media but even within my own family.

"Simple answers to complex problems," Scott said, "have galvanized large numbers of people in this country for hundreds of years."

Next, Phyllis and I took Robert Bray's four-hour media workshop. In a crammed afternoon he tried to teach people about the function of the press, how to do interviews, write press releases, and organize media campaigns. Throughout he was very supportive of the Avengers, recalling our Zap of the Mayor of Denver and what an impact it had had on the Colorado media. Then it was time for the participants to come up, on the spot, with creative actions. Both Jan Welch and Paula Aboud were sitting in the room and the air between us was quite tense. Robert called on me to make a suggestion off the top of my head, and I remembered the anti-gay brunch we had read about in the paper that morning. "How about a Freedom Picnic to compete with their Anti-Gay Brunch?" I suggested, and relief seemed to come across the room. Finally our hosts could see concretely that we had creative ideas that would be appropriate to their area and, also, upbeat and fun.

But the final test came at the end of that long day on a panel on Direct Action with Scott, myself, and Bee Bell from ACT UP Portland. This was the time when the Avengers would either go over or be rejected. I prepared a very careful presentation basically summing up the Avenger philosophy—that all strategies can be valid because people can only respond politically on a level that makes sense to them. I argued that the healthiest movement would be one that employed a wide range of strategies and gave examples of the other ways we had assisted Oregon, Tampa, and Colorado during the previous year. And I offered our concrete services to Lewiston.

As Scott and Bee were presenting, I was filled with fear and anxiety. I had no idea as to how my presentation had gone over and still did not have any indication from EPL as to whether or not they wanted to work with us. Although that day had underlined how much they needed our support, I still could not measure their receptivity. Feeling like a failure, I sat through the other presentations in a kind of daze and so was totally surprised when Jan Welch stood up as the first speaker in the question-and-answer session. She said how suspicious she had been of us at first, but how excited she was to work with us now. And then she made a statement that I will never forget. "Lewiston can accept Direct Action if it is done in a loving way."

This marked the beginning of months of intense work and wild activity. We came up with a two-part strategy that ended up involving over fifty Avengers, on-site organizing, and a Freedom Ride.

On-site, Sara Pursley, a white woman and Chanelle Mathews, a black woman from Nebraska who had recently come to the Avengers from the army, rented an apartment in Lewiston and did full time organizing for EPL during the six weeks before the vote. Armed with beautiful banners by Lydia Medina, these two women came up with the most creative and incredible organizing projects. In general EPL decided to take what they perceived to be the "safest" route. Their literature had virtually no mention of lesbians and gays and they emphasized a "Vote No on Discrimination" campaign including hiring a heterosexual campaign manager. As a result, many resources and treasures of support were overlooked.

For example, Sara and Chanelle went into the underground gay community of Lewiston. Even though only a handful of gay people there were out enough to organize against the measure, the town had enough queers to support two gay bars. The Avengers did voter registration in the gay bars, held special fundraising and organizing events with gay sports and motorcycle groups. When EPL refused to include the two poorest districts in town in their massive literature drop claiming that "those people won't come out for anything but free food," Sara and Chanelle organized a pot luck meal in those districts. When the campaign manager claimed that people who had not voted in the two previous presidential elections would not vote on November 2, the Avengers insisted that these people were forming the base of the right wing's support because no one else paid any attention to them. Throughout there was a belief that helping gay people register and vote to protect their own basic rights is a huge step towards gay and lesbian self-empowerment and is a crucial political act.

The second part of our campaign involved a Freedom Ride, organized by Ann Stott. The purpose was multifold. We wanted to start more lesbian direct action groups directed against the Christian right and we wanted to create a climate of outrage among New England gay communities about the vote in Lewiston. Up until this time, because there was no nationally coordinated effort, the only way that gay people would find out about the existence of ballot measures would be to read about them in the gay press up to a month later. This was a situation we wanted to change. Finally, we wanted to emphasize the importance of a federal gay rights bill— which had to come from Clinton. Only a federal bill would really help this crisis situation because it would render all these ballot measures moot. Basically I believe that it is the responsibility of people with power in America to use that power to protect lesbians and gay men, just as I believe that heterosexual family members are equally responsible to use their societal power to protect the gays and lesbians in their own families. The Freedom Ride was planned to go from New York to Boston to Northhampton, Albany, Syracuse, Burlington, Vt., and end in Lewiston two weeks before the vote.

Organizing this was in many ways a lesson in how far we have to go for lesbians to value their own work and take themselves seriously. Ann, Sara, and I all had people blow off their responsibilities in the most infantile and pathetic ways. Also, I took on the responsibility of fundraising for the entire project and was shocked to see how little interest or support we could muster from the lesbian community. Women who were professional fundraisers for gay organizations were unwilling to raise money for this project. Avengers themselves were afraid to ask other people for money. Professional fundraisers working for expressly lesbian foundations were entirely unhelpful. In the end we raised about $3,000 in twenty-five dollar donations and about ten house parties—mostly cajoled through people like Carl George, Kathleen Conkey, Peg Byron and Marissa Cardinale. We also received a $1,000 donation from David Becker, a very helpful fundraising letter from Laurie

Linton and an $8,000 bequest from David Patierno, a gay man who died of AIDS and instructed his sister Mary to contribute some of his estate to the Avengers. As fundraiser I found that I had to use every personal connection and friendship that I and house party coordinator Sally Chew had in order to raise the minimum.

The only major political obstacle came in Albany where a small political group organized by the writer Barbara Smith objected to us using the name "Freedom Ride," which they said would be insulting to black heterosexuals. The Avengers discussed this criticism with the utmost seriousness and came to a unanimous decision among sixty women to continue with the name "Freedom Ride." Some of our reasons were as follows. First, the black, Latina and Asian women in the Avengers all wanted to keep the name. We recognized that there is as much difference of opinion among lesbians of color as among white lesbians or any other group, and, while Barbara had her reasons for her objections, the women of color in the Avengers felt that we were using the name legitimately. We said that if people were offended by lesbians placing ourselves firmly in the tradition of the other freedom movements then they were homophobic. We knew that this argument had taken place in other parts of the gay movement all through its history. Adjusting strategies so as not to offend those who basically have a problem with accepting gay people for who we really are did not make sense to the Avengers. Finally we felt that our Freedom Ride was in the best tradition of the Freedom Rides of the sixties because it involved people literally moving geographically to defend a community that they identify with when they are under siege. At stake are basic civil rights protections that could not be denied.

However, we were able to turn this event into an action by coming away from the conflict with an increased desire to address the complex racial issues raised by the Christian right. And so we incorporated a component into the Freedom Ride where we showed the Christian video "Gays Rights, Special Rights" at each location. This video, whose primary attack is on black lesbians and gays provoked a lot of distress and confrontational discussion whenever we showed it, but that was preferable to sweeping racial issues under the rug. And it gave us at least a chance of short-circuiting the Christians' attempt to further racially divide our movement by taking their propaganda on directly.

As far as Lewiston went, the vote on November 2 was a disaster. We lost by a margin of 2 to 1, as did gays and lesbians in

Cincinnati and in New Hampshire. But, after the vote was counted we could see that the districts in which Avengers had gone door to door lost by a smaller margin than those in which there was no gay or lesbian visibility. In an evaluation with Jan Welch later, she felt that the Avenger strategies of being out and going door to door were, in the long term, the right strategies. However, she felt that moderate Lewiston gays were not ready for those strategies and she opposed having them carried out by radicals alone.

The differences between moderate gays in Lewiston and radical gays in Lewiston—between assimilationist campaigns and openly gay campaigns—are being debated all across the country. But so far, no campaign that has chosen the closeted strategy has been able to defeat an anti-gay ballot measure.

Even though we lost, our presence gave gays and lesbians in Lewiston a chance to be out to their friends and neighbors—often for the first time. There were gays who registered and voted on their own behalf for the first time. There were people who spoke face to face with out lesbians who never had that opportunity before. In short, even though we lost the vote, we were extremely proud of our campaign.

CONCLUSION

Conclusion
UNPOPULAR CULTURE AND THE LURE OF NORMALCY

In the 1950, the titles of lesbian novels could have been catalogued in the science fiction section. *Twilight Lover* and *Odd Girl Out* indicated the existence of a shadowy parallel world of creepy aliens doing their dirty otherly thing. Today, in Bill Clinton's America, surprisingly little has changed. We are learning the hard way that the visibility that we long craved and fought for has made very little impact on our social position. Our visibility has not made us more acceptable, it has just created an above-board recognizable ghetto in addition to the old secret underground one. And so we now have to ask some very hard questions.

As this volume comes to a close, the euphoria of Clinton's election has quickly faded. It is amazing how much territory gay people gave up in such a short time, how willing we were to relinquish so much of our voice to an administration that has repeatedly failed gay people and people with AIDS. Because the official gay leadership has capitulated to the White House, our best strategy is to ignore them. If we have complaints with Clinton or with the Pentagon, we need to address those institutions directly, not let the liberal leadership—gay or straight—serve as a stand-in or go-between for real power.

The military debacle said it all—America has reiterated its most consistent position on homosexuality: separate and unequal. Back into the ghetto for you. They know we exist, but, so what? Don't ask. Don't tell. The new visibility is an illusion. It has no inherent concrete social gains accompanying it. Those are going to have to be won county by county, action by action, and conversation by conversation. Usually social transformation is achieved by a very small group of people. Most others just stand by and let it happen. But, because the battles happen often on the most personal fronts, gay people have been an exception. Huge numbers will have to continue to stay active in order to keep moving forward.

Probably Bill Clinton will not be re-elected and will be replaced by a Reagan/Bush type of guy. Probably the Christian right will continue their already too successful campaign against us while the rest of America stands passively by. Probably the AIDS crisis will not end. Probably science will continue to argue that our homosexuality is a genetic defect, and the right will continue to argue that homosexuality is freely chosen and therefore punishable. Probably the nature of homophobia will never be widely interrogated, while we will continue to be excluded from school curricula, subjected to vicious media distortions, or entirely ignored, denied basic civil rights while our demands are ridiculed and derided. But in the midst of all of this only one thing has changed for certain. We have changed. We will never go back in the closet.

INDEX
ORGANIZATIONS, PUBLICATIONS, AND PRODUCTIONS

INDEX

A-Socials, 77–78

Abandonment of lesbians and gays, 92, 236, 256, 258–63

Abortion, 24, 36–40, 47, 69, 85, 196; abortion rights movement, 3, 4, 28–31, 70, 125. *See* Reproductive Rights National Network, Committee for Abortion Rights and Against Sterilization Abuse; Clinton and, 15, 283; Friedan and, 26; illegal, 30, 37, 72, 73, 212; Medicaid funding of, 4; parental consent for, 4, 76; role of media, 2; spousal consent for, 4, 31; states' rights and, 4, 15; women of color and, 29, 30

Aboud, Paula, 314, 315

Acker, Kathy, xviii

Ahwesh, Peggy, xviii

AIDS, xviii, 5, 12, 14, 16, 17, 24, 49, 55, 56, 62, 65, 70, 94, 131, 149–52, 194–97, 202, 206, 207, 209, 210, 238, 254, 255, 258–63, 269–76, 220–25, 256, 261, 275, 319, 324; activism before ACT UP, 11, 93, 115, 116, 118, 120–24, 174, 175; alternative treatments for, 157–60; AIDS related complex (ARC), 176, 180, 182, 188; Centers for Disease Control definition, 6, 7, 181, 189, 211–15; cures, 159, 160; dance, 266, 267; Dinkins and, 164; discrimination and, 111, 112, 114–119; Dolan and, 22; education, 60, 65, 103–10, 122, 235; experimental drug trials, 176–79, 188–90, 213, 214; film,
228–32; gay male and lesbian relationships and, 9, 120, 121, 122, 124, 186; Germany, 80–82; homeless and, 120–24, 152, 153, 170–73, 180–84, 223–25; hysteria, 10, 59, 102–11, 113–19; insurance and, 111, 115; IV drug users and, 176, 177, 181, 182, 188, 215; Japan 244, 245; lesbians and, 67, 68, 120–24, 172, 173, 216–219, 286; needle exchange programs, 116; organizing and, 31; pediatrics, 188–90; testing, 171, 224; transmission of, 117, 170–73, 223–25; tuberculosis and, 223–35; women and, 7, 10, 45, 113, 121, 171, 175–179, 211–15; writing, 194–97

Alexander, Vicki, 29, 212

Allen, Paula Gunn, 24

Allison, Dorothy, 247

Alpert, Rebecca, 39

Altman, Robert, xv

Ampligen, 176–79, 195

Anarchism, 125–27, 141

Anderson, Rafita, 30

Anshaw, Carole, 169

Anti-abortionism, 3, 15, 24, 36–40, 65, 71; clinic attacks, 2, 36, 37, 40; electoral politics, 21, 24; feminists and, 37, 38; harassment of women seeking abortion, 2, 36, 37; Holocaust references, 37; rape and incest, 22; freedom movements, references to, 37